THE GIANT CLAM AND OTHER VISIONS

A Traditional Allopathic Physician Explores Non-Ordinary States and Reconciles with Joy

By
Bart W. Balint, MD

Paperback ISBN: **978-1-963100-69-3**

Hardcover ISBN: **978-1-963100-70-9**

TABLE OF CONTENTS

ACKNOWLEDGEMENTS

I want to give special thanks to Rebecca Job, Catherine Marjoribanks, and Lily S. Blodgett for helping me with editing. Each of these women brought a different perspective to my process. Warm appreciation to Fiona Robertson for her guidance on the inquiry chapter and editing. Many thanks to my book writing group including Katie Curtin, Alex Baisley, and Michael Clark for their thoughtful and constructive suggestions.

I am deeply grateful to my children, Chris and Tyler, and my first wife, Sharon, for inspiring me and making all this possible. I have profound gratitude for my life partner, Melanie Balint Gray, PhD, for joining me on this internal exploration and assisting me in expressing the journey in this book. I wonder if I would have even traveled this path without her constant companionship.

DEDICATION

This book is dedicated to my sons, Chris and Tyler.

CHAPTER 1
MISERABLE, BUT AT LEAST I KNEW WHO I WAS

I was dead sure who I was—an anesthesiologist in my mid-forties running my own lucrative pain management practice and a Mensa-grade intellectual with a sharp, mercurial mind. I had a strong body that I enjoyed using for tennis, scuba diving, farm work, martial arts, and many other corporeal endeavors. My mental and physical attributes enabled me to breeze through my professional world. Most people who knew me then might have considered my outward demeanor, accomplishments, and acquisitions a sign of success. What was there not to love about my life?

Though often stretched thin by my professional duties as a doctor and entrepreneur, I still managed to carve out time with my sons, Chris and Tyler. Awkwardly, I tried to be open and available to my wife, Sharon.

However, I felt incomplete, disconnected, and obsessively critical of myself and others. I could barely acknowledge, let alone celebrate, the achievement of healthy success. Something told me that I would be arrogant, self-centered, and too much of a showoff if I expressed pride, joy, or appreciation for what I had become.

Despite everything positive I had, I could always find something that wasn't exactly right: something flawed about my medical practice that could spoil my mood in an instant, something to be irritated about on airplane flights that were actually on time for a change, or something not right about how the roofers lined up the new shingles over the awning. Anything could be described as lacking once it came to my attention.

Underneath so much of my life also lived a simmering jealousy of others who appeared happy in whatever they were doing.

I felt a layer of emptiness inside but had no idea what to do about it. While I could align my home telescope towards the moon and the stars, a feeling of beauty and amazement in the night sky escaped me. I loved my wife and children but could not reach beyond my emptiness to express that love. I had some friends, but I was convinced that anyone who was friends with me would eventually be disappointed. Jealousy, anger, and finding shortcomings fostered my disconnection from everything.

My habitual tendencies included accumulating possessions, shutting out who or what caused me irritation and overeating that I purposely mischaracterized as some warped sense of gratification. I tried hard to associate those tendencies with a feeling of justification and false satisfaction—one more convoluted layer to hide my inner pain.

Karate: An Accidental Doorway

Like many fathers, I wanted to be the best dad that I could. The boys seemed to thoroughly enjoy any excuse to wrestle with each other around the house, so it only made sense that they and I would enjoy the world of martial arts. We started karate lessons in a nearby town. The boys took to it like ducks to water, and the big grins on their faces every time they ran onto the mat delighted the father in me. Secretly, I also hoped they might find karate as a tool to foster the confidence and sense of discipline that is such a gift for young folks.

Figure 1 Just Starting Out in Karate.

Karate class, as I hoped, broadened their exploration of the world. Aside from being happy for the boys, I found satisfaction by progressing up the belt rankings. However, I didn't experience some sudden quieting of my mind, as I had imagined occurred in karate masters. On the contrary, I could always count on my ongoing mental chatter, criticizing or judging myself and everyone else.

During each visit to the dojo, I, an outwardly successful and accomplished physician, stood at the threshold of meeting my suppressed but pervasive feelings of lack, inadequacy, and fear.

When the internal mental prattle got louder, avoidance using physical activity was the quick path to relief every time.

My life changed one day when my right foot stepped onto the dojo mat.

I was paired to spar with my son's friend, John. Smiling at the sinewy sixteen-year-old standing before me, who was half my size, I was suddenly alarmed to hear the instructions. For the first time in our karate training, our instructor yelled, "Take your opponent to the ground!" We had indeed practiced all kinds of karate kicks, stances, blocks, and blows, but never before were we to dominate our sparring partner by throwing him to the mat.

These new instructions thrilled me. There was no way this teenager was going to beat me, and a voice inside screamed,

"This kid is going down!"

With a nod, John and I acknowledged the instructions and quickly returned each other's cold, snarly stare. As the match began, the black mats, the red-colored curtains covering the front windows, and the thirty other students in the dojo blurred. Even the ubiquitous body odor smell that wafted from the locker room faded. As far as I knew, all the other students were focused on John's and my encounter. Grunting and circling, punching and kicking, we worked toward the inevitable—the moment when one of us would take the other down.

And then, my moment came. It was perfect. Slightly crouched, fists raised, eyebrows bristling, and on the offensive, I rushed John and grabbed him in a way that frankly didn't resemble anything we had been taught! Locked together and somewhat off-balance, a command in my head said to give one more forceful thrust. I gave it all my gut-groaning strength. As I threw him to the ground and landed on top, the twisting of my body overpowered him in a way that could never be called skillful. Rising from the mat, I straightened out the sleeves of my white uniform, and the instructor declared me the winner. I won! The match ended as quickly as it started. I had used the physical brawn of my body to prove that I was not the loser.

The evening's instruction continued uneventfully, and the boys and I packed our things in the car and headed home. I was quiet on the drive back, however. Instead of feeling elated, I felt ashamed and guilty. What kind of person was I? A grown man getting pleasure from taking a kid down? I was startled by my behavior, but as soon as I parked the car in the driveway, my thoughts wandered away from these feelings to a logistical issue at work and the grass that needed cutting around our farm.

Ignoring the Signs

I awoke the following morning not to troubling thoughts about my behavior the day before but something entirely unexpected—shooting pains through my right wrist. Rather than receding over the following days, the pain progressed to a continuous, throbbing, toothache-like sensation, accompanied by gradually increasing weakness in my right hand.

It continued to get worse. Eventually, I realized I must have tweaked something in my neck and arm during the karate sparring match. Soon, my tennis backhand suffered, and no matter how much I tried to "work it out" with repetitious court drills and an additional karate practice each week, this annoyance kept getting worse. I passed the test for my brown karate belt during this time despite being barely able to control several of the karate weapons routinely used at this stage.

It didn't cross my mind to take a break from physical activity or to get it checked out. I had programmed myself early in life to block out things that I didn't want to pay attention to, a strategy that had served me well in the past. Keeping with my nature of pushing through life in general, I continued to do physically taxing work like renovating our home. I thought little about holding up each 16-foot paneling board with my head and neck while nailing them to the apartment ceiling. Of course, my medical advice at the time to any patient in this condition would have been to rest, talk with a physical therapist, and *whatever you do, don't carry around 16-foot paneling boards like they're some silly evening hat!*

Over two months, the aching gave way to something more concerning. Sharon and I had just finished lunch and cleaned up in the kitchen. As part of a worn-out vaudeville routine, I would routinely yell out some Viking battle cry, "Lay Waste!" and crush with my bare hand some defenseless empty Coke can, victoriously tossing it into the recycle bin. But as Sharon watched intently, I couldn't even dent the aluminum can this time. After several miscues, I finally gave up and crushed it under my foot. I had complete wrist drop, a sure sign that something was wrong, but I did not acknowledge it or stop to look at it.

The weakness in my arm started to show up elsewhere, in places far more vital to me than demolishing an empty can of Coke. I began to notice that it was becoming difficult to administer pain-reducing injections at the office, and I could hardly tolerate the pain in my wrist when writing a prescription. This scared the shit out of me, and I was determined not to let this weakness show. I talked to no one about it. A voice of survival kept telling me to keep this quiet so as not to display frailty to the outside world.

I kept quiet for another month. Then, one morning, after a particularly restless night of sleep, I woke to such intense pain that I broke down and decided to find out what was happening. Who was I comfortable enough with to confide in? This wasn't an easy question for me, but I finally made an appt with Dr. Mathe, a neurosurgeon to whom I had referred patients for several years. I trusted him. This time, I referred myself as a patient.

Getting a quick appointment was easy, as I knew Dr. Mathe's entire staff. His nurse, Patricia, checked my vitals just as Dr. Mathe entered the exam room.

"Good afternoon, Bart. How have you been?" said Dr. Mathe.

"I'd love to say I'm great, but this wrist and arm have been giving me problems ever since an injury in karate three months ago," I confessed.

"Yes, I see on the exam that you have profound weakness in several nerves in your arm. Have you participated in any physical therapy or had any injections?"

"No, I haven't," I replied sheepishly. "But I have kept up all my sports and been extra busy with some interior woodwork that needed completing on our barn."

Dr. Mathe smiled and shook his head in a *Bart; I thought you knew better* type of motion. "Let's start with an MRI of your neck, and if appropriate, we will have one of our pain doctors do some injections in that area."

The MRI showed several herniated and degenerative discs correlating with my pain and wrist weakness. I tried some steroid injections to help the pain, but sadly, they didn't change the intensity of the nerve injury. Dr. Mathe and I agreed that I needed surgery. I noted some mild nervousness around the recommendation of surgery, but mainly about time off from work and whether I could return to karate. I consented and soon went under the knife to receive a two-level cervical fusion. While I approached the whole experience matter-of-factly, I appreciated the antianxiety medicine the nurse anesthetist gave me in the pre-operative room.

Technically the surgery went smoothly, as Dr. Mathe replaced the injured discs with bone implants, securing all of this to my neck with screws and a metal plate.

"Dr. Balint, don't worry, as everything went well, and you are just waking up," I heard one of the recovery room nurses say.

"Yeah, everything might be okay, but what in the name of blazes is this intense, throbbing, burning pain in the back of my head and neck?" I exclaimed in a voice markedly hoarsened because of the breathing tube needed during the operation. "I didn't have this before the surgery!"

I didn't ask for pain medications as I did not want to seem needy or weak. Moreover, even though the intensity and risks of the surgery merited an overnight hospital stay, the insurance company declared that this surgery was strictly outpatient. As soon as I could urinate, I was sent on my way down the interstate!

My wife Sharon brought our car to the hospital entrance and picked up her just-operated-on husband for the two-hour ride home. Every bump and turn along the drive sent tsunamis of pain through my head and neck.

Maybe a few pain pills would have been a good idea.

I chose not to drive, either from the front or back seat.

Dr. Mathe instructed me to wear a stiff cervical collar for two months. Dreaded in every way possible, the collar contributed to the intense burning and pain in my neck and the back of my skull and became a symbol of everything going wrong in my life. I couldn't sleep properly, woke up constantly at night, and felt exhausted in the daytime. Day after day, I woke up in the dreary light of early morning, in intense pain and increasing depression, neither wanting to get up nor stay in bed. From my experience as a doctor, which sometimes was a detriment, I knew the pain should improve as each day progressed. For me, it worsened. And I would never have predicted my descent into a deepening hole of despair, sleeplessness, boredom, and misery. The days endlessly revolved around a minimal, bland liquid diet since I couldn't swallow normally because of my neck's extreme swelling and tenderness. Reading wasn't an option, as I couldn't look down or bend my neck forward or backward. I couldn't work on my computer or get into any comfortable position to watch TV.

At the flick of a knife, my active life turned inside out, and I grew increasingly dispirited and morose, staying in bed for more of each day. Although I had seen this in several patients, the surgeon and I had never discussed post-surgical pain, depression, or an emotionally dark hole as possible outcomes of cervical fusion. The surgery was supposed to repair the damage, not create more pain.

Three weeks after the surgery and still wearing that rigid cervical collar, I felt and heard a squishing sound that my medical experience told me could be the collapse of the surgically placed screws or plates in my neck. (This collapse was confirmed five years later in a series of X-rays.) As it became my pattern, I did not contact Dr. Mathe and instead took this as just one more reason to feel demoralized. I decided that unless something drastic changed in my overall symptoms, I wouldn't tell anyone about it, not even my neurosurgeon. *What could have been done at that point anyway?* I thought. *Another surgery?* That prospect did not excite me in the least.

Meanwhile, the surgical neck wound, the severed neck muscles, and the ligaments and tendons infiltrated with scar tissue, the way that all tissue heals after being cut. When I moved my neck forward, the muscles in the front of the neck spasmed, miserably contributing to the ever-growing pile of depression piled on top of the mistake I had made by consenting to surgery.

Emotionally, I felt crushed. I couldn't even look up at the stars outside on a clear spring night. While never deeply inspirational, I usually found that looking through my scope was at least quieting and relaxing. After the surgery, I couldn't look up past the roofline of our house. Every time I tried to adjust my head to look through the viewfinder, my neck spasmed. I tried this way and that, and I couldn't do it. In its current state, my neck made it impossible to look anywhere except straight forward. I wheeled my telescope back inside and went to bed.

I did have some progress, however. Gradually, over several months, the achy pain in my hand, wrist, and forearm subsided. Before the surgery, it felt like someone was routinely whacking me on the forearm, sending shockwaves into my wrist and hand.

The numbness also began to improve, though it never ultimately resolved.

For the first time in my life, I felt incapacitated and at a complete standstill. I couldn't work or drive a car, as my head wouldn't rotate to see to my left or right. I couldn't mow the grass or bend to clean our cat's litter box. Many of my routine chores became Sharon's for the time being. I could barely swallow. Even reading or watching TV hurt. Taking pain medications helped with the physical pain, but their downsides rotated around constipation, extreme irritation, and a certain amount of shame that I needed them.

Through my misery, I began to admit that I had always felt an uneasiness beneath the surface, no matter what I achieved. I never became too excited or allowed myself to feel anything but a faint whiff of satisfaction in whatever I accomplished. I never allowed myself to feel complete or confident, except when I could distort those positive emotions into some passive-aggressive behavior, trying to manipulate the world. I always lived with these negative background thoughts but avoided examining them in depth. This negativity was just who I was.

I never felt convinced that I could ever be happy or fulfilled in this lifetime.

The Angelfish Appears

One day, upon partially arousing from an endless string of naps and having sunk lower than the most miserable, I saw a sight that changed my world forever. Unexpectedly presented with an amazing moment, my mind came to a full, silent stop, and I had no time or thought to suggest that I might be hallucinating. I blinked, sat up, stared, and blinked again because a sizeable eight-foot-tall angelfish swam through the air at the foot of my bed. This marvelous creature radiated with the colors I had previously seen during my many scuba diving trips. Whether it was a hallucination, a dream, or an actual angel, the fish was clothed in yellows and brilliant blues, with orangey-red speckles like freckles dotting its face. As I watched, spellbound, the angelfish moved effortlessly and gracefully. It occupied nearly half of the bedroom, its eyes locked on me while its body undulated from right to left, and its bright yellow tail swished from side to side.

O-kayyyyy, I thought, *What IS this?*

It felt so close that I could have reached out and touched it. This visitation seemed to last about 15 seconds (though who knows for sure), and then it vanished. The fish was so real, so big, and so wondrous. It captivated me, and all thinking ceased. I abided in peace and had no neck pain for a while. It took days for me to start grasping the nature of this fish's visit, as it differed from the dreams I'd had sporadically. At the time, it didn't even occur to me that I had to find some deep meaning in this fish. The fish just was. Though I didn't know it, this was the beginning of my inner world taking a foothold in my conscious awareness.

One day, after the angelfish came to me, I got out of bed and dragged myself downstairs. A mirror reflected the ever-deepening despondency settling around my eyes in the form of dark circles. Frankly, I felt like shit, and it showed.

Still off work and instructed to remain inactive while sporting that despised stiff collar, my thoughts ran a loop. "If I can only get this collar off, I will be okay." Or, in more general terms, "If *this*, or if *that*, then I will be fine." I bet heavily on the future as the answer to all my problems—an old habit and a practice that never seemed to help.

Two months after the surgery, the collar did come off. Not surprisingly, I couldn't move my neck as there were so many spasms. I asked myself, "Who was the asshole who said the pain would get better when the collar came off?"

My neck issues multiplied, my pessimism deepened, and the pain ruled my world.

Figure 2 The appearance of the angelfish

Many factors bore down on me all at once. The neck surgery and subsequent chronic pain challenged my belief in my invincibility that any illness could be treated by ignoring the symptoms. Emotionally, I became ever more miserable and irritable. The surgery, depression, and unpredictable reactions to pain medications took a toll on my relationship with my wife, so we slept in separate bedrooms. My inability to have a calm discussion with her illustrated the dysfunction in our relationship at every turn. I stopped all physical activity as I could not move my head and neck without excruciating pain. I watched as everything in my life fell apart.

My outward success had always veiled my inner belief that I was neither worthy nor capable of feeling lasting peace and happiness. Internally, I had felt fractured and torn into pieces. But I had hidden behind my intellect, my many physical hobbies, and the ability to make money in my chosen profession. So, if you asked me back then what life was like for me, I would have said, "Great!' but a sinister jokester lurked in some dark corner of my mind, laughing his head off! That judgmental voice told me I didn't deserve happiness, and unfortunately, I believed it.

Now, with my external activities grinding to a halt, the only things I had left were the negative points of view that had dogged me since I was a teenager. Up to this point, I had always been able to ignore these thoughts. Still, my devastating situation brought me to my knees, pushing me into an unavoidable confrontation and reckoning with how lack and negativity were constant tapes playing in my mind. I was miserable now, but I realized I had ALWAYS been miserable. And I couldn't distract myself from that feeling any longer.

Some of this pessimism showed up as an inwardly directed disgust characterized by constant criticism, irritation, and impatience with everything inside and outside me. My habitual mindset had been to bury these emotions and thoughts and act like everything was great. It might have been a constructive relief to share my misery with someone. But that was impossible. I refused to admit to anyone, even myself, how unhappy I was now or how low I had always been. Part of my mind kept reassuring me that after more recovery, I could go back to chasing success and more achievement. More of that would make me happy!

Sometime after encountering the angelfish, a woman visited me in a dream.

I find myself in a room, unaware of any walls or windows. Soon, a woman comes up to me. I don't know her, but she hands me a piece of paper about the size of a Post-it note. I accept the paper and turn it sideways so I can read the writing on it. "Would you just stop and look at this place you have made?" I easily read the clear, simple block lettering. The woman disappears as quickly as she came. I am puzzled, and then I awaken.

I can see now what wasn't entirely clear to me then—that the neck surgery, severe pain, extreme depression, and the angelfish all asked if I would "just stop and look at this place." But what *was* this "place" that all these pieces asked me to look at? Where was I even to start? And what should I do once I start looking and paying attention?

I knew that my inner world was not a pleasant place. I had seen some hints of internal dissatisfaction with my life, but I refused to look at this directly, as I reasoned it was everyone else's fault, not mine. I refused to see that my intellectual approach to problems only contributed to a more significant disconnection and discontentment. If I only worked on my defenses and said a few more affirmations occasionally, I would be happy, and all those negative thoughts would finally stop. Perhaps …

Something, however, told me that strengthening my defenses would only lead to more pain and suffering. Meanwhile, the angelfish vision mesmerized me and kept calling me as if it were still in my room.

Getting to where I found myself in my inner world contained many moments of despair, victimization, and finger-pointing. My internal misery and desperation pulverized any good I could find about anything. For instance, during this lowest period of my life, the flash of an experience long past that I had labeled as ugly and something to be avoided at all costs. It came without warning. I couldn't bear to acknowledge it superficially, let alone in a more profound, meaningful sense. Associated with a young picture of myself, this timeless glimpse of a child's joy and innocence occurred when I was barely a year old. A memory so joyful that as my mind started analyzing the incident, I shut it down and locked it in some cave with a creaking, heavy steel door. I so wanted to believe that this joy never happened, and my fears demanded that I only generate self-hatred whenever the memory or picture arose.

One more thing to add to that rotting pile of total, overwhelming defeat. With that, I hit rock bottom. As painful as it was to explore my childhood, a look into some of the events of my upbringing will help paint a picture of my early adult mindset and the passive-aggressive traps in which I wallowed as I worked my way toward my karate injury and subsequent surgeries.

CHAPTER 2
GROWING INTO ME

Our family consisted of numerous male members, including George and Michael. One of my grandparents, Michael Balint, immigrated from Slovakia at the age of 15 with his two brothers in the 1920s. Two other grandparents, Anna Mizok and George Komar, were born in the United States soon after their parents immigrated from Slovakia around that same time. My fourth grandparent, Delores Paulman, was the granddaughter of Emma and Edward Breakwell, who came from England in the 1880s.

All four of my grandparents eventually moved to Weirton, West Virginia, to raise their families. Eventually, both grandfathers, one grandmother, two uncles, and my father would be employed at Weirton Steel Mill. Started in 1909 by Earnest T. Weir, the mill gradually grew in size so that by 1915, Weirton Steel was the second-largest tin-plate production facility in the world. Weirton Steel and the steel mills located throughout the Pittsburgh, western Pennsylvania, and eastern Ohio areas became centers for employment for thousands of families, primarily European immigrants. The mill in Weirton offered hope of a stable future for generations, including many of my high school classmates. The workers' grueling days began just a few feet from the numerous entry gates along Main Street. The startling blast of an air horn heard throughout the town announced each shift's end, and the mill's exit gates funneled exhausted men into the streets lined with numerous, dingy, dimly lit bars with blacked-out windows. Mill workers, including my two grandfathers, frequented the dismal bars, trying to transition from their jobs to their home lives.

While my parents knew each other while enrolled at Weir High School, they didn't start dating until after graduation. Their marriage at the time gathered some controversy as my dad's family practiced Catholicism, while my mom's family loosely followed Episcopalian beliefs. Soon after their marriage, my dad, George Edward Balint VII, enlisted in the United States Air Force, which required a temporary move to Ohio. My older brother, George Edward Balint VIII, or George Jr., arrived in 1958, just 11 months before me. My umbilical cord was knotted and cut on August 28, 1959, in the event that physically separated me from my mother, Marlene Komar Balint. In the late 1950s, the television show *Maverick* captured the attention of many US households every week with its tales of the American Wild West. One of the figures in the show, Bart Maverick, became one of my mom's heroes for his honesty, good luck, and good looks. And thus, I became Bart Wesley Balint. Wesley was the name of the man who drove my mom to the hospital when her labor began since my dad was on active duty in the US Air Force.

In a time of relative peace for this country, my father's four-year military career sent him away to Greenland and Newfoundland for many months. We lived outside Columbus, Ohio, near the base where my dad was assigned between those deployments. After his honorable discharge from the service, my dad's name was chiseled into the Veteran's Memorial wall in Weirton.

Earlier, Happier Days

We moved back to Weirton about a year before my younger brother Bruce's birth in 1963. At first, we moved into a small apartment off 10th Street, home of my first childhood memories. I recall the small living room with a door leading to a tiny outdoor porch, and I remember relatives visiting a couple of times. My first and most joyful memory occurred here.

My dad used a detached shed as a makeshift woodshop at the far end of the small backyard, just outside a lower-level door from the apartment. One day, my mom opened that door and pointed me toward my father, who was working on his latest project. Off I started across the green grass of the little yard towards the shed. Oh, the joy I felt as I quickly ran, my shooed feet pounding on the earth as much as two-year-old feet can pound. A distinct sense of watching myself run over to my father washed over me while I wore an enormous smile and laughed as I ran. It was that incredible feeling of joy that included a feeling in my face and the sound and feel of pounding my feet on the earth. I experienced it all and watched it from slightly outside my body. Joy carried me like the wind to my destination, where I marveled at what my dad worked on that day. The shed's dirt floor greeted me, and the smell of freshly painted plywood creation wafted through the air. As I watched, my dad worked on a cut-out figure of Scrooge McDuck, taller than me. He let me stay a while, and then, with a head pat, he pointed me back to my mom. Eventually secured to our bedroom wall, this playful wooden figure became a coat hanger for my older brother and me.

My dad's love for woodworking led him to conceive, develop, and create many wooden crafts and pieces of furniture throughout his life. Years later, tears came to my dad's eyes as I told him my remembrance of this joyful day.

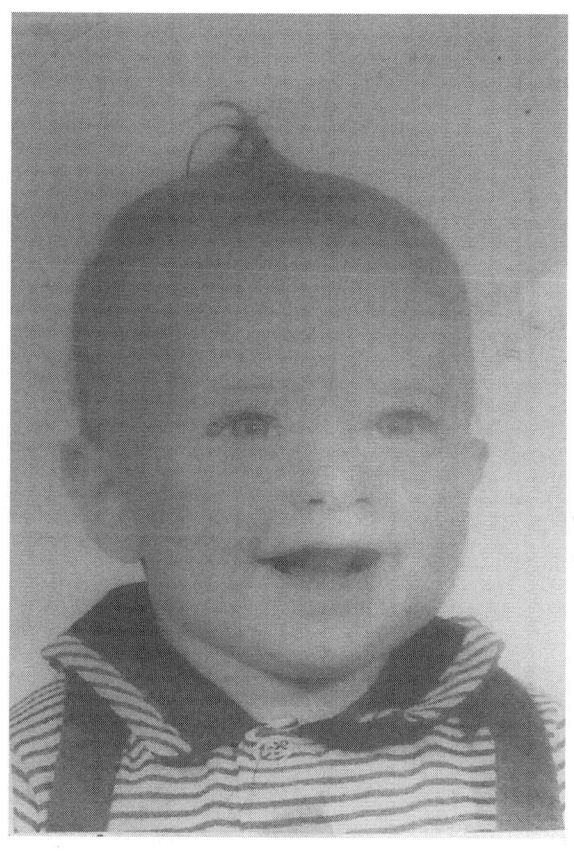

Figure 3 Bart, under age 1

My dad's first job in Weirton involved driving a tractor-trailer and delivering new and used mobile homes. With that connection, we soon moved into a small, used, red-and-white 2-bedroom trailer in the Pleasant Valley Trailer Court. The modest fenced-in yard easily accommodated two toddlers, as long as we avoided the dog droppings deposited by our aging cocker spaniel, Cookie. Located in the country outside Weirton's city limits, the small trailer park had graveled, nameless streets. The air in that part of Hancock County maintained a refreshing quality, as we rarely experienced the smoke and pollution from the larger-than-life Weirton Steel.

Figure 4 George, Jr, age three, on the left, and Bart (me), age two, on the right

My father's parents, Anna and Michael Balint, lived on Weir Avenue, one of the older streets in Weirton, just a stone's throw from the growing mill. As a preschooler, I went out into my grandparents' sooty front yard to survey the remarkable changes when another huge building or furnace rose in the not-so-distant skyline. The proximity of my grandparent's house to the mill also guaranteed that another coat of white paint, soon speckled sooty black, needed to be applied to the little wood fence around their tiny yard every spring.

I also remember many happy and exciting Easter egg hunts my brothers and I had at our grandparents' homes. During one of these, when I was not more than two years old, I learned the art of taking the easy path. My enthusiastic older brother and I were dressed in matching Easter suits that only a two- and three-year-old could wear without being teased, complete with hats. My mother took pride in wrapping the two of us in identical outfits, especially for holidays.

As we scrambled around my grandparents' yard searching for eggs, my brother took the lead but was not careful in keeping his unwieldy basket level. As his basket tipped, plastic eggs filled with small treats fell onto the ground, and I quickly realized I could follow him around, picking up the easy eggs he had dropped.

Figure 5 Bart's Easter presents at age one and a half.

Having birthdays one month apart, George and I celebrated on the same day for a few years. Several pictures showed a cake with half the icing in one color and the other half in a different color and age. This was standard procedure until I turned four and my brother five. On that day, my brother had a special birthday celebration all to himself. My heart sank when it hit me that it was my brother's special day, not mine. As my earliest memory of a tantrum, I started trembling and crying and quickly crawled under the nearest folding chair in the tiny living room of our trailer home. Overtaken with the pain of the event, I wailed in protest as I huddled under the chair.

"Why is it George's special day and not mine?" I screamed as I clutched the metal legs of the chair. From that moment, a life theme expressed itself: Why does someone else have happiness and not me? This theme of being shortchanged on happiness would take many forms in my adult life, such as "Why is Jesus the only son of God and I am not?"

My mom reached down and pulled me out from under the chair, promising me some cake. I felt separated, left out, and excluded for the first time. This is my first memory of being bribed with something sweet in exchange for less disruptive behavior.

Changes for the Worse

After a brief stint working in a tire retread shop, my dad landed a coveted full-time position at Weirton Steel. He started as an entry-level laborer, which consisted of all manner of hot, sweaty, filthy jobs. While this brought a definite pay increase, his job hours varied weekly as he cycled through daytime, afternoon, and midnight shifts. Rough on both of my parents, my father never adapted to the constantly rotating work hours. This left my mom in charge of keeping us young, playful boys quiet during daylight hours as my father tried to sleep before an afternoon or midnight shift.

With my younger brother Bruce's birth, three children and two adults now called our tiny trailer home. The trailer sat fifty feet from the slow-flowing water of King's Creek, the dividing line between the city of Weirton and the surrounding county. A small berm separated the trailers from the adventures along the banks of King's Creek, which constantly called to us. We played in a refuge of clear water, with countless climbing rocks, many types of fish, and abundant crawdads. The creek allowed us to escape our family's physically cramped and increasingly emotionally charged trailer. Whether summer or winter, we played by and in the stream many days a week, seeking our next escapade.

We left home in the morning with clean second-hand clothing and returned spattered in mud, dirt, and leaves at day's end. But what three boys wouldn't get dirty and wet if a creek with lots of minnows meandered just outside their front door? The numerous dams we constructed in the water were only temporary, lasting until the next heavy rain, but it didn't matter. My brothers and I laughed and had fun there, two things not found daily inside the trailer.

The graveled streets of the trailer park doubled as our football, basketball, and whiffle ball fields. We never egged houses, stole anything, or instigated fights. Still, we soon learned that even simple outdoor fun often resulted in punishment, delivering a clear message that enjoying ourselves in nature came at a cost. Perhaps disciplining came intermittently at first, but gradually, it appeared that misery always followed any laughter.

Sharing the same 6 x 8-foot bedroom, George slept on the top twin bunk and I on the bottom, while Bruce slept on a pullout mattress that fit under the lower bed during the day. As we started grade school, mornings became chaotic as George and I earnestly tried stepping over our youngest brother without waking him. This was an impossibility for a six- and seven-year-old, and Bruce screamed each time our movements jostled his bed.

This morning ritual of avoiding a sleeping younger brother became one of my earliest memories of failures for our young family. The situation quickly turned into a scream-fest, with my father yelling at us for not following instructions. I explained that avoiding the lowest bed was impossible; our little legs could not straddle Bruce's roll-out mattress. That may have been one of the last times I tried to explain myself to my parents, because it was like stepping into a minefield. A father on an ever-revolving shift schedule in a strenuous job at the steel mill (who might have just gone to bed after a long midnight shift), a three-year-old sleeping on the bottom day bed, and two young grade-schoolers trying to make their way across their younger sibling's bed without disturbing him were a recipe for disaster.

"You kids are trying to irritate your brother on purpose!" my father yelled as he stomped towards us from the kitchen just a few yards down the hallway. "Why can't you follow simple directions to avoid stepping on Bruce's bed when you get up?" he continued, his anger mounting, face contorting, arms tightening, and fists pounding on our closet door. With the small bedroom window still shaking from the reverberations of his voice, my father would huff off and grumble some instructions to my mom.

Even if we did something to perfection, my father's best positive reinforcement was a monotonous, disconnected "That's nice," said from a mind that was always elsewhere. Occasionally, the flat "That's nice" became a flat "That's different."

I gradually felt a disconnection from my parents as I became aware of their propensity to anger and inability to speak, not only to each other but also to their children, in any rational conversation. In addition, a suffocating, smoky wall separated us, characterized by the perpetually lit cigarette dangling from my father's pursed lips as he tried to smile sarcastically. The few times I remember him laughing were after he'd ridiculed someone or called them derogatory nicknames.

Neither of my parents cursed in front of my brothers and me, and I never heard a racist remark towards any of the black people in Weirton. However, I heard many offensive jokes about Polish and Italian people. My parents and extended family also thoroughly enjoyed poking fun at my brothers' and my physical features. My curly hair attracted particular ridicule since it curled more than anyone else's in the family. My father also laughingly entertained himself by never calling me by my real name. He always called me Bret or Bert, and I can say that I hated the fact that my dad never really saw me. Mom didn't chain-smoke like my dad, but she contributed to the obnoxious smoke inside our family car as we drove to outings with the obligatory rolled-up windows. She always had a drink in one hand and a cigarette in the other at all family gatherings.

School: Both Haven and Dividing Line

I remember when my older brother attended kindergarten, and I visited his classroom when we dropped him off on his first day. It was exciting to see—shelves filled with colored paper, little chairs at each table, and marvelous pictures and drawings on the walls. I could also feel his teacher's gentle and caring presence. I couldn't wait for the day I would go to this fantastic place. Sadly, that day never happened. With our one-car family and finances so stretched, kindergarten was out of the question when I was old enough to attend. I remember my disappointment when my mom told me I would not participate in kindergarten. I may not have cried or wailed, but the weight of those words settled into my chest and shoulders as I stored them away in my little body.

When I reached the age of six, I headed off to first grade. My mom walked George and me to the bus stop at the top of our short trailer park road, and Bus 33 arrived to pick us up—driven by Homer, my bus driver for the next five years. Excitement filled the air. My preoccupation was so high that I didn't even say goodbye to my mom. As we arrived at the school after a 40-minute bus ride, I grew frightened as I stepped off the bus and watched my brother walk away to his classroom. Many strangers suddenly filled the space. Most of the kids were from local neighborhoods and stood in small groups excitedly chatting with one another. I knew no one. My teacher, however, pinned a small piece of paper on my coat that said "Bus 33." A thought tinged with fear went through my mind: *Hopefully, this means someone cares enough to ensure I get home.* Symbolically, life attached characteristics to me, all in an effort to help give me an identity.

After entering the main doors at Broadview Elementary, I slowly walked down the long hallway toward the 1st-grade classroom. I don't remember assigned seats, but my gaze immediately fell upon Sheila, another 1st grader already seated on the far side of the room near the windows. For what seemed like an eternity, I looked at her, unaware of any of the other children. The hustle and bustle of a new school year summoned me back into the full activity of the classroom. While Sheila and I attended the same schools for the next twelve years, I rarely saw her, and we never spoke to each other. It would take fifty-seven years before I reencountered her.

I liked Miss Volgarakis, my first-grade teacher. Since I didn't know how to read, Ms. Volgarakis introduced me to the *Tip and*

Mitten books on the first day of school. Quickly, reading became second nature. At the end of the school day, we all lined up in the parking lot outside our respective buses. Absorbed about why so many students left the school grounds before me, I learned of the "walkers." I thought the walkers had many advantages over us kids who rode Bus 33 beyond the boundary dividing Weirton from the countryside. The walkers arrived at their homes of bricks and shingled roofs in just a few minutes after walking through one of the finer neighborhoods in town. Oh, to be a walker, walking to a big house in a fancy neighborhood! The thought both tantalized and saddened me. From that first day at school, I concluded that every other kid had more friends, came from a happier, more loving family, and probably didn't have to crawl over their younger brother's bed, trying not to disturb the giant monster masquerading as their father. Resentments grew as the differences between my family and others became apparent.

Only a few families with children my age lived in the trailer park. Most came for a year or so, and just as I got to know the kids, their parents moved on to a different job or home. Through grade school, I got to know some kids who lived across King's Creek in the newly paved streets of Pleasant Valley Estates, where the houses were huge, expensive, and out of reach for families like ours. One of these children was John, and we became good friends. I was even permitted to visit his home several times to prepare for some school projects. Sadly, he and his family eventually moved, and I felt a sense of aloneness in my chest with his absence.

At first, the dividing line between our trailer park and the Pleasant Valley Estates didn't mean much to me, but as time passed, "this side of the creek" and "that side of the creek" became one of those resentments reflecting my perceived economic disparity. Many of my classmates lived on that side of the creek, and I was too ashamed to invite them to our trailer.

I especially loved third grade because of my teacher, Mrs. Karpinski, a bright spot in my life. Kind and caring, her math instructions lit up my young mind. Math came naturally to me, and I marveled at how simple addition and subtraction could be expressed through multiplication and division.

I think now that Mrs. Karpinski saw something special in me. "Bart, do you know how to play chess?" she asked me one day.

"No, ma'am, I don't," I answered, shy about admitting that while I had heard of the game, I had never touched a chess piece.

"Would you like to learn?" she continued.

"Yes, please, Mrs. Karpinski," I answered, smiling a little.

"All right then, during our daily lunch hour, let's meet at this table. We'll explore chess together."

For months, she took time out of her lunch hour to sit with me and teach me how to play a game that required planning and strategy. Sitting with her caring attention while we played chess became a haven of calm and wonder for me. I remember the happiness that silently played in my heart as I moved chess pieces around the board. And at those lunch games with Mrs. Karpinski, I remembered the joy I felt as I ran across the yard as a 2-year-old to see my father's woodworking!

Trouble at Home

Meanwhile, cyclical upheavals filled our trailer home. Physical punishment became common as I entered grade school, as my father regularly disciplined us for even the slightest transgressions. Mom verbally reprimanded us early on, but gradually, her tack changed from personal intervention to a declaration of, "Just wait 'til your father comes home!" And while my brothers and I would have long forgotten our earlier misbehavior, my mom quickly recounted the situation to my dad. Upon hearing this, my dad immediately proclaimed my brothers and me guilty. We were given no chance to explain, as any justification amplified my father's anger to the boiling point. However, it was a catch-22 because if you didn't at least make some feeble attempt at an explanation, my father's anger rose as well. It didn't matter either way. My father's rage and abusive actions regarding punishment were pre-determined.

"Why did this happen?" my dad would scream, and the whole trailer would shake as his voice rose in volume. My mom would stare into the distance, get up, and walk out of the room, leaving her three young kids to face their dad alone.

My brother George occasionally would sputter, "Because...," and my dad would immediately cut him off, "Because is NOT a reason!"

The trembling tension in the room became ever more palpable, and at this point, while I may not have been the direct target of this interrogation, I would feel fear rising through my entire body. I'd hear the words in my head, "*Do not respond. Do not dare move or show any emotion. Do not help your brother. Do not get yourself further into this mess.*"

By this point, it was already too late. I imagine that the whole trailer park knew it was too late. My father's deeply held fear, anger, and disgust were about to unload on this trio of young humans who could not fight back. While my dad interrogated one brother, he always punished all three. At this point, my mind tried to make sense of this. There was none to be found. A ball of thoughts churned in my head, and deep sadness lay underneath it.

The beatings went on for years, sometimes every couple of weeks. Frankly, they mostly blur together in my memory now, but one stands out.

I was about seven years old and had no idea what we three boys had done that called for punishment. Regardless, my mom told us earlier in the day that a spanking was imminent when my father came home. Hours passed, and the situation lightened as I hoped our pending whippings were forgotten. Sadly, the need for punishment was something my parents never forgot.

Before learning of our alleged disobedience, my father came home in his typical dark mood and lit his usual foul-smelling cigarette. Grumbling in the next room and exaggerated footfalls warned the rest of us of his already aggravated presence. He stomped around the house and threw down his jacket and keys. His sulking, angry silence cast a heaviness over the entire trailer. My father had just worked another rigorous shift in the hot, polluted, noisy steel mill that gave our family at least a subsistence-level existence. Most of the time, my father distanced himself from us kids, and when he did approach us, he often did so out of anger.

"Your boys purposely ignored me today," my mom said in her usual way, deflecting my dad's anger from herself and onto my brothers and me. Dramatic exaggeration dripped from her every word.

"I had to call them twice before they agreed to come in for lunch. I sent them outside in clean clothes, and their clothes were filthy when they returned to eat! I've told them a million times not to play in the creek!" she fumed.

She only stopped ranting upon recognizing the awakening of my father's wrath. I saw it, too. His eyes narrowed to pinpoints, first on her and then on us children. The seriousness and tension in his facial muscles were entirely evident, as I had seen them countless times before. His tightly clenched fists were raised as if being pulled into some street brawl with another angry grownup.

We three children sat silently on the small, worn couch in the dark-paneled living room of our trailer home, shaking, full of dread, eyes riveted on the floor. I did not feel guilty, as the offense was minimal, but I feared the pending beating. I hated that feeling of doom, trembling, and fear coursing through my body. I hated that I could not even imagine some fairy tale ending to the whole drama. And before my father said anything, I felt apprehension welling in my eyes. Having played it out many times before, we all knew how the situation would go. As soon as any of our eyes showed that first tear, my father would holler, "You want something to cry about? I'll give you something to cry about!" I lost count of the times I heard that.

"This is going to hurt me more than it is going to hurt you!" bellowed my dad, now almost entirely out of control and maniacal, as he reached for the wooden paddle that carried the obnoxious saying, "For the cute little deer with the bear behind." Every word from his mouth was emphasized to induce maximum fear in my brothers and me. Neither his yelling nor the actions that followed made any sense to me.

"Pull down your pants and bend over!" he demanded, glaring at me with fire in his eyes.

Whoosh-Crack! This time, I remember writhing with intense pain and crying while he thrashed me on the rear. The louder my crying became, the more chaotic and overtaken my dad became. Whoosh-Crack!

"You want something to _really_ cry about?" my father screamed. Whoosh-CRACK!

I don't remember what I said in response to his threatening rant, but I felt something I had never felt before with the next few swings of that paddle. Waves of sensations progressed from my head down to my toes, and I felt a clenching like a fist inside my chest and abdomen. This seemed to move inwardly from my skin into deeper areas I had not felt before. In the next moment, I became emotionally and physically numb. I now realize I witnessed and felt a significant bodily contraction accompanied by a withdrawal from all other physical sensations. With each wave of contraction, I withdrew into deeper and deeper places inside myself as I felt the physical pain less and less. Unlike any other time before, with each paddle swing, I felt the progression of the movement of "me" into my chest and abdomen. I decided the outside world was insane and that little, if any, of what I saw out there would ever be understandable.

It was as if my packet of joyful being had been dropped into a bottomless well, gone forever.

Events passed in slow motion, and the physical punishment no longer hurt. I no longer heard my father screaming at this point, and thoughts quieted in my mind. Complete numbness took over.

I realized my dad could beat me all he wanted, but I wouldn't feel it any longer. I stopped crying.

The beating continued for a few more hits, but I felt a profound change within me. I knew that no matter what physical punishment he gave me, I could almost block it entirely. A large part of my playfulness was also beaten into submission that day, but at the same time, I experienced clarity in my mind. While my mistrust of the outside world grew with each beating I endured, this particular beating cemented an inner distrust combined with a touch of contempt.

It marked a huge turning point in how I felt and dealt with my family and our relationships. I still felt things physically, but there was now a separation between the physical aspects of my emotions and the mental aspects. It was as if I had withdrawn out of my body and into my head, where I found safety and security for the next 40 years, even if the tradeoff turned out to be an attitude of negativity towards everyone. I still ruminated on all my fearful thoughts like anyone else, but the physical part of my humanness, the felt experience of fears (and of joys), was almost gone. It was as if I had emotionally flatlined.

Soon, family gatherings became increasingly irritating and painful. I envied other relatives who, unlike us, lived in regular houses. They laughed more and appeared happier because they didn't live in a trailer, and their fathers didn't beat them with wooden paddles. I also detested the "Smile for the camera!" command before Christmas family pictures. I resisted this pretense of happiness until someone pointed to me and forced me to oblige.

I still enjoyed being around some family members, especially my mom's brother and father—both named George! However, I held myself back, not giving even them my full attention and trust. If any love resided inside me, I knew it was too dangerous to find.

Physical abuse occurred at any time, even in the most innocent settings. For example, one time, I was looking forward to attending Scout camp the following summer. My maternal grandfather, a Scoutmaster years before, visited our trailer. I innocently asked him if he had any extra footlockers I could use at camp. I don't even remember what he said, but my question to my grandfather raised all sorts of insecurities and rage in my dad. As soon as my grandfather left, my dad angrily demanded my presence before him.

"Why were you even talking to your grandfather about Scout camp?" My father raged.

"I only asked him about his old footlocker," I said, shocked by this sudden, furious reaction. "I saw one in his basement the last time we visited his house."

"Why did you ask him about borrowing a footlocker when I specifically told you I would build you one?" my father screamed.

I saw his eyes narrow and his fists clench in anger, as if he wanted to destroy something. Then he hauled off on me and landed his fist on my face. This confrontation took me by surprise, as I felt a sharp, stinging pain from my father's clenched hand on my right cheek. I didn't remember any promise of my father making me a footlocker. Perhaps he'd thought of something I said to my older brother. After only a few pleasant moments with my grandfather, this sudden outburst destroyed everything—as if God had sent a lightning bolt from the sky.

I immediately ran back to the tiny, three-mattress bedroom and slammed the door, burying my face in the pillows, crying more in shock than from pain. Soon, my mom came to the bedroom and apologized for what happened—the only time she ever admitted my father might be wrong. My face was red and swollen, and immediately, my mom announced that I wouldn't be going to school the next day because I was "ill." She left the room for a few minutes and returned with a model tank kit she said she had been saving. I only felt contempt for both of my parents as my mom handed me this worthless plastic consolation prize. Any attempt at soothing me fell flat, and without my father returning to apologize, material gifts like this model only reaffirmed my growing distrust of and disgust with the outer world. After this incident, I viewed Scouts and model building adversely, two activities I associated with my dad. While I still went through the motions, both became chores and something else I was expected to do. I continued to be shown that any fun, happiness, interest, or joy only brought painful physical and emotional punishment that needed neither justification nor explanation. Being punched in the face by my dad further pushed me towards disconnection from myself and others—one more excuse to retreat into my head and my thoughts.

CHAPTER 3
CLENCHING MY FISTS TIGHTER THAN EVER BEFORE

In fourth grade, my friend David and I started drawing our favorite comic book characters at the lunch table, and I found a hero I could relate to—the Marvel comic superhero Iron Man. Iron Man became my idol and mental companion. He was a human with extraordinary intellect, protected by an impervious metallic suit he designed and built himself. He outfitted it with a wide array of defensive and offensive weapons, a manufactured wall of near-perfect impenetrability. The Iron Man persona seamlessly melded with my nine-year-old psyche, valiantly shielding me from the emotional and physical onslaught swirling within and around me. I often imagined myself in that iron costume as I woke up each morning.

Sometimes, a loud argument concerning money had already commenced in the kitchen when I got out of bed. Paycheck-to-paycheck explosive shouting matches occurred between my parents on schedule nearly every two weeks. The money always ran out a few days before my father's next paycheck. Even though he was never willing to take over the finances, my dad always accused my mom of deliberate mismanagement when the funds fell short.

My mom bought a cake to mark my brother George's First Holy Communion. But the celebration never started as my dad angrily confronted her about spending money on a stupid cake rather than cigarettes. And with that yelling, my brothers and I were served another slice of guilt instead of feasting on the commemorative cake. My brother absorbed most of the shame that permeated the trailer that day, and it took him years to realize he didn't need to carry the burden of his parents' arguments any further. The implication of guilt trickled down to me as well. Verbal abuse flew back and forth in front of the whole family, all in the name of not having enough money to feed my father's addiction. These kinds of money arguments increased my embarrassment around my parents. One good thing emerged from this situation—I learned that my older brother vowed never to smoke after this incident!

Not only did my siblings and I face regular physical abuse, but also a constant dismissal of any point of view that didn't correspond with my parents' opinions. "Just who the hell do you think you are?" they often yelled when I questioned their reasoning or seeming lack of sense. This rhetorical question, which they never really wanted us to answer, was really a command to shut up. It signaled the end of any give-and-take, leaving me feeling dismissed and disregarded. Angrily questioning anything he disagreed with, my father never opened for reflection or pause. My parents weren't looking for any conversation with their children—they wanted us to be silent and compliant, punching bags. It worked; we usually shut up, not offering our perspectives, as a response invited verbal or physical punishment.

While a wealth of violence and criticism existed, there was little positive modeling or guidance. My mom was jealous of people who had things she didn't, especially relatives with more self-confidence or material possessions. She also struggled with addictions and weight; I was ashamed of her failings. Neither she nor my father knew how to talk with children neither about growing into adults nor about the issues young men face in relationships with females (or anything else). The best dating advice my mother could come up with stated that I was forbidden from connecting with girls or women my age, as those females would only lead me "to a life of misery and ruin." I always wondered if these were her feelings and thoughts on her life. She told me it was my job to become a doctor, make lots of money, and care for *her* until she died. I hated these one-sided conversations as I felt guilt pile on top of my disgust.

A Few Brighter Spots

My mom taught me how to drive. While my dad lacked patience, my mom was very different in that regard. And for that, I am thankful. It started because, at age fourteen, I occasionally helped my mom load, unload, and fold the newspapers she delivered for extra money.

One day, she said, "Hey, Bart. With nice weather and dry roads, it's a perfect time for you to learn to drive a clutch car. Would you like to try?"

Taken back for a split second, I immediately said, "Drive? Of course, I would!"

We switched places, and my mom helped me adjust the driver's seat in her sky-blue Volkswagen Beetle so I could reach the clutch, brake, and gas pedals.

"Now, push in the clutch with your left foot, and then place the car into first gear," she instructed. "Keep the parking brake on for now as you learn to do this."

Her route took her on the back roads of Hancock County, way beyond our trailer park. Very little traffic traversed those roads;

on this occasion, my mom stopped in someone's lane with an uphill incline.

"Left hand on the steering wheel. Your left foot with the clutch fully depressed," she said. "Put the stick shift in first gear. Right hand on the parking brake, ready to click the release button."

"Now, put your right foot on the gas."

The engine roared to life as I excitedly stomped on the pedal.

"Not too much gas. Just enough to keep the engine going. Now, let out on the ..."

The car lurched forward, and the engine quickly stalled.

"Yes. That was a bit too fast. Go a bit slower with the clutch next time, and don't forget to let off the parking brake as the engine starts to connect with the transmission."

In this instance, my mom's patience and calm instructions helped make the entire situation fun. Sure, it took a few trips out into the country, but mastering one more machine convinced me I was claiming more control over life.

My dad did get us started riding a motorcycle. He scraped enough money together to buy us boys an underpowered mini-bike. It only had a centrifugal clutch gearbox, but we found delight and cutting-edge freedom while riding on it. Despite all the fun I had on this mini-bike, I noticed I continuously compared our bike with the three-geared, regular clutch Honda mini-bikes owned by a few friends who lived outside the trailer park. Later in high school, I purchased a small Suzuki motorcycle to get me back and forth to school.

My older brother started playing trumpet in the junior high school band, so I thought I'd try the saxophone. That didn't last long, as the instrument rental costs increased quickly. Soon, my mom picked me up an entry-level guitar and paid for a few months of guitar lessons. The lessons ended when my teacher unexpectedly landed a more lucrative steel mill job. Though I picked up a few bad habits when teaching myself, plucking the strings eventually took on a life of its own. Through many passages, I didn't need to think about the notes my fingers played.

My father also piqued my interest in scuba diving. His older brother, Mike, started a pool construction company and needed someone with an underwater breathing apparatus to help clean the pools. He and my dad rented one, and soon, we all learned beginner scuba 101. My dad even took us out to a nearby lake to try out this device, opening up part of an underwater world that, later in life, I would rather enjoy.

Relationships and Shutting Down

I had crushes on several girls in high school, including Layla. While I knew her distantly, it wasn't until she came down with mononucleosis and needed help carrying her books from class to class that something sparked between us. I offered my services and began carrying her books. Pretty, intelligent, and funny, I noticed in her the first voice that ever entranced me. She knew I played some guitar and asked if I wanted to join a 4-H acoustic band. I eagerly agreed.

We were both sixteen and going from 10th grade into 11th when we agreed to meet at an old diner in New Cumberland, West Virginia, just up the Ohio River from Weirton, for my first taste of fried onion rings with ketchup. We then went to one of the latest movies to hit the screen, *Jaws*. Afterward, we were both a bit rattled, and I quickly concluded that horror films might not be the best movies for young dating couples.

We spent most of our time together at Layla's house, about ten minutes from the trailer court. One day, I had my first real kiss while walking with Layla in her backyard. Delightfully lost during this encounter, I felt surprise, elation, and wonder, all with a splash of guilt. As the kiss ended, I heard a maternal voice warning me of severe consequences.

For months, I snuck in telephone calls on evenings and weekends to hear Layla's voice. After an evening's visit to her home, I raced along back county roads in a calculated effort to avoid violating my parent's strict curfew.

Unfortunately, Mom openly disdained Layla's mother. My mom incoherently retold her yarn that they had disliked each other since attending the same high school 20 years prior. I didn't know the particulars of those ancient interactions, but my mom carried them with her for years. Mom said, "You are never to see Layla again, as her mom pissed me off in high school." It never made any sense to me—one more impossible situation where any constructive conversation was immediately crushed under anger, fear, and misunderstanding. I suspected my mom would find some excuse to find fault in anyone I dated.

Gradually, Mom caught on to the frequency of my calls with Layla and did her best indignant child routine to end that relationship. She started screaming at me every time I called or took a phone call from Layla. Finally, I couldn't take my mother's constant bullying. Instead of fighting back, however, I caved. Layla and I had a minor disagreement one evening, and I used that as an excuse to end the relationship. I shut down our fledgling romance with little conscious thought and no explanation to Layla. I went deep into my seclusion hole, just like so many times with other relationships. I blocked out my feelings for Layla behind some iron wall that I definitely felt and could even describe if someone ever asked. No one ever did. I could never allow myself to deal with the discomfort of having a mother with overwhelming jealousy issues and the terrible pain of breaking up with someone I liked.

When I was the one who broke off a relationship, it was as simple as turning off a light switch. One second, I held good feelings toward someone and the next, I would be as literally cold and disconnected as a dead lightbulb. Of course, if the *other* person cut off our connection, I ruminated endlessly on how that stupid, inconsiderate person had wronged me. I never hesitated to create some incoherent, pain-driven response. In this situation, and with many others, I lacked interpersonal relating skills. Sadly, I had no role models for conflict resolution, as the adults in my life could never get past their own pain stories, let alone see any other possible points of view.

I also abruptly ended relationships in multiple workplaces. When I had trouble at a job, I easily walked out and never looked back, believing that the iron box closing around my heart protected me. For instance, lifeguarding at the local pool gave me work for several summers in high school. At one dollar an hour, the paycheck did not inspire any employee loyalty in me. Right in the middle of one of the busiest weeks of the second summer, I landed another job at a bowling alley that paid three dollars an hour. Circling the troops and cutting off any feelings despite the pleas of the pool manager, I gave 24-hour notice at the pool and walked away without thought of responsibility.

As my parents' marriage issues continued in a recurrent pattern, I shared less and less with them about my social interactions, school activities, or any anecdotes from my day-to-day life. Thankfully, they rarely, if ever, asked. The last thing I remember Mom asking about concerned my ninth-grade French class.

"Bert, tell us some of the French you're learning," my mom prodded. My defenses entered full alert mode whenever my parents addressed me as Bert.

What? Since when have they ever asked about school, or anything for that matter? I heard in my head. After trying to escape the situation, I finally said, "Je n'aime pas les bean soupe! That means," I continued, "I do not like bean soup." And I frowned at her.

Her face fell in disappointment, and she did not achieve the ridicule she intended. Two points for Bert. After all, I did hate it when my mom made bean soup, and I had no qualms telling her that in as many languages as I knew.

The less we talked and interacted, the better. I tried to ignore the continual dysfunction, but the constant yelling and fist-pounding reverberated throughout our home's thin walls. Occasionally, the yelling carried outside, and one evening, I returned from my part-time work to find my father and mother in a screaming match on the side porch. My father had just raised his fist, and I recognized that fist as the very one that had once punched me. His eyes said he was about to pummel my mother. I yelled, "Hey!!! What's going on here?" They stopped, turned toward me, and then walked away from each other. Again, one more incident, never to be discussed or even acknowledged.

Creating My Inner Dialogue

During those years, numerous repetitive phrases started cycling through my mind. Concerning my parents, I heard the thought: They beat my happiness out of me. When I saw anyone else having fun, this phrase changed to: They stole my happiness from me. It didn't matter who they were; I usually didn't even know them. Angry and accusing thoughts overwhelmed me, and jealousy arose at the slightest demonstration of their happiness. I immediately saw them as enemies.

Why is everyone always trying to take something from me? I often heard it in my head. This arose when classmates were celebrated for their social, academic, or sports achievements. I especially felt disgusted and hateful towards any couples displaying affection.

Such a fake, I'd think. *How dare they display such disregard for my inner pain?*

Outwardly, I usually made some attempt to cover my contempt, but I felt my pursed eyebrows displaying my inner dialogue. The other person's happiness, success, or laughter obviously came at my expense, either directly or indirectly. And I had every right and even a distorted responsibility to respond to it, even if that response came out in a twisted, passive-aggressive manner.

One very threatening thought that floored me was when I heard a voice announcing that joy would be punished by obliteration.

Once, while enjoying something at home, my mother yelled for me to stop and attend to her wishes. Irritation surged through my neck and radiated around my head like a helmet, quickly becoming a full-face expression of wrath—my eyes closed to stealthy-looking slits, and my eyebrows quickly squeezed together. Even more rapidly, my fists clenched.

"Put this up on the door, Bert." Mom first asked and then demanded, "Put this up *now*!" She stepped smack on a landmine with that command since she had just finished complaining about me going out on a date.

"Right now?" came the words from my mouth, *"I'm in the middle of playing Pong, for Christ's sake! I deserve some quiet time to myself before I head off to work. Geez!"*

"Yes!!! Right now. I'll show you where I want it."

I watched her point to a spot on the living room side of my parents' bedroom door.

A grotesque heap of emotional baggage surfaced instantly as I approached the door. I hated going in there. For years, we three children had had the duty and punishment of going through that doorway and waking my dad from his "snore-orama," unequaled in the modern world. Each time my turn arrived, it felt like being served up as the freshly slaughtered calf in the daily religious spectacle called "Go Wake Your Father and Tell Him It's Time for Work."

Each time, I read my death sentence on the door and realized I had no option.

"Dad, it's time to get up and get ready for work." I'd say softly, hoping the first and least obtrusive announcement would be met with a "Sure, son, thanks so much."

But instead, my dad would turn from side to side, struggling with his pillow. Soon came the perfunctory low grumbling "Grrrrrrh!" that rivaled any grizzly protecting its young.

"Ahgggggggr, what the ahrgggggggagrr!" he'd exclaim.

"Mom sent me in here. It's time to get up for work," I'd say, noticing a little pride that I'd added that this was all my mother's fault.

"Ahgggrrrrggrrr," came the next semi-vocalization, even more threatening than the first.

I then felt confused. *Why do we do this every single day? He knows he has to get up for work, but he acts like it's the first time his alarm clock has ever rung.*

Damn! Why do I have to be here? I'd think.

Bringing me back to this hell hole of reality, "I want a nail placed in this door so I can put that knickknack right here!" Mom yelled. "What? You don't want to do this simple thing for me?" Ironically, the knickknack was a little sign that said something like "Peace" or "Love." *Yeah, right.*

"No, I don't," I replied. "Why couldn't you just put that nail there?" And I wanted to add, *why don't you ask Dad to do that?*

"All right. Move out of the way," I finally grumbled back, not reaching the lower cavernous tones that Dad naturally growled.

As I lined up the nail over the specified spot on the brown plywood, I took the hammer in my right hand.

Then I heard a male voice in my mind, just as loud as any everyday conversation. Sternly and convincingly, the voice said,

God will allow you to experience joy for a fraction of a second, and then He will obliterate you for the fun of it.

I stopped, hammer poised in the air. *What? Who was that? Where was that?*

I heard it one more time, slightly differently: God will allow me to experience joy for a split second, and ***then he will cruelly take it away from me.***

I suddenly felt some twisted confirmation: *Yes, God does want to obliterate me.*

A decision formed. *I should never allow myself to feel any joy; that is certain. If I do, I will be obliterated.*

Not wanting to be eliminated, I knew I must never allow joy to surface. And so, I held back celebration about anything. External celebrations without prior approval weren't welcome in my family, so that wasn't a big deal. Soon, however, I didn't allow myself any good confirmatory feelings, inward or outward. After a while, I had so buried my sense of innate happiness that I didn't have to pretend it wasn't there anymore.

Disappointment lurked around the corner whenever I experienced happiness, like over a new bike tire or getting a date with a young woman I liked. Happiness may not have ended in annihilation, but it ended for some stupid reason, such as my dad hauling off and hitting me after a joyful time with my grandfather, my mom screaming incessantly over the part-time work I chose, or the persistent feeling that I never did anything right.

I repeatedly learned that misery soon followed any happiness.

The critical judge in my head always found ways to make joyful experiences seem meaningless. It also sent me into circular thoughts, scheming to regain the joy that had been stolen.

Figure 6 shows the Balint family males. I am in the middle back row, and my father is in the back row, far right.

I always hoped that things would be different. I wished I wouldn't awaken to either of my parents already smoking cigarettes in the trailer. Their smoking continued.

I repeatedly hoped my parents would see their insanity and stop fighting over money every two weeks. It persisted.

I desperately hoped my father would come and apologize for his stupid comedy around never calling me by my proper name. He never apologized, and the name-calling continued even into my forties.

I hoped, again and again, that the many embarrassing aspects of living in a trailer park would change and that perhaps we would move to a real house. Things never changed.

Since my achievements in academics and Scouts thus far only evoked a "That's nice" from my dad, some of me still longed to please him and gain his approval. My mind searched for any endeavor that might accomplish this. Anything. I wanted to hear, "I am proud of your accomplishments, Bart!" The emerging desire pointed toward the Air Force and learning to fly planes. While my dad was a specialized mechanic when he served, I sensed that if one of his children learned to fly, my dad might even break through his stone wall of never letting his appreciation show.

But just like many things, that was not going to happen. In ninth grade, I went to an optometrist for a recommended well-check documenting perfect vision in both eyes. The day after this visit, I woke to searing pain, redness, light sensitivity, and discharge in my right eye. This soon became a diagnosis of a topical viral infection of my right cornea, which caused a localized deformation and permanently left me with 20/80 vision in that eye. Topical drops, eye patches, and no swimming for two weeks preceded the astigmatism that followed. I didn't have the viral infection before visiting the optometrist, but I certainly did afterward. I knew that flying in the Air Force would not be my future. I was crushed.

This hopeless hope—that someone or something outside of me would change and allow me to be happy—seemed to be what I pinned my contentment on, and it was a losing game of continual disappointment. I practiced this ritual repeatedly, but each time, the actions or inactions of others let me down. This youthful hope gradually transformed into its opposite. The innocence initially found in that hope became a tarnished narrative that always expected something negative, and through that, I fostered cynicism. It gradually became an entrenched, rigid, and recurring part of my thought stream. The hopelessness attracted a new layer that demanded that I separate myself from others in one way or another. Either through an intellectual superiority or a jealous rage, I arrived at the immovable, futile point of view that things would never really change.

Brief Brushes with Something More

Another casualty of living such an emotionally thwarted childhood is that I was punished for and repeatedly felt discouraged from developing a playful connection with nature, even though our family camped regularly. Each beating I endured affected my fleeting harmony with the natural world. All the fear and misery of life in our trailer followed me into the wilderness, so I couldn't fully appreciate what nature or life had to offer. I distrusted anything that stirred in me a sense of beauty, appreciation, uniqueness, or respect, including the great outdoors. While I had once been a small, enthusiastic boy in love with playing in the creek, it became routine to confine myself emotionally and only to experience nature as something separate from me. And sure, I could go for a casual hike into the woods, but I felt I'd better not lose myself in the wonders that might unexpectedly find me there.

Each summer during my dad's extended vacation, we loaded up the station wagon, attached a pop-up camper to the hitch, and headed just east of Pittsburgh to a small Pennsylvania state park called Shawnee State Park. On the way, we stopped at a small store in Bedford, PA, and we three boys were allowed to buy one comic book apiece. This was a special event, as we purchased comics at no other time during the year except if we earned a few bucks cutting the trailer park grass lots. At the state park, the campsites were private, shaded, and quiet, and there was a sandy beach, but the black-biting flies took a lot of the fun out of beach time.

For three summer trips in a row, I experienced a curiosity while sitting in the back seat, taking in the old country music my dad played on an eight-track tape as we traversed Route 40 into rural Pennsylvania. For a split second, I watched everything happening inside and outside the car from a perspective different than my day-to-day perspective. I found my mind silent as I watched from a position just slightly outside the body and somewhat distinct from my usual thoughts. Mesmerizingly quiet, untouched by the banter of the others in the car, a feeling of the perfection of everything washed over me. Not a thing was out of place.

All too soon, however, I felt a slight tremble and a voice that said, *this is too dangerous, being out here just watching. You are defenseless. Put an end to this!*

And with that, I felt a jump back into my body, and the perspective changed. Back as quickly as they had gone were all the thoughts of danger, punishment, and guilt of being somewhere I should not be.

I had no one I could trust with this experience, and I had no idea what it all meant. Rather than look further at these episodes of extreme peace, I shut them down, just like I eventually shut down that remembrance that I was joyful as a small child. For whatever reason, the voices in my head convinced me that my only safety lay in the isolated world I constructed.

Godzilla-Sized Guilt

While my family didn't corner the market on guilt, it was a defining feature of my childhood. From non-religious events to Catholic Church-related indoctrination, the production and maintenance of guilt permeated everything. This guilt felt like a dark, lurking presence: a threatening, religious dogma that non-believers or non-repenting churchgoers would be forever separated from God and their loved ones upon death. Declared a sinner, church doctrine maintained my eternal shortcomings in the eyes of God. Around every corner lay a reminder that I was not good enough, would never be good enough, and deserved the punishment of God despite all my begging and praying.

I could not even relieve the guilt when going to confession every other month in the Catholic Church.

I entered the confessional booth as discreetly and quietly as I could. The sliding divider that symbolically separated me from God and his emissary opened, revealing a latticework barrier that kept us both unrecognizable to the other. That was my cue to begin.

"Bless me, Father, for I have sinned," I'd say, as instructed by the nuns during Saturday catechism classes.

"Yes, my son. Tell me how you have sinned against God and his creations," the priest responded.

What? Sinned against God? I heard it in my mind once. *I am only here because the Catholic ritual says I must go to confession to receive communion.*

And immediately, I drew a blank. Frankly, I had been pretty good all month and had nothing to confess. Many times, I also experienced a blank space in my chest.

"Go ahead, my son. Tell me how you have disrespected your elders, family, or brothers," the priest prodded me.

Gosh, I got to get this over with already! I thought. *I must confess to something; otherwise, I will never get out of here!*

Just make something up! Screamed the voice in my head.

Usually, at this point, I blurted out a lie. "OK, well. My brother made me so mad one day that I hit him."

Lying in confession just to get it over with only brought on more guilt. Not having any sins to confess was just as blasphemous.

"I understand," said the priest, who knew I was just making something up. "Go and say three Hail Marys, and be sure never to lie again."

The Catholic dogma said I was a sinner no matter what I did. For years, nuns taught me that my "given nature offended God."

Family gatherings heaped a whopping dose of guilt and shame on everyone. I certainly felt unlucky and ashamed to have my family as my family; most of my extended family had intolerable characteristics (in my opinion), so I avoided them whenever possible. However, many family events were mandatory to attend. These seemingly endless family get-togethers always had photos I didn't want to participate in or celebrate, and this wasn't a passing teen aversion that resolved when I transitioned into adulthood. I made it all into much more than that.

All family events inevitably included some form of guilt. How could the family's matriarchs keep things together and justify their attacks on everyone else? Even with the most uncomplicated visits, I'd hear from one relative or another, "Why haven't you called or visited before now?"

But I'm standing right in front of you now! Doesn't that count for something? I'd hear myself shout back in my head while trying to pull off an insincere smile.

Not only did this produce guilt and shame for what I did or didn't do, but it also pointed out that even being there at that moment never sufficed. In the future, I'd better feel the full extent of any guilt and let that guilt guide my decisions.

The guilt felt like a colossal lead stone chained to my heart, a constant dark presence that God or any adult could see at any time, ready to be summoned to shut down any glimmer of relaxation or joy.

Coincidentally with all this heavy religious dogma, the Japanese monster, Godzilla, arose in my frequent early childhood dreams as a significant symbol of guilt and shame for me. Bedtime was usually 8 PM, but gradually, our parents allowed us to stay up late on Saturday nights to watch Chilly Billy's *Chiller Theatre*. Chilly Billy featured various monster movies and performed silly skits during commercial breaks. One late Saturday, my brothers and I watched the Americanized version of *Godzilla* featuring Raymond Burr. Godzilla searched the entire world and always found whomever he wanted to destroy with his radioactive breath.

A recurring dream:

I find myself in a valley surrounded by mountains, and often, I am just outside a cave entrance. I feel dread and doom, and I know something or someone is looking for me. Suddenly, the figure of Godzilla comes peering up over the mountains. As he scans from left to right and back again, his eyes pretend they do not know what or who he is searching for. But I know for whom the monster searches—me! I feel more and more scared every second. I could go into the cave, but Godzilla would find me regardless. I then awaken in a slight sweat and panicky breathing.

The same dream scenario repeated until one night when I was about 14 years old.

Godzilla, once again, is looking over the mountain ridges. This time, something inside me tells me to stay where I am and look the monster in the eyes when he zeroes in on me. I do just that. I stare into Godzilla's eyes, and suddenly, the beast changes into a figure of my father. With that, I suddenly awaken in the familiar panic that doom awaits me around the next corner.

*What? My dad is Godzilla? O*nce again, I felt clammy and shaky upon hearing this. I awoke with the sense that I must have done something wrong or bad and punishable. I felt alone in my misery. Other children seemed to have it good, and I constantly envied them for their position above me. *Why do all the other children have caring and supportive parents, and I equate my dad to Godzilla?*

Figure 7 Godzilla is always just over that next mountain.

Cold Shoulder to the World

Of course, I had very little idea what my classmates' home lives were actually like, but that didn't matter. I made up stories about how much better things were for them. King's Creek represented a Cold War wall, separating the haves from the have-nots.

Relationally, I gradually became colder. I rationalized that I didn't need others and reacted to classmates' hurtful words or actions with equally insensitive, rude, and uncaring comments. I could be as nasty and cold as I thought the world was to me. Not only could I be crass and hurtful to fellow schoolmates, but I could also be downright revengeful toward my parents. Anything inconsiderate or demeaning they said about me triggered embarrassment. It drained me. Dad's compulsion to purposely call me a different name than my given one was no different from him calling me an asshole.

Once, a buddy of mine and I were asked to play some simple guitar tunes at a Boy Scout awards dinner. I agreed, but my friend backed out just before the event. While at a different meeting prior to the dinner, my dad came over to where I sat amongst a few friends and offered to learn some chords so the show could go on.

"Hey, Bert (yes, he addressed me as Bert even in these settings), I see Dean can't make it on Tuesday. I could learn a few chords and play along with you."

Immediately on the defensive, the urge to strike back arose very quickly. Instead of softly answering, I intentionally yelled "No!" to ensure others heard me. "I WON'T play any songs with YOU!"

I slammed that door shut as quickly as he had tried to open it. The issue was never open for consideration.

And then I snickered.

My dad looked at me with surprise and stopped. He turned and silently walked away. I felt gloriously victorious on the battlefield—slightly pulling in on my belly and lifting my chest, feeling quite inflated.

Then guilt swept through like having all ten fingernails painfully screech on a chalkboard.

Unfortunately, while I tried to set some limits between my parents and me, I could be as obnoxious as anyone. I never owned up to any loathsomeness. Each failed encounter proved my belief that only a significant change in the world's actions toward me could make these wrongs right. Repetitive thoughts of my past cycled repeatedly like an old player piano playing the same worn-out tune. I hid my inner conversation from everyone, hoping my intellectual achievements blinded them to the turmoil below.

Another habit of rumination developed: trying to predict the future.

If I do this, then this, this, or this might happen, was a running internal monologue. I thought that if I refined my ability to predict the future, I could at least tell when the shit would hit the fan. Of course, I was oblivious to the fact that often, what happened had nothing to do with what I'd predicted or demanded.

. While I hid most of this and never talked with anyone about the repetitive, pessimistic thoughts, my attitude often emerged as apathy towards events and people. I defiantly walked instead of running to the outfield as instructed by the coach when playing baseball. I rarely smiled at the camera. I quit a small musical group I'd joined when another spoke critically of me rather than simply discussing our disagreements.

One Foot Out the Door

I moved like an automaton towards college and medical school under the urging of my family—not out of any desire to save lives or make the world a better place, nor with any idea of what being a doctor meant. I'd barely talked with anybody in the profession, and nothing inspired me about it. At least going to medical school would allow me to escape from the trailer park and the misery of my life in Weirton. Achieving academic success in high school made the transition to higher education relatively easy. Leaving our trailer seemed a good enough reason to do just about anything.

However, I never realized that I would be taking myself with me, no matter what level of education I achieved.

I left school at noon each day during my senior high school year, not needing any additional academic credits to graduate. This gave me plenty of time to get to my job at a local bowling alley. At times, the hours dragged, waiting for that stuck ball behind alley number 9, and I often arrived home after midnight. However, I enjoyed driving through the deserted streets of Weirton at that hour, and my bowling arm got quite the workout as we got unlimited practice time during non-working hours. My mom complained about these late hours and how they were a setup for getting mixed up with alcohol and women. As with other topics, she threw tantrums and screamed at me until I agreed to quit, disappointing myself, the owner, and my friend who worked there, reinforcing my belief that enjoying something always came at a high cost. After getting home from school, I moped around the trailer for a week with little to do.

Soon after quitting, my mom snarled, "Just how long do you expect ME to pay for your gas and car insurance now that you're not working?"

I knew that further debate would go nowhere. I was talking to a lunatic. I suddenly yelled back,

"YOU are making NO sense."

"I can't believe you just said that! Just wait till your father comes home!" she hollered as I slammed the door to my room. My older brother had gone off to college, and for the first time in 17 years, I had my own space where I could retreat. When my father came home, my mom dramatically told him how I yelled at her. Never one for a calm exchange of views, he came storming to the rear of the trailer, pounded several times on the door, and threw it open so hard that the doorknob cracked the fake wood paneling that made up the small closet.

"How dare you yell at your mother?" my father bellowed with the usual rage in his eyes, clenched fists and spit spewing from his mouth.

That did it. I finally had had enough of their abuse. I was ready to fight. My hands clenched into fists tighter than ever before, and I found them instinctively raised in front of me as I stepped toward him. My shoulders assumed a forward posture, and my entire body slightly crouched into a fixed and determined stance, ready to defend myself against anyone who came into my space.

"THAT woman once again yelled more incoherent nonsense earlier today!" I complained, refusing to acknowledge her as my mom while my eyes threw daggers to complement my words. "Last week, she criticized me for working too much, making me quit my job. And this week, she's whining about me not working! This makes no sense! She IS totally insane!" Even though my dad was still markedly more muscular than me, I took another step toward him, ready to punch. At no time during this confrontation was backing down an option.

We glared angrily at each other for a few seconds. My dad turned to look down the hallway at my mom and shook his head just a bit. *Then*, to my unequaled amazement, my dad *walked away*. He walked away, as simple as that. This was one more confrontation that neither my dad nor my mom ever spoke of again. However, after this hostile encounter, my father never physically corrected or manhandled me again.

The following week, I started a job at an Italian grocery store downtown. As a high school senior, I worked 40+ hours a week, and I was more than happy to avoid going home as long as I could every evening. I worked even longer hours the summer before heading off to college.

I excelled academically in high school and was named valedictorian of my graduating class, along with three other students with 4.0 averages. Asked to give a short speech at commencement, I quite consciously titled my speech "Apathy," discussing how I had little interest in anyone else's speech and felt every person attended only for themselves. I stated that numbness ruled most of our relationships. At the practice session a few days before the ceremony, with the faculty as our audience, my speech landed like a crashing lead balloon filled with toxic gas. Almost all the teachers stood up and forbade me from giving the address I had written. One teacher, from whom I had never taken a class, said it was one of the better and more honest speeches he had ever heard. Towards this teacher, I smiled and felt a confirmatory sensation deep in my belly, a confirmation I seldom let myself experience. In that instance, I knew that somehow, and somewhere, it was okay to have a different perspective than most. I silently thanked him. Two days later, I gave a contrived, generic, meaningless, and unmemorable speech.

By the end of high school, the repetitive, pitiful, defensive thoughts in my head were pretty well set to go off whenever I felt threatened, compromised, confronted, accused, or whenever I saw someone else had something I didn't—namely, happiness. I made it my unconscious mission to continually justify my personal brand of victimization. By now, I had assembled that iron mask to cover any happiness or joy that might accidentally emerge. I had also locked my heart in an iron vault, vowing never to show it again except in minimal and controlled ways.

CHAPTER 4
HEADED OUT

I always enjoyed the idyllic drive on the backroads of northern West Virginia approaching Bethany College. On the day I started my college career, my mother drove me with a suitcase of my belongings to an open parking space in front of the freshman dorm. I don't remember any conversation on the way or how we parted. I probably thanked her for the ride and gave her a cursory hug, which was all I could muster toward anyone by then. I went home several times that semester, but neither of my parents returned to Bethany until my graduation four years later. The college was 23 miles from Weirton, but it felt like light-years away.

At first, college was a breath of fresh air, away from my father's violent temper and my mother's constant guilt-tripping. As a chemistry major, students on the pre-med path surrounded me. Many of us joined the same fraternity. Along with classes, I immersed myself in a jazz band, intramural ping-pong, and the local AM radio station run by the college as an on-air personality—dare I say—with little personality. My side voyage into radio started with the alluring voice of a female DJ, Tory, whose lyrical intonations captured my attention like never before.

"Joe, what station is that on that radio?" I asked, putting down my anhydrous chemistry book.

"WVBC," Joe replied, "And the announcer is a student named Tory Talley."

I sat utterly silent for a few seconds, taking in every last drop of her silky-smooth delivery. If you could fall in love with a voice over the radio, I just had. I had no idea who she was or what she looked like.

"She mentioned a party tonight at the Kappa Alpha house. We have to go and meet her!" I exclaimed.

An hour later, Joe and I grabbed red plastic cups for the keg at the KA house. No one cared that I hadn't reached the legal drinking age of 18. Almost immediately upon arriving, I gagged at seeing several students swallowing live goldfish. *This is what college is all about.* I said to myself. Finally, my ears tuned in to that voice that had called to me over the airwaves. Circling the outdoor patio, we spotted an attractive young woman chatting with other students. With a burst of nervous laughter, I went to introduce myself.

"Hi. Um, nice party? My name is Bart. You wouldn't happen to be Tory, would you?"

"Yes. I am Tory Tolley. Good that you, and …"

"Joe," said my friend.

"Good that you and Joe could make it."

"I heard you on the radio and wanted to come down and meet you," I said as my heart beat out a rhythm I had experienced just a few times.

"I love the radio station," she said. "In a few months, when I graduate, I will have worked there for four years. You and Joe wouldn't be interested in something like this, would you? We are always looking for good people."

Graduating ... in a few months ... shit! I thought as my heart dropped into a puddle of disappointment. Not wanting to end our brief encounter, I would have feigned a slight interest in just about anything.

"I never thought about radio. What would I even do there?"

"Call the station manager and arrange an interview!" Tory explained. She suggested a start in the WVBC newsroom.

I went on to host a radio show every Friday evening and Saturday morning for most of college. It was a great distraction from science and mathematics and loads of fun while it lasted. Once, I indulged in a passive-aggressive tendency and repeatedly played the same tunes for weeks to annoy a fraternity brother. While my voice extended on the airwaves throughout the small town of Bethany, the actual control room was small, secluded, quiet, and inviting to me. I could be by myself, yet everywhere, all simultaneously! I had moments of comfort and great pleasure sitting behind a microphone, cueing up the next record, or reading an important public announcement. The administrative staff asked me to do a daily show, but necessary schoolwork took precedence.

While I occasionally heard Tory on the radio, I never saw her again. Immersion into college life soon drowned out her voice. Years later, I still imagine her voice and that wondrous feeling that resonated inside me as I heard it.

As a private school, Bethany College's tuition is a bit higher than that of that of public universities in West Virginia. I thankfully attended this "small school of distinction" through a significant scholarship, several grants, and an educational loan. I wanted to be at a smaller school, as I would have been unseen at a much larger institution like West Virginia University. To help with college expenses and earn a little spending money, I worked part-time at the local Bethany hotel and monitored basic chemistry labs for first- and second-year students.

During the summers between my first and second years in college, I applied for and accepted a position at the Weirton Steel Mill, where my grandfathers, father, and several uncles worked. The mill generously offered local college students employment for a few months. My $15 hourly wage at the mill far outpaced the $1 an hour I made as a lifeguard at the local swimming pool and the $3 per hour I earned at the bowling alley and Italian grocery store. I lived at home but didn't see my parents much during this time. We spoke little, even when I did see them.

Assigned to the coke plant and perpetually drenched in sweat, I shoveled coal and coke to my boss's content while wearing long winter underwear and heavy flannel shirts to protect myself from the extreme heat of the 1800-degree ovens. During midnight shifts, I was continually awestruck by the contrast of the darkened sky and intense flames as railroad car after railroad car full of blazing coke traveled the rails barely a yard below me. My lack of fear amazed me as I stood on a three-foot ledge between the open oven doors and the railroad cars. I frequently cleaned the oven door seals with an air chisel—requiring me to stand directly in front of the hot oven opening, hoping that the operator of the giant machine that removed and replaced the doors kept a good eye on me and didn't accidentally crush or entomb me in the ovens themselves.

The experience offered me a different perspective on the work many of the males in my family had performed for 50 years since emigrating from their home countries.

Figure 8 Coke Plant worker cleaning the seal around the door of an 1800-degree oven.

Awkward Brushes with Grief

My paternal grandfather passed away from liver cirrhosis and alcoholism during my sophomore year in college. After I arrived at the nursing facility where he died, my eyes welled with the beginning of a tear as I watched my grandmother mourn his lifeless body on the hospital bed. The local priest who came to administer the last rites quickly brought me back to my senses as he told me, "You need to stop that crying and be here for your grandmother." I nodded and silently thanked the priest, as part of me promptly agreed that crying made me too vulnerable. However, as I wiped my nose, I became aware of a profound sense of emptiness about how to console anyone. Comforting another was not something I wanted or was prepared to do. And with this, I felt a terrible uneasiness. To my relief, other supportive family members quickly entered the room. I was grateful for them. My flatline emotional response contrasted with the family member who became hysterical and required a shot for sedation.

That year, my father's brother also passed away. In his mid-forties, Uncle Mike, as we knew him, developed amyotrophic lateral sclerosis, an irreversible degenerative neurological disease. Uncle Mike was a big, strapping man who showed little emotion. His symptoms started with persistent hoarseness, quickly advancing to total muscle atrophy. I froze with fear each time I visited him before he passed, not knowing what to say to him. I didn't even know how to put my hand on his shoulder in some gesture of comfort or connectedness. The last time I saw him alive, his mom, my grandmother, cared for him. I walked into his room and quickly noticed all his skin sores from being unable to shift positions. We looked at each other, and he started to cry. So did I, but I couldn't deal with any emotional expression, let alone crying. I softly said that I was sorry and quickly exited the room. Life had not prepared me for any interaction like this.

After that, I quickly returned to Bethany, never speaking to anyone about my uncomfortable feelings. I buried all of that under academic studying, weekend drinking, and a bit of frisbee golf. All to further separate me from these pesky emotions.

Work and Beyond

Just before the end of my second college year, Weirton Steel announced the suspension of the college student work program, with little hope of reinstatement that summer. With the possibility of not getting a steel mill job that year, I applied to the local radio station in Weirton as a newsbreak announcer. That would have been fun, but the day before I started that position,

Weirton Steel called and said they had a job in the coke plant if I desired. *Of all the places in the mill, back in the coke plant?* I thought. Still, the money at the mill doubled the radio station's wage, making the decision very easy.

So, for one more summer, shovel in hand, soot covering my face and clothes, I ventured into the furnaces that morphed raw materials into finished steel products. My assignment took me to the unloading dock along the Ohio River for one of those weeks. I thanked my supervisor for my week on the Weirton Steel French Riviera. Calm, dry, cool weather greeted me as I went down to the quiet riverbanks, attending to odd jobs. Located west of the primary mill, the river docks offered fresh, clean air. I helped align the massive steel sliding doors that covered the barges brought in for unloading. Sitting three stories up in the control room, the crane operator laughed hysterically during my "initiation" on the river, including the "accidental" descent of a 10-foot-diameter magnet used to help open those doors. The door fell just inches from my feet. The magnet hit the steel cover with such force that I dropped to my knees as the barge violently rocked back and forth. The operator did not unexpectedly receive a nice view of my middle finger in return.

Figure 9 Hot coke being pushed into a waiting railroad car from the coke battery oven.

During that summer, my girlfriend at Bethany decided to go to another college. She felt strongly that a long-distance relationship wouldn't work and broke up with me. Her sound reasoning mirrored my thoughts, but my wounded, defensive--self insisted on an angry meltdown. The unflattering letter I wrote to her should never have been mailed. After that news, I once again moped around Weirton, sulking while at my job at the mill as well. My immediate supervisor noticed this, and he carefully asked me how I was. For whatever reason, I let my usual guardedness open to his compassion. For the first time, an adult male had the time and interest to talk with me about relationships. He did not judge and mostly listened as I told him my tale of woe. While I can't remember his name and never saw him again, his genuine concern opened a small crack in my armor, allowing me to recognize a place of peaceful contemplation in my mind.

Right around this time, I learned of the organization Mensa, which required proof of having an IQ in the top 97th percentile for membership. I had a qualifying ACT score the year before, and after being accepted, it felt like I could hold my head higher for a short time. Membership became one more thing I pointed toward and said, "I belong; you probably don't." I liked Mensa's monthly magazine, but I found that socializing with these mentally endowed contemporaries threatened me in a way that I found hard to pin down. Mostly, I didn't want to admit that many Mensa members exuded more intelligence than I did.

The following summer, I accepted a research job in Wilmington, Delaware, at Hercules, Inc., a national company specializing in explosives and mining-related chemicals. While I loved the weekend beach trips, the extended lab hours convinced me that doing chemistry research was not a long-term option for me.

"Why Do You Want to Go to Medical School?"

Late in my college career, my professors sat dejectedly in their office chairs as I told them my plan to apply for medical school and not a higher degree in chemistry. While the research aspect of chemistry didn't interest me, a passionate desire for a career in medicine also eluded me.

"Hello, Bart. Good to finally meet you. I am Mr. Smith, your friendly neighborhood college advisor. What brings you in today?"

"Until now, I haven't needed your services, but several of my professors felt it important I run this medical school application by you before I submit it to West Virginia University," I answered.

"Let's take a look at what you have."

I handed my application to Mr. Smith, who had a master's degree in counseling. I felt uneasiness around my application as I had liberally used white-out on several lines.

"Okay," Mr. Smith said as he reviewed the manuscript. "I see here that most of this is straightforward. Your academic performance here at Bethany has been top-notch, and your extra-curricular activities are good. But I do have a question about your answer as to why you want to go into medicine. While you probably will have a decent salary as a medical physician, I strongly advise you to rewrite this. Medical school admission boards do not, under any circumstances, want applicants to talk about money."

My jaw dropped just a few inches, but I tried not to let it show.

Not talk at all about money? I thought. Then came a sarcastic follow-up: *Yeah, right! How hypocritical! I bet all those docs on the admission committee are happy to work for free!*

I struggled to answer the "Why do you want to go into medicine" question on the application. But honestly, anything I went into post-college needed to provide me with adequate income. I got the sense that, just like my "Apathy" speech in high school, only specific party-line answers were allowed in these situations.

"Bart," the advisor continued, "You must rewrite your response, and I suggest you say that you truly want to help people and promote good health for the citizens of West Virginia."

Ugh, I heard my mind say. I saw the logic in his proposed rewording of my "goals," but this did seem all too hollow, even for me.

I thanked Mr. Smith, and he wished me well.

All applications at that time were completed with either a pen or a manual typewriter, so after another trip to the school store for more white-out, the US postal service delivered the form to my state's medical school.

From College to Med School

Bethany required all graduating seniors to take a comprehensive oral exam in front of a panel of five professors who had instructed them. Navigating around some complex genetic questions to some involved physics of chemical reactions, I did well on that exam and received the highest evaluation possible. Eventually, I graduated second in my class with honors in chemistry. Not first, just second.

"That's nice," my father said when he and my mom came to the graduation ceremony.

The few months between college and medical school seemed quite a blur. I needed to find housing in a whole new city, and I experienced the ending of one more romantic relationship. I said goodbye, wished a few fraternity brothers good luck, and then happily blocked out most of the fraternity experience. My maternal grandfather helped facilitate my move as he borrowed a truck big enough for all my things. His presence during that transition comforted me.

Unfortunately, I found medical school deeply disappointing. The required reading doubled, but I found little of it challenging.

My interest in learning new things evaporated when tasked with pathologically memorizing endless lists of bacteria. My initial excitement drowned and died when I heard the teaching staff mantra: “We had to do this, and so will you do this.” This included the ongoing scut work of collecting labs and test results while working long hours without breaks or even lunch. Many medical rotations required 80 to 110-hour work weeks. In my mind, most professors acted like gods to their patients and demanded that students worship them. And some students did—especially the ones entertaining an academic career in that professor’s field or those going into orthopedics and cardiovascular surgery.

Even with green and red decorations tastefully decorating the nursing stations, I found Christmas Eve dismal as I went on late afternoon rounds with a group of four students, a resident, and the chief of cardiothoracic surgery. (Residents had their MD degree and chose to specialize in a particular medical field for three to five years.) A middle-aged man with severe cardiac issues lay semi-comatose on his hospital bed, oxygen mask in place and monitors displaying his heart rhythm. His wife and children stood beside him as the cardiac surgeon spoke.

“Mrs. Johnson, I am Dr. Ushallbow, and I reviewed your husband’s tests. He has severe problems with his heart and needs immediate surgery.”

“What did you …,” started Mrs. Johnson, but the surgeon immediately interrupted her.

“Regardless of what I saw on the test, Mrs. Johnson,” Dr. Ushallbow said, getting louder so everyone in the room heard. “I am the only person in the world who can save your husband tonight. You would be advised to stop asking questions and sign the consent allowing me to do this surgery if you want to see your husband alive tomorrow."

What I had just heard shocked me.

Is this what medicine is all about? I thought. *Sure, the guy needs surgery, but is this how we are supposed to act in front of patients and their families?*

I said nothing about it, and no deliberation ensued amongst students or residents about whether this was any way to talk with patients and their families. We all understood the unwritten rule that students and residents must mirror and never question their professors' thoughts and actions toward patients, loved ones, and hospital staff, no matter how demeaning. I witnessed multiple events similar to this, and they further chilled my enthusiasm for medicine. I lacked the courage or imagination to do anything about this mistreatment other than retreat further into my head. We eventually accepted our professors' attitudes as the "normal" to emulate.

Death arrived at any turn. During the first cardiac procedure I watched on my first rotation, a patient died as their heart suddenly stopped. One week into a pediatric cycle, a group of students and the resident physician walked into an infant's room, only to find that the child had died minutes before we arrived. During a psychiatric rotation, a resident physician tried to resuscitate a patient who seized during a routine injection into the back of her skull. Unfortunately, the medication had gone straight into an artery.

Experiencing the deaths of patients—or worse, seeing them mistreated and experimented on in the name of education—

hardened my shell, forcing a retreat even further from my emotions. How else would anyone deal with this sort of thing?

Medical learning came down to "See one, do one, teach one." Perhaps that should have been rewritten to "See one, try to do one or two, then teach one." Whether it came down to an invasive procedure or simply talking with a depressed patient in the psychiatric clinic, it embarrassed me to admit that I had little idea of what I was doing most of the time.

I did well academically in medical school and studied very little to pass my exams. All courses were pass/fail in an attempt by the administration to lower competitiveness. Hilariously, I was the only student in my class to graduate with a 4.0 grade point average. I earned an A grade for participating in a volleyball and Frisbee elective! I enjoyed the class and am still proud of that achievement. The course introduced me to volleyball, and I started playing with the crazy psychiatric residents during my spare time in my third and fourth years.

Lighter Times Abroad

I wanted to study overseas during my senior year of med school. I had two specific requirements in reviewing options: an English-speaking country and rotations without evening or night calls. I chose to attend the University of Newcastle-Upon-Tyne in northern England, where I took courses in dermatology and endocrinology. I expected to see patients in the clinic during the day, with evenings and weekends free for pub crawling and visiting local sites.

After an overnight flight from the US, what I heard as I stepped off the train in Northumberland surprised my ears. The local dialect and accent were Geordie, the dialect spoken in the

British *Andy Capp* comics first published in 1957. Though I got my wish of an English-speaking country, I barely understood a word anyone said—especially the newspaperman yelling in the central city square!

Had I just arrived in Czechoslovakia?

For a week, I struggled with the regional vocalizations. Wandering into a local shop, I bought a small portable radio to listen to music. When the shopkeeper realized I was from America, he proudly exclaimed in his Geordie accent that he had recently visited "Colorado!" With that one word, "Colorado," I finally connected a word and its spelling with its Geordie pronunciation. Such a Rosetta stone moment for me! My ears had gotten a foothold in the local dialect and were good to go.

My medical rotations at Newcastle University proved different than my experience in US hospitals. The English afternoon tea break surprised me; I remember my first thought being, *Afternoon tea? What an arbitrary waste of precious clinic time that could be spent seeing more patients!* Newcastle University also had no private patient rooms, barring the few set aside for patients with uncontrolled infectious diseases. All other patients shared space in a ward with 10 to 15 beds. Only vaguely familiar with the word "queue" before arriving in England, I quickly learned that almost everything in medicine involved a long line. Patients knew to expect a six-month wait even for something as simple as a new prescription for their glasses.

I received wise advice from a dermatology professor who stated, "If you don't know what the skin condition is, don't touch it. If you know the skin condition, you don't need to touch it."

I enjoyed my experience quite a bit: no one knew my past, no one asked about my history, and most of all, I was the only American student in my department. I felt unique that way, and I didn't have other Americans around to remind me of "home." Along with finally getting used to the local warm beer, I visited many parts of the British Isles and even made side trips to Paris and Ireland. On that trip to Paris, I wandered into Notre Dame. I don't know if it was the time of day, but I encountered only two other people in the cathedral. Sitting in one of the pews, I became so aware of the lack of noise that, for an instant, I imagined myself in the back seat of the family station wagon again, experiencing a slight out-of-body peacefulness. An eternity could have passed, except my mind jumped back, saying, *Not too much of this. It could become dangerous.* I returned to my senses and exited the church as quickly as possible.

By the time I left, I had absorbed so much of the local accent that an American couple sitting next to me on the flight home asked if this was my first visit to the States. I wanted to say, "Yes, this is my first visit, and I know no one." I secretly loved their comment, and the temptation to lie only needed to wait for my next breath. A sinking feeling in my stomach appeared, and in the end, I told them the truth.

Life seemed lighter during my Northumberland period. I had a reprieve from my most negative thoughts for a short time, and I allowed myself to fully enjoy my days. A welcome breather, I traveled 3000 miles away from every responsibility I ever had. I even ignored the fact that I had other family members.

Back to the Grind

Returning to the US, I faced six more months of medical school before graduation, and I needed to make a significant decision. Which field of medicine did I want to go into? I took several elective rotations early on in school to try out different areas, including psychiatry, anesthesiology, surgery, and pediatrics. I quickly ruled out any surgical field as the teaching staff and professors acted more obnoxiously than anyone I had ever met.

And there it arose—anesthesiology. I kept telling myself that anesthesiologists displayed intelligence and self-control. But the real reason was quite symbolic. In psychiatry, you deal with patients face to face, including all their repetitive mental stories and emotions. In helping them, I would eventually have to face my own narratives. I neatly avoided getting personal with patients in anesthesiology since I put them to sleep. Numbing and anesthetizing each patient suited me internally and externally.

Despite training under several kind and compassionate professors, my four years in medical school showed me a system that turned caring students into non-feeling clinical robots trying to hide their struggles. I grew weary of the unending daily rounds on hospital wards. The frequent night calls meant we students stayed in the hospital for 36 hours without a break, a grueling schedule that did not bring out the best in practitioners. Twelve hours later, we did it again. Never taught to deal with patients and their family members' emotions when facing significant illness and death, I conveniently kept a bottle of ether between me and my patients.

As one of my last electives in medical school, I worked in the university hospital administration department, shadowing the CEO. This was an eye-opening 30 days. I discovered grown adults in administrative roles who kept running lists of doctors or hospital employees who questioned or opposed their policies. It shocked me that the CEO, once named "Hospital Administrator of the Year," kept a little black book with the names, dates, and offenses of all who dared cross him. Administrators and accountants manipulated patient data, billing, and receipts to one day make it look like the hospital prospered, only to use the same data to document a significant loss the next. It all depended on the audience to whom they were playing. If you need more money through West Virginia or federal grants, report a considerable loss. If trying to woo a potential donor, show them a spreadsheet profit documenting how well the hospital is doing. All with exactly the same figures! My first exposure to the business side of medicine intensified my already robust cynicism. Corporate America wallowed in its own pain, and money provided the only consolation it could imagine.

During this rotation, I met my future wife, Sharon. She worked as an administrative assistant to one of the executive department heads. Attractive, slim, and in control, I took to her almost immediately. Our relationship blossomed quickly.

We bonded over a mutual love of tennis and physical exercise and gradually spent more time together. I admired her for her independence, work ethic, and knowledge of administrative workings that she had acquired while working for the hospital.

Beyond School

I tried to have a life outside of medicine. Also, as a medical student, my roommate Charlie and I played basketball with the chairman of ophthalmology one afternoon each week. We occasionally frequented bars around town when off duty. One day, out of the blue, Charlie and I decided to ride some go-carts. It had been years since driving any machine other than my car, as I had sold my motorcycle after college. Soon, we raced around a small oval track, the sound of a two-cycle engine straining as I attempted to gain an advantage over Charlie during one turn. With the warm wind on my face, I instantly experienced the joy I had briefly encountered as a toddler. Wow! I hadn't felt it for such a long time. The pleasure almost overtook me when, once again, the mind returned in full force, telling me that this behavior bordered on foolishness. Sheepishly, I returned to the go-cart's seat, finished the next few laps, and relegated that feeling of joy to an inaccessible vault. I conceded to that voice that demanded I lock things back down.

In my last year of med school, my parents divorced. I imagined that the yelling matches finally overtook any reason to stay together. My contact with them was limited, but I knew they had been separated for some time. Mom never called to tell me this news, but Dad did. Rather than give the facts, he wanted to talk about his new social life and the women he had started dating. I never really knew what to say, as I had never considered myself an expert on male-female relations. I felt that under my external façade, I was entirely sucked at all those interactions.

During this time, several thoughts repeated in my mind. They followed a definite pattern.

Once I get through this, things will get better.

Once I get through this surgery rotation and away from those stupid surgeons, things will improve.

Once I graduate and get on to residency, things will look up.

Once I have a life partner and a stable home, I will have a purpose.

Once I get a real paying job, I will be happy.

And in fairness, perhaps things did get better for a minuscule period with each of these steps, but I soon found myself no happier than before—just more stressed, pressured, and squeezed for time.

The day after I graduated from medical school, I returned to England as a gift to myself. For a month, I slept on a friend's couch and played the part of a busker in the London Underground, strumming my guitar and repetitiously belting out "American Pie," receiving enough money to buy lunch. A thought pervaded me: *Yes, I can do something crazy and irresponsible!* And a warning followed: *Don't think that too loudly!* Regardless, the lightness I felt during my previous trip to England returned. For that month, someone else visited England, not the negative Bart, who lived in the United States.

Sharon and I had formed a growing relationship during my last six months of medical school, and this decision to travel across the ocean for a month to visit friends did not sit well with her. But I would have gone regardless of her ultimatum. When I returned, Sharon and Charlie met me at the airport in New York City, and I got to meet Sharon's mom and her stepfather. Sharon and I developed a bond that gradually became a love for each other.

Residency and a New Family

With my MD degree now secured, four more years of an anesthesiology residency lay ahead before entering private practice. After interviewing at three programs, I chose an anesthesiology program in Pittsburgh, a familiar city about 20 miles from my hometown. While I looked forward to progressing in my career, I wasn't thrilled with the Pittsburgh traffic. At least I avoided the morning rush hour, as I needed to leave my apartment before 6 AM daily. Driving home in the evenings often turned into a congested nightmare.

While we were not ready to marry, Sharon asked to move in with me as I relocated to Pittsburgh, and I agreed. We initially shared a three-bedroom apartment with Jeff, a dear fraternity brother from Bethany. Conflicts with Jeff's girlfriend occurred almost immediately, though, and to top it off, a previous girlfriend of mine, also from Bethany, moved in just two doors from us.

The anesthesiology residency continued the veiled oppressiveness I had found in medical school as, once more, I encountered domineering staff with little business in teaching positions. I felt several of the team members cared and were genuinely interested in the wholeness of each resident, but most staff saw residents as cheap, disposable labor.

The department chairman, Dr. Berkebile, made me feel at home when I occasionally spoke with him. He gifted Sharon and me a weekend at his Seven Springs ski resort condominium a few hours east of Pittsburgh. There, while enjoying a rare vacation, Sharon and I decided to get married, have children, and start raising a family.

Because of my demanding schedule, we arranged a wedding at the local justice of the peace. Spooky orange and black decorations adorned the office walls since our private marriage ceremony occurred on Halloween, the only time I could get off duty. Our first child, Christopher, arrived nine months later and soon took up my only free time, but I felt happiness as this child reset our lives. Having no idea how to raise children, I felt overwhelming nervousness and responsibility. I didn't want to follow in my parents' childrearing footsteps.

Our second child, Tyler, arrived during my last year of residency. Around the same time, we moved to a slightly larger apartment in Dormont, a suburb just south of Pittsburgh. Familiar with Mennonite churches in the Shenandoah Valley where she grew up, Sharon suggested we attend services at an urban Mennonite church in Pittsburgh. A few other young doctors in residency training also participated in the church. I loved the community lunches served following services on Sundays, and the fellowship allowed Sharon and the boys to meet and make friends.

With two beautiful children, Sharon and I did our best to create a stable environment for their early years despite all the pressures of starting a family and my medical training. While I found comfort in a familiar city, being geographically closer to my parents developed into another minefield.

My dad visited us occasionally in our small Pittsburgh apartment. However, these visits drained Sharon and me. "Why are all these walls only painted white?" he exclaimed. Why did you choose that car? What made you live here?" he asked. My dad poured out a stream of constant criticism without ever an encouraging word. Occasionally, things in my life were so stressful that I asked him outright for support, but he could never give any.

Post-divorce, Mom burned through several relationships with men I couldn't stand, let alone allow my children to be around. My mom's second husband, Ralph, purposely sat on their couch in his underwear, endlessly chain-smoking. Visits while Ralph lived with her did not last long. Mom also started to play me and my brothers against each other, saying how Bruce said or did this, while George said or did the opposite. With little truth behind it, every phone call or visit to her apartment further reinforced my feelings of disgust and failure. My whole family seemed focused on making one another feel miserable and guilty.

Eventually, for my sanity and my family's well-being, I stopped talking with or visiting either of my parents. Other family members also taxed us, prompting a complete withdrawal from them. Eventually, I distanced myself from my brothers and missed their children's young adventures. Sharon and I often disagreed about handling these dynamics, as she faced similar issues in her family. She might have a pretty good conversation with her mom one week but a complete meltdown the next. Avoidance seemed to be my best option.

Clashes with the Chairman

After my first year of residency, the anesthesia department's chairman moved to a different position, replaced by Dr. Notsokind, a man who irritated me from day one. (I've changed his name to protect his identity.) He defied the hospital's no-smoking rule and lit up in his office whenever he chose, a habit that disgusted me, reminiscent of my parents' nicotine addictions. I never attempted to foster this hopeless relationship with Notsokind; I would never have considered the Pittsburgh residency program if Notsokind had been chairman when I initially interviewed.

Called into the chairman's office one afternoon during the last year of my training. Curiosity and apprehension filled my mind as both Notsokind and his second in command, Dr. Canoe (again, I changed his name), sat sternly waiting for me. Notsokind let Canoe lead the conversation as if in a training exercise.

"We hear that you have been moonlighting at a small hospital in the area," said Canoe.

"Yes," I responded. "I worked two days up in Altoona when I had a few days off. Another resident gave me the contact, as they have been doing the same thing for over a year …"

Cut off from speaking further, this whole interaction reminded me of being reprimanded by my father while growing up. I knew these two men had the power to dismiss me from the program for just about anything and that the best course of action was just to shut up.

"Dr. Notsokind reflects the best that any chairman could be, and I agree with him that moonlighting, while not directly spelled out in our residency manual, could easily be grounds to have you terminated," said Canoe. "Besides, you are obviously not a team player, and frankly, if I were chairman, I would never have hired you in the first place. Don't ask either of us for a recommendation, as it won't be very nice."

It was true that I wasn't trying to gain favor with either of these physicians, as a few other residents did. And I wasn't about to start. They had two stipulations going forward: one, never to moonlight again while a resident, and two, never talk to anyone in the department about this conversation.

Scoring in the 94th percentile on the national anesthesiology board's written exam a few months later, no congratulations or acknowledgments ever came from the chairman or his staff. Finishing my residency couldn't have come any sooner. Like my parents, the staff did not see or value my gifts and achievements.

Life in "Dreary Erie"

Upon completing the residency, I moved with my wife and kids to Erie, Pennsylvania, and walked into day one of my new job as a staff anesthesiologist in the city's Catholic hospital. The nuns who ran the administrative aspect of the hospital had a much kinder and more holistic approach to treating patients. Overall, the environment was much more relaxed than the cutthroat, academic, demeaning attitudes I had encountered in medical school and residency. Relief. Joining a large anesthesiology group, I specialized in open heart anesthesia but did the whole gamut of anesthesiology services, including pain medicine. Overnight calls rotated every third or fourth night, but occasionally, I had additional calls if a case required my expertise in open-heart surgery. I never knew when I would get home on any given day, and all my colleagues said that was just how the practice worked.

This added more stress at home, as my wife was primarily responsible for the children. While we could now afford to buy a house and pay off all my student loans, my profession dictated most of my life schedule. Complexities and frustrations occurred with specific partners in the anesthesiology group, and just being in dreary Erie by the lake soon took its toll. While Lake Erie offered some summer recreation, low-lying clouds and a lack of sun for over 300 days a year dominated the rest of the time. We saw several company outings in the middle of June, shortened by 45-degree weather and blustery winds that quickly blew picnic blankets in every direction. Every Halloween, snow covered the ground. Those conditions and the depressing flatness of the Erie countryside soon gave us all a progressive seasonal affective disorder. On the other hand, amazement overcame me as I watched the violent waves of Lake Erie as a severe low-pressure system covered the area. I didn't connect the dramatic crashing of waves to my growing inner turmoil, but I see it now.

Dissatisfied with living in a subdivision, we started looking for other properties. After spending many hours of my little free time on the search, we found a small farm not too far away with an 1840s farmhouse. Along with the installation of vinyl siding outside the home, the previous owner had muddled the original interior look of the place. I took it on as a weekend restoration project to recondition the old house to its rightful look and feel. Several contractors helped me, but I found their work ethics questionable and soon terminated them.

My blood pressure crept up, and my weight also rose. I constantly worked at one thing or another. At the hospital, I cared for newborns and their moms, folks needing new arteries to keep their hearts functioning, and teenagers needing emergency tonsillectomies. At home, I mowed, cleaned, and restored the old farmhouse and property while trying to find time for my children.

Fulfilling Sharon's long-standing dream, we bought three Arabian horses and a pony, thinking we could all take riding lessons and share in the stall mucking. The boys lost interest in the horses after the pony named Treasure bit Tyler in the stomach. I took some riding lessons but never felt comfortable on the feisty horses. The horses knew I had no idea how to control them, and several times, I found myself sitting in the mud after being thrown off. They became expensive pets, and I became the designated muckraker. However, I found solace and a silver lining when investing in a new tractor with a front loader to help with all the sawdust spreading and manure collecting. The constant shoveling reminded me of my coke plant days.

As my medical career began to demand even more of my time and the farm activities took on a life of their own, my wife and I gradually grew apart through misunderstanding, jealousy, and inability to form relationships with other families. We stopped going to the local Erie Mennonite church because of miscommunications with the pastor. I lacked any healthy skills to deal with my immediate family demands, and I certainly didn't have any beneficial tools to help my wife deal with her loneliness and growing depression.

I found myself acting exactly like my dad under stress: moody, demanding, and intolerant, like no one knew as much as I did. Impatience dominated my interactions with my children, colleagues, and work staff. Poor Sharon encountered agitation in me as she struggled with the advent of personal computers. Irritation even followed me on vacation if things didn't go perfectly. The slightest mistiming of flights or longer lines than usual brought out my worst headaches and behavior toward others, including my family.

The boys loved living on the farm and being outside for much of their day. Once the hayloft filled with the horses' food for the winter, they jumped from the highest points in the barn into the waiting hay piles. Christopher's love of nature delighted me as he explored the reaches of our woods and a small creek. Their love of sci-fi of all sorts blossomed during this time. With limited interest in this genre, Sharon's frustrations soared if the boys spent too much time on the computer. Despite my fearful childhood dreams of Godzilla, I felt compelled to introduce the boys to him.

Time for a Job Change

Increasingly weary of night calls and the never-ending workdays, Sharon and I looked for a different work opportunity. By this time, I had made a name for myself in pain management in Erie. In residency, I learned to do injections by touching external landmarks on the patient, and I gradually added more advanced injections that required X-ray guidance. While I was still unwilling or unable to look any deeper into my negative characteristics, X-ray guidance techniques at least offered me a chance to look deeper into my patients' pain.

We found a possible job in my wife's hometown of Harrisonburg, Virginia. Sharon had some misgivings about moving back to where she grew up, as I could well understand. Still, the allure of not having to get up in the middle of the night for an emergency open-heart surgery or a labor epidural beckoned me to apply. It seemed like a good move for me, especially regarding hours.

Desperate to make a change, I put on blinders to the exaggerated egotistical tendencies of Dr. Neverstumped, my potential new boss at the Mountains of Pain Associates, with branches in several small cities in Virginia. (I have changed both his name and the clinic's name.)

To move forward in negotiations with his company, I felt the need for him to concede something in his routine contract with physicians. I didn't care what it was. I just wanted some say, no matter how minor the issue. Dr. Neverstumped declined to change the sign-on bonus, salary, or profit-sharing structure. He refused to change the hours or scope of my work. Finally, he agreed that the standard non-compete clause would be changed to a ten-mile circle around each office out of which the company operated. He gave in to changing something! That's all I wanted. I never bothered to see what that change even meant; he had changed *something*.

After meeting Neverstumped and against my wife's intuition, I took the plunge and signed the contract. For the first time since I'd started medical school 15 years earlier, I could guarantee leaving the office at 5 P.M. every evening. While required to take emergency telephone calls on weekends, there were no in-house calls. Best of all, I stopped clinic at noon on Fridays and enjoyed two-and-a-half-day weekends.

Unable to find a suitable property in Harrisonburg, Sharon and the boys remained on the Erie farm while I commuted seven hours by car every other weekend. My wife's brother-in-law, Harold, who lived in Harrisonburg and had his pilot's license, regularly flew planes out of the local airport and offered me flights to Erie and back.

"Thanks so much for flying me up to Erie, Harold," I told him. "I really appreciate this, as it saves me about ten hours of driving time."

"No problem," Harold responded. "I love flying, and this gives me a chance to return to the pilot's seat again. Did you ever want to fly a plane, Bart?" Harold asked as the plane's engine propelled us down the runway.

"I always wanted to fly a plane," I said as the aircraft's wheels left the earth and Harold lined us up on an almost due north heading. "In high school, my neighbor Ron, who lived right next door to us in the trailer park, had a single-engine Cessna, and he took me flying every now and then. Ron loved to land on open backcountry roads, and occasionally, he handed the yoke off to me for some simple turns. He even allowed me to land the plane one time!"

"Yes, Bart," he agreed. "Love of flying. It seems to have always been in my blood. I love getting up and over the clouds, as the rolling landscape provides some beautiful scenery."

At that moment, the earth beneath us disappeared as we headed into a dense stormfront. Immediately, heavy, steady rain obscured the cockpit window—no ground for any reference anywhere. A thundercrack filled our ears as the precipitation intensified.

"Crap!!!" Harold exclaimed as I looked over at him. His hands shook, and the fear on his face completely grabbed my attention. The sweat rolling from his forehead paralleled the pummeling downpour outside our small craft.

Harold quickly glanced at his phone and dialed in for the latest radar conditions. Sure enough, the bright yellows and reds of a thunderhead cloud occupied our exact position.

"No big deal, right Harold?" I asked hopefully. "We just follow the quickest route out of the cloud and back into sunny skies."

"If it were that simple," Harold said. "You see, I only have my visual flying license as I have yet to complete my instrument training."

"Wait a second," I said. "Only your visual license? You're saying you have never flown before with just instruments?"

"True," he admitted as his legs began uncontrollably twitching. "I haven't started training yet for instrument-only flying."

The radio crackled to life. A local air traffic controller out of Pittsburgh noticed that our plane's radar signature had just passed into the heaviest of the surrounding thunderstorms.

"Flight NG132454 out of Shenandoah, please respond."

"Flight NG132454 here. This is Harold. And yes, our visibility is zero right now."

"Harold. We have you listed as having a visual flying license only. Why are you in the middle of a raging thundercloud?"

"I realize that fact. This totally came as a surprise. Can you help direct me out of this mess?"

"Please turn towards a heading of 179.34. Stay at your current altitude, and in about 15 minutes, the weather should clear. Once you reach your destination, you must file a flight incident report because of your license situation," the air traffic controller said calmly.

"Thank you," Harold replied. "We will be in touch."

About 15 minutes later, the clouds dissipated, the little roads and fields on the ground reappeared, and we visually confirmed our position. Not to be outdone, our plane's engine stalled two hours later as we approached Erie International Airport. We had a non-refundable glide of about 20 miles onto the tarmac.

My feet never so loved the feel of the earth as when we finally landed. I spent the next several days with my family, and Harold returned on Sunday to fly me uneventfully back to Shenandoah.

Several more times, Harold and I flew side by side. We discussed buying a plane together and trading alternative weekends for our flying time. I thought about this, but a few weeks later, Harold's radio failed while crossing the Allegheny Mountains on our way back to Harrisonburg. We heard incoming radio communications, but Harold couldn't send any. As he descended close to the mountains to avoid another last-minute thunderhead collection, the airport assumed we had crashed. As rescue squads prepared search teams, Harold used his cell phone to call the FAA on an emergency access number. Luckily, cell phone towers were just being placed along those mountain ridges. After that, I decided to skip flying in small planes.

The Long, Slow Move to Virginia

Sharon and I eventually found a small property with an 1890s farmhouse full of the original character. Its charming personality included a minimal 15-amp electrical service, bare wires hidden in the walls, and three rooms supporting only one light bulb each. A cistern served as the sole water source. Neither the walls nor the attic contained insulation. The septic overflowed, and the wood rot on the barn predicted imminent collapse. But it was the best we could find, so I undertook the restoration with the help of a good electrician and several other workers. I slept on a mattress on the floor in one unfinished room and had a barely functioning rustic toilet and bathtub on the outdoor porch. Room by room, I sanded and reconditioned all the floors myself while the electrician updated the electrical wiring. For three months, I worked 8 to 5 in the pain clinic and, most evenings, three hours on various aspects of the house and barn.

The impending move of Sharon and the boys stressed everyone. She had second thoughts about being so close to her family, and our children had difficulty adjusting to the new location. Christopher never wanted to leave the farm in Erie. While our Erie property took some time to sell, we discussed returning to Pennsylvania, no matter how dreary the weather. At that point, I would have done whatever my wife wanted, but staying afloat while changing her mind stressed me.

I negotiated with the Erie Hospital to return and open a new pain clinic separate from the anesthesia group I worked with. I even went to the extent of finalizing the paperwork and driving six hours to Erie to sign it, only to have Sharon call me in the middle of my trip, declaring that she no longer wanted to return to Erie. Flooded with confusion and disgust, I thought of gunning the car and driving off the highway into a ravine, though I recognized that as a fleeting thought. I ultimately acquiesced to her most recent change of mind and canceled the move back north, embarrassed by this turn of events.

The hospital administrator in Erie understood my decision and asked that I return my signing bonus, which I promptly did. The next week, I returned to work at Neverstumped's office with the heaviest of hearts, although I couldn't tell you where my heart was.

Dr. Neverstumped didn't make things easier. Flirtatious with all the female patients, he thought it hilarious to demean the patients' husbands when checking out at the front desk. I tired of hearing for the hundredth time how he honed his exceptional business skills while working as a high school employee at a hamburger joint, salvaging mayonnaise powder in plastic bags. Neverstumped easily alienated most physicians in the area with his condescending attitude. Thankfully, most of my colleagues recognized that I was a different and separate person from

Neverstumped. I tried to work seamlessly alongside the hospital staff and its anesthesia department.

Another stress of working in the medical field is malpractice. I was sued once in Erie because a lifesaving procedure on a young woman left a visible scar. The anesthesia and surgical teams saved her life, and she sued us all in return. The stress around these cases felt real, as most of the proceedings were out of my control. Eventually, that case was dropped as the patient's attorney could find no physicians willing to say we had made a grave medical mistake.

While employed at Neverstumped's office, a patient I saw sued the practice and me. My professional assessment concluded that the patient had developed an addiction to pain medications. I recommended admission to a local rehab center for inpatient detox and psychological counseling. The patient's employer got wind of this and promptly fired him, and the patient blamed me. The suit went nowhere, but I had to list any malpractice suit, whether valid or not, on every application for hospital privileges and medical insurance coverage for the next ten years. The feelings of frustration and anger due to being falsely accused lingered.

Starting My Own Practice

I earned a modest income and had reasonable working hours while working for Neverstumped. Eventually, though, I felt the environment was becoming too toxic to work. So I quit. Immediately after, Neverstumped filed a lawsuit alleging that I was the worst employee ever hired at Mountains of Pain Associates and that he fired me because I had an affair with one of the office staff. With no truth to any of these statements,

Sharon still angrily accused me of indeed having that affair. We had a running argument for several days until we both got tired of the endless circles.

Amid this madness, I decided to start my own pain management office. The changes I requested in the original non-compete clause allowed me to stay in the area and open a small office in a local town called Weyers Cave, Virginia. I hired a knowledgeable and seasoned office manager and support staff. With one ad in the local newspaper, I resumed seeing pain patients, this time at my clinic. While some things about running my business were easier, stressors still reared their ugly heads.

Neverstumped owned a historic building in a local city, and prior to my beginning employment, he asked if I would like to divert part of my salary to purchase an ownership share. The deal sounded good, but my intuition sent up a flag that literally felt like a giant stop sign in my belly, begging me to decline. Luckily, I did.

"Dr. Balint. Would you please come to the front desk? There is a registered letter here for you," announced my office manager one day.

Soon, I was reading a letter from the OIG (Office of the Inspector General) requesting an interview concerning the Astoria building I knew was owned by Dr. Neverstumped. I quickly called my attorney, and in a week, another letter appeared stating that I was not the target of their investigation. The federal government only wanted to talk with me.

Reassured by my attorney that everything pointed toward an interview only, I attended a meeting with one representative from the FBI and one from the Office of the Inspector General. Both men carried side arms. The cordial meeting ended after about 45 minutes, but I had nothing to add to what they already knew. My initial gut reaction helped me avoid getting tangled up in this scheme.

Several years after I left Neverstumped's employment, federal law enforcement officers arrested and convicted him of illegally removing asbestos from this building. Rumors circulated that Neverstumped had hired homeless men to remove asbestos at night without protective equipment and then bury it on a local farm. After pleading guilty, he spent a year and a day in federal prison.

Bonding over Scuba

A hugely positive aspect of running my office was that I could arrange my time as I saw fit. If I wanted to take a vacation, I merely scheduled a month or two ahead. Utilizing this perk of being the boss of the practice, I started scuba diving classes with Christopher. Too young, Tyler had to wait a few more years before I took him to Nevis and St. Kitts to get certified. Chris and I traveled to the Bahamas for our final certifications, and the following year saw us 150 miles offshore of Eastern Australia, floating over the Great Barrier Reef!

As Chris and I finished two morning dives, the temperature hovered in the low 80s Fahrenheit. The crew quickly reviewed the upcoming afternoon dive checklist, which included an overall summary of the dive site and descriptions of some of the marine life we might encounter. While waiting for lunch, we enjoyed refreshing drinks and rested in the main lounge area of the ship.

Too excited to sit, Chris stood and described the fish that greeted him in the morning dives. "Wow. Did you see those clownfish swimming in the sea anemones? I've seen pictures, but clownfish are much smaller than I imagined. These latest dives took my breath away, and not because I ran out of oxygen in my tanks!" he grinned playfully. "What's for lunch?"

"I don't know about lunch yet," I answered. "'Amazing' still describes last night's dive. Sure, we got separated from the main group, but those sea cucumbers' colors made the whole trip worthwhile! Ok. So, we did surface in pitch blackness 100 yards from the boat, but with our orange inflatable sausages, waterproof flashlights, and the quick actions of the crew, we were fine!"

Suddenly, an announcement broadcasted over the loudspeaker.

"Captain here. We're about to face a bit of unexpected trouble. We must pack up and move towards shore immediately. This morning, the weather service reported a tropical cyclone forming to the north, and predictions said the storm would miss us. Instead, the cyclone turned south, heading straight toward our position. Crew, prepare for immediate departure." His voice sounded concerned and slightly apologetic.

Chris and I looked at each other with extreme disappointment about this disruption of our trip. "This could get rough. Let's make sure all of our gear is stowed. Lunch may be on hold for quite a while," I said to him as calmly as possible.

In just 30 minutes, the weather turned from a relatively smooth ocean to six-to-eight-foot waves as the background sky darkened with ominous thunderhead clouds.

The loudspeaker blared one more time.

"Because of this turn of events, we have about 12 hours of racing this storm back to port. Expect large waves. But don't worry; we will make it back safely. Our satellite phone is available so guests can call home to notify their families of the plan change."

Damn, I thought. The sudden rocky movements of the boat made staying calm in front of my son more difficult.

"Let's get in line and have you talk to your mom, Chris. Only say the diving is great, and we are doing well. Lots of sunscreen."

Chris understood the raging anxiety his mom might feel if we told her the truth, so he kept his comments short and cheery. "Mom, hey, Chris here. Yes, it is late. No. Nothing's wrong. Diving has been great. And we are well and using lots of sunscreen! Can't talk long! See ya soon!"

I thought to myself, *Kudos to you, Chris, for that upbeat delivery!*

Chris and I nodded to each other, knowing he had expressed the little lie perfectly.

Sure, the weather turned rough quickly, but the boat and its crew handled it all very calmly. But no sleep was to be had as we stayed just ahead of the most severe weather the cyclone could offer. Each unannounced wave threw Chris and me off our bunks when trying to rest. A rumor circulated that everyone on the boat, crew included, was experiencing seasickness. And I couldn't just go on deck and lean over the side like I had on previous dive trips.

Saddened by the abrupt ending of the live-aboard dive excursion, Chris and I made the most of our remaining ten days in Australia by visiting a crocodile farm and taking several day-long outings to do some local diving offshore of Cairns. A few administrative items required my attention back at my new pain practice, but for the most part, I could leave the rest of my business obligations behind as Chris and I explored Australia. In a way, I didn't want this trip to end, and I believe Chris shared that sentiment.

More Troubles with Neverstumped

The sharks that enjoyed our company in the ocean seemed loving compared to the creatures that swam in the murky legal pit I needed to extricate myself from when I returned home. I filed a countersuit against Dr. Neverstumped, demanding the salary he owed me. Stress accumulated in every waking hour, but we finally agreed to settle the suits just as my legal expenses added up to my back pay. Neverstumped laughed at that one! Sharon continued to fret over my supposed affair. I couldn't convince her that the allegations were totally contrived. Then, I mistakenly hired one of Neverstumped's old employees for the new office. My wife tolerated this for a short time and then, in a fit of jealousy, demanded that I fire this female employee without notice. I sheepishly agreed to her demand in a futile attempt to preserve the peace.

Soon, my wife's jealousy of all female employees and patients took more control of our relationship. She instructed me not to treat female reproductive pain issues under any circumstances and not to take any calls after hours from female patients. Sharon often demanded that I quit medicine as some magic cure for her insecurities.

In Sharon's defense, I recognize that I sometimes displayed a front of false compassion with my patients yet acted as cold as a stone with Sharon and our kids. Neither of us had any tools to talk calmly about our fears and anxieties.

One day, while relaxing outside our home beneath the leaves of an oak, I received a call from one of the attorneys who assisted with the Neverstumped suit.

"Dr. Balint, Mike here. We just received a letter from the Yellow Circle insurance company demanding $60,000 to settle several issues they found with Neverstumped's billing."

In an instant, the warm sun fell behind some large clouds, chilling me and raising goosebumps on my arms.

"Mike, I didn't have anything to do with that. Neverstumped took my bill sheets, and I never saw them again."

"Well, apparently, he increased the charges on the Yellow Circle insurance patients you saw. They revised return patient visits to look like new patient visits."

New patient visits paid almost twice as much as established patient visits, as a physician always needed to spend much more time with a new patient than with a return patient.

"Mike," I said with a wavering voice, "I coded all those patients as return visits. I didn't change those. Neverstumped did."

"Doesn't matter, Bart. Your name is on the billing sheet, and the YC insurance company assumes you approved it. A few of YC's comments are just fishing in nature, but in my opinion, you should offer 50% of what they are asking and allow this to go away. Otherwise, as the major insurance carrier in Virginia, they can make your practice very non-profitable."

"Shit!" I said out loud, as I thought, *Just one more freakin' thing!*

"OK, I'll offer them 30% of what they ask, and let's get this resolved!"

Mike agreed rather quickly, which raised a red flag in my mind.

"Sounds reasonable, Bart. I'm having lunch with the CEO of YC tomorrow, and I will offer this to him."

All sorts of thoughts went through my mind. *Is YC going after Neverstumped as hard as they pretended to go after me? Have lunch with the CEO? All conveniently arranged ahead of time? Was my attorney on my side, or was he shaking me down?* I cursed YC and Neverstumped so loudly that the woods echoed with expletives. While I never knew what happened to Neverstumped and his billings to YC, I eventually paid the agreed-upon 30% refund to get this unpleasant episode behind me.

Successful Business, Troubled Mind

Most of my former patients from Neverstumped's practice transferred to my new office. Doctors consistently referred patients based on my reputation alone. Most professionals would have been thrilled to be in my position: I had minimal debt, a new flourishing medical practice, a steady income, a solid reputation in the local area, and positive outcomes on the treatment I recommended and performed. However, a spiral of negative thinking consumed me at times. If I saw nine new patients in a week, it disappointed me because I didn't see ten. "Never good enough, and never fast enough" became my motto.

I could never rejoice if my treatment reduced the patient's pain; my long-standing conditioning said I could only respond with, "That's nice."

Sharon despised my "That's nice." I never understood why back then. Now I do.

I never allowed myself to feel accomplishment or satisfaction. I believed it would all be taken away if I celebrated any part of it.

Sharon and I moved to a property less than four miles from my new office. The house was new enough that I didn't have to rip it apart and restore everything like I'd felt compelled to in the last two places we owned. There was a lack of outbuildings on the property, so we enlisted a local company to build a 40x80-foot barn with an attached apartment in case one of our aging parents ever wanted to live there. I found plenty to do in the attached apartment, plenty to lift, and plenty of things to buy at the local Lowe's store. I hoped that the manual labor would numb me mentally and emotionally. While some people may find it peaceful driving a tractor across a gorgeous landscape, I experienced my pessimistic, ranting thoughts that ran a mile a minute. My mind recounted all the previous bad contractors I had ever dealt with, administrative challenges at work, marital conflicts—anything but quiet, even with the best hearing protection on my ears.

Over the years, I let a few employees go because they were less qualified for certain positions than they claimed on their applications. I fired a few others because of insubordination. The constant headache of governmental regulations regarding Medicare billing, employment, and confidentiality followed me around like undigestible fast food. Luckily, I had an office manager who loved reading through and interpreting the laws that changed yearly. Starting in January, the federal government could prosecute a doctor for the same thing he did legally in December. I always loved the letters from Medicare stating that I, as the practitioner, "should have known that Medicare would be changing its rules concerning this or that subject," even though the new rules were never published or advertised. And, no, Medicare was not obligated to instruct practitioners on the correct coding or wording that needed to go into the next cryptic box or the following non-existent line. Medicare implied that we were to keep guessing until we got it right or ran afoul of the law.

I had control of many aspects of my life. I controlled my practice regarding hiring, firing, and what positions employees filled. I had control of my finances and could afford anything I wanted, whether a trip to scuba dive on the Great Barrier Reef or a new car paid for with cash. Emotional and physical satiation fleetingly came and went with each new thing I bought, but money never soothed the long-standing discontent and disconnection I felt. I explored nature, from 120 feet deep in the ocean to 14,000 feet in the Rocky Mountains, but I felt disconnected. I found an excuse to be dissatisfied everywhere, even while smashing a winning overhead in tennis or achieving the next belt rank in karate. Even underwater, the sound of my breathing annoyed me. Countless times, I wished I could stop breathing and be one with the ocean.

I never felt comfortable sharing my recurring judgments and criticisms with friends over a beer. I didn't trust anyone enough. I did see a psychologist a few times about my failing marriage, but I tended to blame Sharon and circumstances beyond my control instead of admitting the part I played. At the psychologist's suggestion, I used all kinds of pre-scripted mental gymnastics trying to deal with Sharon's ongoing anxiety and depression, for which she refused treatment. Our relationship at home became a cyclical pattern of blame and dissatisfaction with each other, a refusal to discuss anything calmly until our inner pain exploded in vicious fights. Neither of us could listen reasonably. I usually retreated into myself and hid away for a couple of days, moody around the kids and pets.

Of course, through all this, I continued to work and put on a happy face for the staff and the patients. I now see that this is precisely what my dad did. He would happily help out any neighbor or relative but then come home to complain about everything. His pent-up anger and stress led him to beat his children at the slightest transgression. I didn't hit my children, but emotionally, I often dished out as much anger as my dad did to me. Outwardly successful, brilliant, physically fit, and maintaining a pretense of control, I started karate as another way to try to kick further, punch harder, and throw things out of my way.

Five years into owning my pain practice, and despite all my accomplishments, a wreck waited to happen. The universe was poised to use the karate injury, neck surgery, and subsequent depression as wrecking balls, slamming me with such force that my world came crashing down.

CHAPTER 5
THE ANGELFISH'S INVITATION

Depressed, discouraged, defeated, and exhausted, I suffered through several weeks after the angelfish visit until I admitted I needed help. While one part of me asserted that nothing would ever change as I didn't deserve it, a slightly louder part argued that I couldn't continue on the path I'd trudged thus far in life.

A friend suggested that I try out acupuncture. Skeptical and resistant but desperate to relieve the neck pain, I took their advice. Little did I know that my relationship with my acupuncturist would lead me down a path I could only see in a dream.

I scheduled a meeting with Dr. John, a medical physician trained in acupuncture. His office setup resembled mine but without the usual front desk assistant ready to process insurance. Interestingly, Dr. John had worked with Patch Adams, MD, the renowned physician who took clowning and innovative medical approaches worldwide, bringing lightness and laughter to patients everywhere. The relaxed meeting space contained a table and a small desk with a large cabinet holding medical books and supplies; I don't remember any Eastern medicine-related items, such as a picture of the Buddha or incense. Dr. John and I discussed my inexperience with acupuncture, and we agreed that if, after three sessions, I saw no significant change, we would stop and reassess. While gently placing acupuncture needles into various points about my body, Dr. John asked about things I liked to do and if I'd had any dreams lately. Something about his manner put me at ease, and I started talking about some of my scuba adventures and the recent encounter with the angelfish.

Immediately, he responded excitedly, "Oh, Bart, this fish is inviting you to dive with her into your unconscious."

What a silly idea, I thought to myself. This was followed by blurting out something like, "Really? You're joking, right?"

Dr. John gazed at me thoughtfully and shook his head.

"I am not joking. This fish is asking you to join it in the adventure of your life."

My mind went silent for just a second. Until this time, I never considered looking at dreams a fruitful endeavor. While Dr. John's suggestions intrigued me, I remained leery.

The session with him lit some spark inside me, and before I left, I scheduled another appointment. I wanted to see this through a little further, and after the first few acupuncture sessions, I knew I had arrived at a small crossroads. *Can I overcome this automatic skepticism I always feel toward self-help fixes? Should I even consider some of the dreams I've had?* I quietly listened as this line of questioning went through my mind.

One thing was sure: the depression that engulfed me wouldn't give up easily.

I continued to meet with Dr. John, whose manner and insights wore small holes in my armor. I slowly opened up to the possibility that my cervical spine's dysfunction called attention to any imbalance in my inner world. I noticed how my neck had become a symbolic iron gate between my brain, where my intellect resided, and the rest of my body, currently used only as a vehicle for my mind to get around in the world. I couldn't feel beauty or love, but I thought that was normal for me. My "thought police" never let anything that might inspire awe or wonder pass from my mind into the rest of my being, where those qualities might be felt and flourish. Residing in the intellect enabled me to bury and forget a long-held question: "*Why am I the one who is punished, and why am I the one who is undeserving of joy?"*

The neck, no longer able to function as a locked gate, finally failed; the entire structure collapsed, opening a floodgate of pain, anger, fear, and depression. Increased emotional awareness terrified me. It threatened my very sense of survival. I imagined that from this point onward, my inner conflict would be slowly and painfully exposed. This was unfamiliar terrain for me.

To avoid looking at my negative and numbing strategies, I had previously filled my life with activity--work, home projects, or sports—each a fail-proof strategy of avoidance. Such physically based tactics no longer worked because of this immobilizing neck injury. Nonetheless, part of my mind wanted to resume my usual game of blaming everyone and everything. Another aspect of me had its toes curled around the edge of the dock – eager to dive into the deepest ocean imaginable to meet the angelfish. At this point, the pull toward resuming busy activity primarily prevailed.

It never occurred to me that my happiness came from within me and not from how much worldly success or wealth I amassed; I had no clue that the rigid beliefs that I clung to, my rock-solid proof that I was right and in control, only served to widen the divide between me and others. I thought that if I were right enough times, just in the right way, I'd finally be happy. Something *out there* had to fill this vast, gaping hole lurking within me.

I decided that my depression and restless, non-restorative sleep needed attention. Visiting another colleague specializing in psychiatry, he and I settled on medications that helped me get some meaningful sleep, though not without glitches. I began by taking Ambien, which contributed to sleepwalking. Several medical journals reported patients on Ambien sleep-driving their cars, going outside and firing their guns, and ending up in jail with no idea how they got there. Thankfully for me, Ambien-induced sleepwalking was confined to unintelligible loudmouth outbursts and drinking alcohol with only a fleeting awareness of my actions. We switched to another sleep aid. The new sleep medication brought a slight relief from depression, but by then, I knew these Western medicine interventions couldn't fix me all by themselves.

At about this time, my dreams took off in vivid frequency. Every night, I dreamt, sometimes of conflict and sometimes of an enticing warmth I seldom knew in waking life. I even began writing some of them down! I thought it was a chore and a waste of time, but I continued.

At two months post-surgery, the painfully rigid cervical collar came off. Sharon and I decided to celebrate by picking up an Airstream travel trailer from a nearby dealer, anticipating future outings and trips with our two children. I should have waited. Scheduling this big outing to buy an Airstream so soon after the collar came off, and then driving two hours home pulling a trailer played havoc with my neck. The first week after the collar removal was just as miserable as those prior, with neck muscles so weak and atrophied after two months of immobilization that they gripped in a constant spasm.

Physical therapy gradually calmed the muscle spasms but did not remedy the severely limited range of motion that had developed since surgery. When the therapist tried to increase the forward movement of my neck with a gentle push, nerve pain shot through my hand and wrist.

Committed to returning to work immediately, I resumed part-time hours at my pain clinic. As a doctor, I knew I needed more time to recover, but gnawing fear and endless waves of guilt told me I was lazy, worthless, and losing control of my practice if I didn't head back to the office.

Everything in my life was a mess. Severe neck pain flared whenever I looked up or down. Migraines hit instantaneously if I even slightly overextended my neck. I felt discouraged with putting pillowcases on pillows and even trying to stargaze, one of my favorite pastimes. My neurosurgeon encouraged me to practice karate and to start playing tennis again, which I tried, but the pain of even minimal neck movements made concentrating impossible. Soon I dropped these sports that I had once enjoyed, as they now took more out of me than I felt I received from participating. I stopped hiking because looking down at where my feet were going was an invitation to a splitting headache. Biking dropped as well. The loss of each of these activities devastated me.

At the same time, my marriage reached a boiling point. Depression and physical limitations affected my interactions with my wife and children. Sharon and I slept apart because of the surgery, and the intimacy in our relationship died. Our verbalizations turned into blame-the-other-person sessions and typically ended with me walking out of the room and not speaking to my children or wife for days. The similarities between my parents' constant fighting and Sharon's and my inability to talk to one another without dumping guilt and blame were all right in my face. We tried several outside counselors, but from my perspective, those sessions mainly consisted of one more person saying it was all Bart's fault. I even tried seeing a personal counselor, but instead of focusing on the tremendous changes inside me, the counselor and I mostly re-hashed the week's arguments with Sharon.

Keep going forward; I heard from within.

CHAPTER 6
DREAMS

One day, Sharon brought me an issue of *The Hook*, an alternative paper from Charlottesville, Virginia (about an hour from us). She pointed out an advertisement for a dream workshop run by a local psychologist, Dr. Len Worley, who specialized in therapeutic dream work. Once we reviewed the available literature, she and I agreed I'd attend and see if Dr. Len's presentation gave me clues about my sudden increase in nighttime dreams. Until my neck injury, I had viewed dreams as entertaining little snippets, annoyances, nightmares, or literal re-enactments of waking life. Dreams were always about other people and how they set themselves up to be problematic for me. As I did with waking life, I used dreams as opportunities to blame anyone but myself for the internal misery I harbored.

Off I went to attend my very first dream workshop. In an ordinary, well-lit classroom, thirty-some people attended, all strangers to me. I sat by myself while Dr. Len spoke of dreams using Jungian terminology, explaining that this approach helped others receive profound realizations about their lives. I didn't buy into some concepts, like the collective unconscious, archetypes, or anima and animus, but something told me to pursue this work. I began individual dreamwork sessions after talking to Dr. Len at the workshop. They still came nightly, and I figured that looking at a few might be helpful. We met weekly or biweekly and usually discussed the newest dream since our last meeting, attempting to uncover possible connections between my dreams, my past, and the depression I felt. These sessions led me into a whole new realm of experience.

Instead of just nightly interruptions, I began to see subconscious messages in my dreams. While many of them didn't provide clues about bridging the gap of disconnection I felt, they got me in touch with other aspects of my mind and world. Based on a Jungian interpretation of dream imagery, Dr. Len's intuitive approach encouraged me to consult my emotional world to begin communicating with dream figures. He often asked, "Is there a different way to see all of this?" In other words, could I see past any literal interpretations my mind automatically provided and intuit more figurative, nuanced, and non-linear explanations? An entirely new way of thinking challenged me to step out of my head and intellect and pay more attention to the feelings in my body. I often retreated into a detached, deflecting, and analytical response to Dr. Len's thoughtful questions. Until then, solutions to all my problems lay in fixing external situations and getting others to improve themselves (to my specifications). I resisted redirecting my attention inward at every turn; frankly, it was just too scary.

However, this dream work slowly changed my relationship with my nightly visitors. At Dr. Len's suggestion, I entertained the possibility that all of the figures in a dream represented parts of me, conscious or unconscious. This included dramatis personae I found aggravating, frightening, or disgusting. Equally weird to contemplate was that dream characters who exuded warm, loving feelings might also be aspects of me. This approach challenged who I thought I was to my very core. My discernment grew regarding whether a nightly actor represented a facet of me or an actual person from waking life—like instances of premonition.

I read a few books claiming to give accurate dream symbol interpretations. If you saw a white sock in your dream, it always meant blah, blah, and blah. While this might help some people, I found that these dream interpretation dictionaries seldom offered more than another way to spend my money.

Talking to the Angelfish

Dr. Len introduced me to an additional dreamwork technique known as active imagination, which provided a method to revisit and interact with a dream that might still hold valuable information.

He instructed me to interact with a dream character as I would a waking-life person, asking questions or accepting assistance. The subtlety of many of the replies made it challenging to make out the actual communication, and I needed help trusting what immediately arose in my mind. I couldn't tell if the dream figure spoke directly to me or if I had made it up in my imagination. Was I manufacturing answers that I wanted to hear? Part of my take on this technique was to trust that the first sensation, emotion, phrase, or image I heard or saw was the one to pay attention to. My domineering logical mind did not like sitting in the backseat.

As I used active imagination, I allowed more significant interactions with dream characters. In several sessions with the angelfish, I started to view my situation through her eyes. The backstory of her visit came to me.

She said, "Doing my best sexy swagger, rolling my colorful hips, I swim into the dark, smoky bar long past closing time. I am fishing for the most miserable and forlorn guy in the bar, the one alone and alienated from others. I know that in this

person, I'll find some joke fodder to use at the next holiday party; telling humorous tales about unhappy humans always brings roars of laughter from my oceanic pals.

My eyes immediately fall upon the guy at the bar ceremoniously wearing the stiff, rank, off-white neck collar. I know immediately that this adornment represents a lack of spirituality and profound disconnection.

The jokes begin forming in my angelfish brain, but something nudges me that telling this guy not to take himself too seriously is pointless. His misery wholly owns him, even to the point of having major neck surgery to prove his victimhood. While I know exactly who I am to connect with, I pretend to look around the room and ask for volunteers."

At this point, the angelfish goes silent, as she knows that profound silence is the only way to reach this guy so caught up in his own legend. No one else's drama matters, just the one he continuously tells himself. The angelfish knows that the man needs to flounder without a safety line in the darkest, uncharted waters in him. Within that experience, a long-hidden buoy of light, submerged beneath all kinds of fearful thoughts and beliefs, will emerge.

Utilizing active imagination, I glimpsed connections I couldn't see before.

The seemingly solid negativity swirling around me thinned each time the angelfish arose in my memories. Instead of a verbal revelation from God, which I would have discounted straightaway that morning, I watched this eight-foot angelfish swirl, dance, and gracefully move at the foot of my bed. Her presence quieted my thoughts.

The angelfish left as quickly as she had arrived, completing her task of initiating a few moments of silence. This angel of a fish demonstrated that peace even lay beneath my most profound feelings of misery.

The angelfish's being radiated the essence of peace. I caught glances of how this peace merged with the stillness I occasionally encountered while scuba diving in various places worldwide.

To the angelfish, peace existed underneath all interactions.

I wondered, "*While I observe the dream, are the dream characters watching me?*"

A direct answer eluded me, but just sitting with the possibility that my dream figures could be conscious poked a tiny hole in my perspective that I alone controlled my world. The angelfish seemed to observe me, and with her kind, intense gaze, she found just the right angle from which to open my clenched fist wrapped around tightly held beliefs. I wasn't simply watching a nightly movie and then drawing conclusions on my own; I gradually learned to dialogue with aspects of dreams.

Each night, I went to sleep intending to watch for that opening to moments of peace that the angelfish had taught me to sense. In doing so, I might eventually remember enough of a different, long-buried part of myself. Perhaps that long-lost part could sit and hold space while other parts of my mind pondered its existence. Apparently, other facets of me existed and might collaborate as guides through this life.

What I Discovered

Dreams took on a life of their own. They became more expressive and vivid, graphic and explicit. Most of my dreams were black and white, but occasional colors populated the scenes. Dream content also reflected inner conflict as scenes from World War I, World War II, and The Vietnam War became the battlegrounds of my nightly landscape. Waking up after nights of skirmishes, gunshots, and battles, some fought from the sky, and others waged in jungles or forests, disturbed me. In several dreams, I found myself hunted by enemy soldiers along the streets of a bombed-out city, my mind on high alert as I searched for someplace to hide and elude them. Usually, I had no weapons, and when armed, I found that each gun I wielded quickly became ineffective. Breathing laboriously, sweating, and terrified, I experienced many traumatic scenes that boiled down to retreating and hiding in some forlorn bombed-out building.

After working with Len, I realized a need to stop running and start paying attention to what I had so long repressed.

Many dreams seemed symbolic of my feelings of disconnectedness.

I dream of swimming up from the bottom of a pool. Coming to the surface, I notice a sheet of ice on top of the water, not very thick, as I quickly break through it. Pulling myself from the water, I see one of my cousins standing on land at the side of the pool. She looks straight at me and says, "He is the one who has seen the giant clam."

I didn't understand this at first. Yes, I had been to Australia, and while scuba diving on the Great Barrier Reef, I saw many giant clams; some of the larger ones could easily contain a person. Magnificent creatures illuminated the surrounding seabed with their beautiful, velvety inner softness *when their shells were open*. Could the meaning of this dream be that simple? I had seen giant clams. My intellectual mind accepted this, but I sensed that underneath this literal explanation churned an ocean aching to provide me more.

Many weeks after this dream, my orange Kubota lawn tractor and I mowed the grass in back of our home. As if preceded by the flashing of a light bulb, I suddenly knew that the symbolism of the giant clam represented me. A human giant clam, if you will. It showed me how I related to the world—my giant clamshell clamped shut, afraid to open and connect with anyone. I also saw that my longstanding role as a giant clam was lost on no one, no matter how carefully I thought I covered it up.

As I followed my nightly dreams, they mostly fell into one of three categories. Some were premonition dreams in which characters and actions in the dream sequence reflected very soon in my waking world.

One night, I find myself in a very non-descript room. There is no furniture, no windows, or even any doors. I see my Aunt Ethel from across the room. Wincing in obvious pain, she limps and hobbles across the floor. She doesn't acknowledge me, and I don't say anything. I awaken.

I had previously cut Aunt Ethel and many other relatives out of my life. After my grandmother passed away 20 years ago, she and her husband, Robert, hosted the annual Christmas Eve family celebration. With the birth of my children, I stopped going to those get-togethers. But after this dream, something inside said I should reach out, and when I did, I asked her how she was doing.

"Hello, Aunt Ethel. This is Bart calling to check in with you. How are you doing right now?"

Aunt Ethel answered," I'm doing just fine, except for yesterday's foot surgery."

I kept the conversation short, and I wished her well.

Asking me to reconnect with her the dream alerted me to Aunt Ethel's recent surgery before I learned of it in waking life.

Sometimes, the battlefield dreams functioned as premonitions, forewarning me of a pending outburst of anger on my part in a personality clash with someone in daily life. At first, I ignored them, but eventually, I acquiesced. These dreams gave me advanced warning that I was about to jump into a real-life skirmish, not so much to change it but to raise my awareness of what I might experience as that conflict played out.

Some dreams functioned like report cards or the status of where things are dreams, revealing an unconscious perspective on some aspect of my life and providing me with little nudges (or full-out bonks on the head) as guidance toward a new, more open view that was far less painful for me and others.

In one dream, I enter a run-down bathroom. I am filled with anger as I look for a functioning toilet. Some debris blocks the floor, and in making my way around it, I see a mirror with my reflection—the reflection of an older man in the midst of an angry outburst. It is hard to look at myself as that uncontrolled anger rises on my face. I realize this is how I look when I get angry; frankly, it isn't enjoyable to witness or feel internally. I awaken.

This dream brought me face to face with my anger.

Some dreams stretched me: the this-is-just-under-the-surface-of-where-you-think-you-are dreams presented clues inviting a questioning of my thoughts and beliefs. Beginning to work with these dreams constantly pulled the rug out from under my feet, along with all the ideas I'd used to prop myself up. The jerking carpet ride continues to this day! One of my dreams in this category was a short segment I experienced early on in this new adventure. From my dream journal …

I am on the deck of a cruise ship with an older woman seated at a small round table nearby. I hear her monotone voice say she is waiting for her dead husband to arrive. At first, I don't see anyone, but suddenly, her dead husband is seated at her table in a white robe. He is stone-faced and silent, with no overt acknowledgment between them. There is nothing positive about their energies; frankly, they both appear dead, just sitting there. A man behind me gets my attention and asks, "Have you noticed how high the price of gravity is lately?" I am puzzled and tell him, "But gravity doesn't cost anything." Looking at me, he says, "Really? Just look around you."

Figure 10 The Price of Gravity

Contemplating this dream, I asked myself: What is the price of hanging onto old, dead stories that no longer speak to me? What is the price of the gravity of guilt and shame called sticking-to-my-story-of-victimhood cemented to the past? And what is the cost of the anxiety and disconnectedness I feel while I try to figure out and control the future? While I had been privately suffering for a long time, I began becoming conscious of the high price I paid to remain in the old definition of who I thought I was.

In another dream, I find myself in Hiroshima just after the atomic bomb decimates the city. A devastated landscape dominates all of my views as I find myself hiding behind a shattered brick wall. A woman in a dark cloak covering her face and head appears to my right. I feel reassurance in her

presence, although I don't know who she is or what she represents. The cloaked woman then reassures me, "Don't worry. It will come again." Puzzled by her words, I look into the distance at the horizon as the brightest of all lights appears silently and proceeds to engulf everything. Then I awakened.

Figure 10 "Don't worry. It will come again."

As with any dream, including being at Hiroshima after the dropping of the atomic bomb, my little mind wanted a definitive answer and something tangible to hang onto so it could relate what I knew to others. Instead, I uncovered more questions. Who is the mysterious woman beside me professing that there could be a hopeful meaning to this incredible destruction, war, and suffering? What, indeed, will come again? Why does it leave in the first place? How will I know that it has come again? And perhaps most importantly, despite all the destruction around me, I still managed to find at least a remnant of a cement wall behind which I could stand. What beliefs or points of view does the wall symbolize? While these questions helped tease meaning out of this dream, they also illustrated my ongoing need to know every situation's cause and effect.

I needed repeated reminders that the meaning I wanted any dream to represent may not be the meaning the dream brought.

No matter what energies arose, including an atomic bomb, I perceived a wall separating me from everything. A wall held in place with the strongest of beliefs. I sensed that the "coming again" pointed toward my remembrance of inner peace. However, I had not yet experienced this peace.

Soon after the Hiroshima dream, a dream illustrated some repetitive thinking from my youth.

I am outside the baseball stadium in Pittsburgh, Pa., with several familiar buildings in the background. A figure running towards me interrupts a lovely, partly cloudy spring day. I recognize this man as Bill Mazeroski, who played baseball for the Pittsburgh Pirates in the 1960s. Maz, also known as "The Glove," is out of breath, sweaty, and tired. He doesn't have any shoes or socks on, and his feet up to his knees are swollen three times their average size, red, blistered, and very painful. Maz sits down, totally exhausted, and asks me to "look at this situation." In the dream, I feel sorry for Maz, but I am unsure how to help him. I awaken.

In the ninth inning, with two outs in the seventh game of the 1960s World Series, Maz hit a home run to win the series for the Pirates. At the last minute, a celebratory smack into the outfield bleachers saved the joy of a whole city that had waited a century for a miracle season. I didn't see that particular home run in person, but I watched Maz and the Pirates repeatedly when my family traveled to Forbes Field in Pittsburgh to watch professional baseball games. Maz's miraculous "save the day" reputation preceded every trip to the plate as countless other Pittsburgh fans and I prayed for another game-winning hit. Sometimes, we were rewarded; other times, not. More often not.

Soon after waking from the dream of Maz, I repeatedly insisted that Maz slug some game-winning pitch out of the park and miraculously change my life at home. In multiple situations, I begged that things not be as they were, that things turn out differently, and that all the turmoil in my family magically disappear. While part of me approached the world cynically, another part pinned my future on the wish that someone outside of me would finally bring me happiness.

The dream with Maz illustrated my circular thinking of wishing one more time that things would be different and finding that they never were. Perhaps I secretly wanted that hope to fail, as the dismal situation gave me one more episode I could point to as the reason for my suffering. I apologized to my internal Maz for believing that he had failed me. Maz pointed towards the circular thoughts and feelings I had held for so long. No matter how repulsive, these feelings asked to be released of the meaning I placed on them so they could be seen simply as recognitions or perceptions.

This was the second dream where someone asked me if I could just look at this situation or place.

The Dream Group

Eventually, I deepened my dream work by joining a group led by Dr. Len. Here, I met my future wife, Melanie, who introduced herself with a hug and became the first person in the group to welcome me. An academic type with a Ph.D. in immunology, Melanie worked in the local Waldorf School, where, just a few years before, I had taken a tour considering the possibility of enrolling my children. Another woman in the group worked on casting for Hollywood movies, and her dreams were long and detailed. One man who owned a local professional cabinet shop often dreamed of retention and elimination themes, especially about his abusive father. Raul, who became a close friend, was a magnificent woodworker who enjoyed his home workshop. I remember his dreams pointing back to innocent, joyful roots in Africa.

Searching together, we met every other week to retell and gift each other our dreams. Dr. Len's profound insights helped us navigate each dream and its implications for our everyday lives. It's one thing to meet privately with a dream therapist and hash through your personal experiences; it's another notch up the vulnerability scale to do so in the presence of others. We sat in a circle on the available chairs and couches and one by one, opened ourselves up just beyond our safety limits. Len's provocative, occasionally subtle intuitions always presented a slightly different perspective than any of us came up with on our own.

Around this time, I often dreamt of natural disasters. I would find myself on a beach and suddenly see a towering wave about to crash onto me. From the inside of a building, I saw as many as six tornados ripping up a town that looked very similar to my small hometown. In multiple dreams, I experienced the earth's rumblings topple buildings and open huge cracks in the ground. And several times, I witnessed fires consuming entire blocks of the same small city. Each of these found me fearfully taking some action to save myself. These dreams reflected the many changes occurring or about to happen in my waking life.

While the dream work was illuminating, I knew that I needed to face other parts of my life in different ways. Part of me knew that all the answers I sought eluded even the most wondrous dream experiences. Despite all the lessons I assimilated, I still felt disconnected.

The honest take on my life declared that things weren't fine and something was still missing.

CHAPTER 7
THERE HAS TO BE SOMETHING ELSE HERE

A few days before the next dream group meeting, I realized Sharon and I needed to part ways. I knew that neither of us would make any emotional changes if we stayed together. Couples counseling didn't provide any breakthroughs, and the pain we held only amplified over time, becoming the dominant focus in our household.

To cope with our separation, I relied on my well-worn approach of shutting down all feelings, and so, without emotion, I moved out of our home. Soon after, Sharon gathered my remaining clothes into black plastic garbage bags and dumped them in my office's parking area. Not too different than collecting the trash to take to the dump, the bags quickly ended up in my car. Two minutes later, back inside my office, I examined patients and wrote out prescriptions as if nothing unusual had happened. Beneath that calm veneer, guilt, shame, and sadness blocked me from even trying to explain the failure of their parents' marriage to our teenage children. I drove them to and from the private school they attended, an hour each way, three days a week; our rides together were mostly awkwardly silent. Sadly, I never asked the boys how they felt about all of this, so I never knew how they managed.

I found stability through distraction by working with patients and their issues—burying my own pain until meeting with Len each week. Around this time, I added more to my workload when the following dream occurred:

I walk up and down an office hallway, looking for my office. I find a room with my name on the door, and as I enter, two nurses say in unison, "There goes that new Virgina (pronounced ver-JI-na) surgeon," in a slightly Southern accent. I awaken.

The "Virgina" pronunciation puzzled me. Did the nurses mean "vagina" or "Virginia"? As a youngster growing up in West Virginia, a grade school friend and I had joked once or twice about Virginia being the land of ***ver-JI-na***. At the time, I didn't think it was particularly funny, and I dared never let my parents hear me say ***ver-JI-na,*** as punishment loomed for saying or alluding to any word dealing with sexual anatomy. After a short active imagination session, the words "verge" and "Enya" came to mind. It turns out that Enya is a Gaelic word referring to "fire" or "seed." Could I have been on the edge of a fire about to consume whomever I thought I was? While I did not know the meaning of this dream, it motivated me to inquire about a position in pain management at the University of Virginia.

I applied for a position, and a few weeks later, I found myself instructing advanced physicians in pain management at UVA one day a week. Early in my career, I vowed not to go into academic medicine, but at this point, I sought any excuse to deflect my attention away from my hopeless marriage. New teaching duties conveniently packed my workweek. I tried to balance the failure of my marriage with the success of adding the title of assistant professor to my list of credentials!

"Hello. Comfy Chair Inn. How can I help you?" answered the hotel receptionist.

"Do you have any rooms with a double bed available for several nights?" I asked, desperately trying to find a place to rest after a long clinic day.

"Yes, we have a non-smoking room, but I can only give you two nights."

"Sounds good," I said, hiding my disappointment at only landing a two-night stay. I started the car, filled with my belongings in glorified black, plastic-trash suitcases, and headed four miles down the highway.

Several pieces of heavy equipment and bucket trucks occupied many of the spaces in the hotel parking lot. Before checking in, I rummaged through my bags, gathering enough clothes for tomorrow's workday. The hotel was clean but very commonplace. Several men, still wearing white construction hats, nodded to me as the automatic doors announced my presence. Paying for two nights, I asked for complimentary toothpaste, boarded a crowded elevator to the second floor, turned left, and used the key card to enter my room. Without room service, the hotel offered warmed frozen waffles for breakfast. Sadness filled my eyes as I started the non-ducted air conditioner to help clear the stale smell. Old and faded flower prints hung on the wall above the bed. I found the only electrical outlet outside the bathroom and charged my phone. Falling back on the bed, I wondered how this had all happened. My life was totally in upheaval; I knew I'd be back in my car looking for the next place to stay in a few days. I wasn't looking forward to breakfast—alone.

Disorientation prevailed when I stopped working long enough to let myself feel. I had never been adrift in life like this before.

However, no matter what happened on this drop into the unknown, I knew this was the only way I could go.

Something Else

I met with Len again while staying at the third hotel since separating from Sharon. Our meeting started as usual, with me settled into the now-familiar tan chair. The afternoon sun faded as I gazed out the window at people walking casually on Main Street one flight of steps below Len's office. Jealousy raised its head, as they were all obviously much happier than me.

"Len, I'm not sure where to start," I sighed. "All sorts of dreams have crossed my path, but none seem that big of a deal."

I shared a dream of conflict symbolized by another WWII scene but gleaned little from it except that it reflected my life's ongoing restlessness.

I didn't think much of the following dream but decided to share it anyway.

Several fraternity brothers from college, who I know are staunchly against illegal drugs, grab and hold me down at the bottom of a stairwell. There isn't any dialogue, and mild confusion runs through my mind. One of the fraternity members takes out a needle and syringe and injects a white powdery substance into the great toe on my right foot as I struggle to get away. I don't recognize the location of the stairway, but I noticed that several of these friends had been roommates of mine. I awaken.

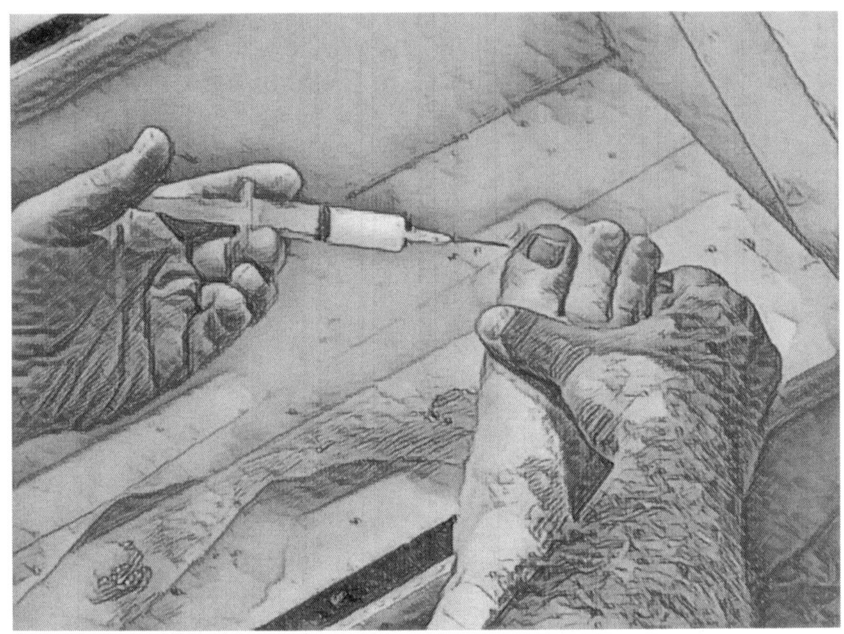

Figure 11 Held down and injected

Before Len spoke, it felt like a thousand thoughts went through my mind. I felt tired and at a total impasse. Hopelessness appeared as I looked towards the floor. I turned to Len, and I said, with the emptiness of an entire universe in my stomach,

"There has to be something else here."

Despite the insights and meanings unearthed in the flood of nightly dreams, a massive disconnection in my relationship with the world, nature, and other human beings felt real. A vast hole inside me spoke up, maybe shouted, declaring that there had to be something else.

Of course, the relentless self-critical part of me took great pleasure in placing the blame on me—that I overlooked that one particular word, elusive thought, or sacred object that would provide me with the missing piece of my life. Or maybe I only needed that captivating and approving glance from someone I admired; all just one more situation where the gift of my happiness lay in someone else's hands. Great.

"There has to be something else here," kept echoing as I waited for his reply.

As he leaned forward and approached the edge of his chair, Len's expression transformed into one more intense, probing look.

Quietly and slowly, he said, "Yes, indeed. There are several ways of approaching this."

"And what would those be?" I quickly blurted out.

"Of course, we can try some active imagination. And have you heard of holotropic breathing?" Len asked.

"No, I haven't," I replied, and with that, Len gave me some information on a holotropic breathing technique by Dr. Stan Grof.

"Another possibility is psychedelics," he said.

"I have read just a little about these, but aren't they all illegal, unobtainable, and just as dangerous as the government proclaims on television?"

"Psychedelics have a rightful place in treating depression, trauma, and anxiety when paired with other avenues of psychotherapy," declared Len. "While psychedelics in and of themselves aren't a cure-all, they can be a first step in helping people get themselves off the basement floor."

"This is perhaps what your dream is about, Bart," he continued. "Your college buddies hold you down and inject a medication that can help you climb up and out of the pits of where you think you are at the bottom of the basement stairs. What do you always lead with when you walk? Your great toe."

I sat there, speechless, for a few moments. What did I have to lose but my medical license and an illusory image I believed others had of me—that of a conservative, compassionate, professional physician who would never veer off the mainstream path? What did I have to loosen but that white-knuckle grip I had on who I thought I was? While dreamwork had helped open me up to different possibilities, I still mechanically went through the motions in life, all the while feeling lost and alienated from a kinder inner world that I hoped awaited me. This brought me to another fork in the road.

Len offered me a referral to a practitioner who used their psychology training and the occasional use of psychedelics to help patients navigate their ongoing detachment from life. I accepted without hesitation, without needing to weigh the pros and cons. I immediately said yes to his offer.

A New Path to Try

All my experiences with drugs, including alcohol, were socially related until this point. I liked certain alcoholic beverages, but aside from a few isolated binge-drinking weekends in college, I never found alcoholic inebriation and post-drinking effects attractive. An adventurous and rebellious roommate in medical school had occasionally brought home some marijuana, but I never experienced the high that others described the few times I tried it. Even the best stuff left me with the same negative, circular thoughts.

Dr. Len assured me that Dr. Sam, a quiet and reflective man, didn't advocate for rave parties. And he, indeed, wasn't extending a quick high to help me momentarily forget my issues. He provided a purely therapeutic experience. Could an opening or insight emerge that broadened my view beyond my current internal landscape?

While not guaranteeing any breakthroughs, Dr. Len referred me to articles and books on psychedelic medications used to treat depression and PTSD, some written by Stan Grof, MD, and others by Alexander Shulgin.

I read these both with interest and a sense of conflict. Many of these substances had regained medical recognition in several countries, allowing clinical trials to resume after a 25-year hiatus. Medications such as MDMA, plant derivatives from certain mushroom species, and ayahuasca could be tremendous therapeutic agents used in the right hands under controlled conditions. Quite a few ape species are known to eat psilocybin mushrooms. A theory developed that our pre-Hominid ancestors inadvertently multiplied the neuronal connections in their brains by eating mushrooms growing on cow dung. This may have allowed us to develop language to describe our inner and outer worlds. I wondered whether this early connection between humans and mushrooms may have allowed the yogis of the Indian subcontinent to channel concepts of worlds beyond what we see here to develop yoga, its postures, and its many implications in spiritual life.

Many indigenous and spiritual communities have used plant medicines and psychedelics as their mainstay of medicine and mind-expanding work throughout recorded history. Canadian psychiatrist Humphry Osmond first coined the word "psychedelics" during his correspondence with Aldous Huxley in the 1950s. It comes from the Greek words for the mind, *psyche,* and reveal or make visible, *deloun.* Research on psychedelics essentially ended when the US government outlawed these therapeutics under The War on Drugs in the early 1970s. Thankfully, many of these substances have become accepted, legalized, and available in other countries for patients to help bridge that body/mind gap.

Considering such information was quite a departure for this previously by-the-book, well-trained doctor from Virginia. What in tarnation was I heading into?

On the day of my first MDMA adventure, I parked the BMW, climbed the stairs, and walked into a plain office with simple decor. A hardwood floor covered with an area rug of basic square patterns in muted colors complemented the two windows looking out into a modest courtyard. Given what I was walking into, I felt surprisingly relaxed, and I sensed compassion as Dr. Sam entered the room.

"Tell me a little about what brought you here, Bart."

"Oh, you mean how I got into the big pit of a hole I find myself in every morning?" I said wryly.

"I don't need every detail, but a quick background would be good."

I told him about my successes and how I still felt empty and fragmented.

"Perfect!" came the response. "You are already familiar with some of these medications. And you have done some interesting pre-journey inner work. Of course, you should continue dreamwork with Dr. Len, especially if you have any breakthroughs today. Are you ready?"

I let out a breath of agreement and said, "Yes, let's get started."

Dr. Sam carefully weighed out the medication and placed it in a capsule. I stared at the small pill for a second, perhaps wishing for future happiness. I felt a slight pang of guilt, saying I shouldn't be doing this. I wondered what Sharon and her attorneys would say if they knew!

He gave me a dose of the medication 3,4 methylenedioxymethamphetamine, also known as MDMA and Ecstasy. We made small talk, waiting for it to kick in. I talked about whatever came to my mind and told Dr. Sam about a few of my recent dreams.

After talking for about an hour, I noted that nothing was happening–no relaxation, no quieting of thoughts, no insights, and no feelings of relief. I felt a very familiar sensation of disappointment settle on my shoulders and chest and gave my approval for an additional dose. But even after more time passed, I still felt nothing. We talked about current events and the weather. We even walked around the block during that calm spring afternoon. No tremendous or annoying insights into my dreams or side effects surfaced; no trembling, no paranoid thoughts, and no visual patterns. While things weren't bad for me, this wasn't anything to write home about. Not that I would ever tell my parents about this.

After four hours, both of us ready to wrap things up. I still felt no change. I resigned, hoping for some interesting dreams that evening. Getting my coat, I stepped towards the door. But suddenly, I felt a tingling in the front of my chest at heart level. I didn't feel like going out dancing or having sex, but the sensation grew from one tiny spot to what seemed like hundreds of little tingles. All I could muster was a distant, vague curiosity. I casually mentioned it to Dr. Sam in a tone similar to describing tomorrow's weather forecast. I drove back to my hotel with little thought concerning the sensation.

Opening the Heart

This chest-level tingling sensation seemed subtle yet calming, like a gentle breeze on a warm sunny day, and it persisted for days, non-stop. Amusingly, it began to annoy me because the sensation demanded that I interrupt my precious train of thought and pay attention to the feeling. I had no clue this sensation could be from the heart until I spoke to Len in his office several days later.

Settling into our usual chairs again, I asked Len to close the blinds as the afternoon sun brought too much light into our space.

"How did the session go with Dr. Sam?" Len asked.

"Uneventful," I said, "But I did get a T-shirt saying, "I took some drugs, and all I got was this lousy sensation in my chest!"

I later learned that Len immediately knew what this referred to, but he allowed me to continue without interruption.

"Nothing happened after two doses of medication, except I started to feel a sensation in my chest as I got ready to head out the door. A night later, I had a dream involving heart surgery."

I went on to tell Len the dream.

I suddenly find myself in an operating room with several monitors. It dawns on me that I am the one who will be having surgery, and yet I'm strangely not alarmed. A close acquaintance, Dr. Art, a cardiac surgeon, approaches me and proceeds to make an incision on my chest. I am awake and unafraid. Dr. Art is a physician I trust and have worked with many times in waking life. I remember he trusted me to give him a spinal anesthetic during a surgery he needed, and now I find that I trust him to open my chest. Once my chest is open, I see my heart beating. I awaken.

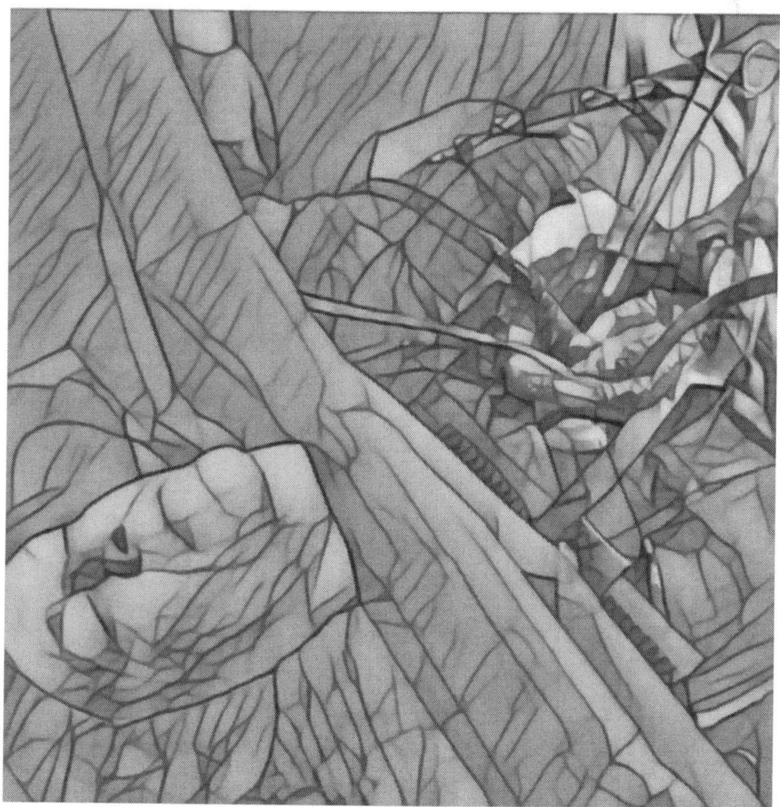

Figure 12 "Opening of the Heart Surgery"

I had dreamt numerous times of operating room themes in the past. This dream didn't seem like a big deal, as I had participated in thousands of cardiothoracic surgeries in the years before I became a full-time pain management physician.

"Bart, it occurs to me that what you experienced at the end of the MDMA session was an initial awareness of your heart chakra," Len said. "I think this dream helps to reinforce that."

I had read little about heart chakras, and I had never heard them mentioned during any lectures in my medical training. Due to their connection to Eastern medicine and lack of laboratory validation, allopathic medicine viewed chakras as less credible than acupuncture. Western medicine didn't deny connections between the brain and various organs, as the nerves were right there for anyone to see under the microscope. But to acknowledge a "mind-body" connection where someone could affect, control, and gain knowledge from their body was just a step too far for my medical school at the time. Most of that kind of thinking was discussed as psychosomatic and delusional.

"Yes, the heart chakra makes some sense to me, but where would I even take it from here?" I replied. "I am not getting anything from it other than an occasional fuzzy sensation, and that has dissipated to just about nothing."

"For that, we must see where things go," responded Dr. Len. "I talked with Dr. Sam, and we suggest trialing a slightly different medication in a completely different setting."

"Doing something like that will need to wait a few weeks," I said. "You know, work."

Dreams of Layla

Over the next few weeks, my high school girlfriend Layla appeared in multiple dreams. I hadn't spoken to her for at least

15 years. While mesmerized by her presence in my dreams, I had many conflicting thoughts about how I had dumped and ignored her when a tiny amount of conflict arose in our relationship. After that unfortunate miscommunication with her in high school, I ran straight back to my clamshell, climbed in, and shut it tightly.

Outside in a parking area, I notice old-style covered wagons. It almost seems like a traveling carnival show. Soon, I notice Layla near one of the wagons. I walk over to her and say, "Hello." I immediately see that she is roundly pregnant and probably, I guess, just a month or two from delivery. Our conversation is minimal but friendly. Without thinking, I ask her who her child's father is, and she unexpectedly replies, "You are the father." This leaves me speechless, and I wake up instantly.

Dr. Len suggested that the figure of Layla in my dreams symbolized my anima, the archetypal source of the feminine aspects of my personality. According to Jungian psychology, each person has a masculine (animus) and a feminine (anima) side; the two complement and balance one another in a healthy human being. One interpretation of this dream brings characteristics ascribed to the feminine, such as empathy, kindness, and creativity, to join with my more masculine characteristics, such as responsibility, rationality, and strength. All bringing different aspects to a new way of seeing the world. A literal interpretation of this dream could never apply, but I wondered if this dream directed me toward rekindling a relationship with her. I considered getting in touch with her and sensed something in me, hoping that she or her companionship would fulfill me.

When I brought this series of dreams to Dr. Len and the dream group, everyone strongly urged me to drop the literal interpretation regarding reconnecting with Layla and consider the dreams as symbolic, representing parts of my inner self. I heeded their advice and did not contact her, although disappointment arose.

Many years later, I spoke to her regarding a proposed high school reunion, and I learned that at the same time she had appeared in my dreams, she had gone through a separation and divorce from her first husband. Deep in my chest, I felt slightly disappointed at not having reached out sooner but immediately shut it down.

Connecting Heart and Brain

Not long after my MDMA experience, Len introduced me to something called HeartMath®, a scientific approach that uses the connections between the heart and brain to reduce stress and balance the nervous system. He said it would help me activate calming areas in my brain. Len purchased a license to use the program on his computer and thought I should try it. It didn't occur to me then that he might have started using HeartMath exclusively to help me expand the potential of the soft opening of awareness in my chest, but I wonder now.

Len gave me simple instructions and put the pulse oximeter on my finger, measuring oxygen in my blood. Immediately, I saw my heart rhythm on his screen. Len then asked me to breathe while focusing on my heart area. The graph color changed from red to blue to green, indicating a certain level of "coherence" and smoothness in my heartbeat variations. After a few seconds, I again felt that now familiar sensation in the chest/heart area that

I had noticed for several days after the MDMA trial. When I placed attention on my chest and brought up mildly distressing thoughts, the graph color went red again, and the variations of my heartbeat became chaotic. This gave me insight into the sensation related to my heart and emotional state, and I now had a tool to help me reproduce it.

The HeartMath technology measures beat-to-beat variations in heart rhythm, but it is not an electrocardiogram device. A smoother heart rhythm gives a person more access to clarity, focus, creativity, compassion, joy, energy, and less stress. In contrast, a more erratic heart rhythm correlates with stress, anxiety, depression, fear, frustration, narrowed thinking, energy drain, and increased pain. Breathing with an intention and focus on the heart area, especially while activating a sincere feeling of appreciation or care, activates local nerves, leading to a pleasant sensation in the chest.

MDMA had not been as ineffective as I'd first thought! It helped me feel a part of my body, my heart, which I had denied and ignored. Len and I later discussed the potential benefits of using HeartMath in my clinical practice. I had plenty of patients with anxiety, depression, and other issues, and felt they might benefit from it.

Len's Vision

"Bart, before we begin today, I want to tell you about a thought that came to me a few days ago," he said in a slightly serious voice.

A captivating anxiety churned inside me. "Ah … sure …. go ahead," I responded.

"Just sitting here the other day, I saw a vision of you and Melanie together. A very simple scene, but it appeared happiness surrounded you both."

I stopped breathing for just a second. "Melanie? Are you sure?" Up till now, I had never even thought of that. A very puzzled, slightly disgruntled look appeared on my face.

"But she lives her entire life in the past!" I exclaimed.

Len stood still, neither acknowledging nor refuting my outburst. "Let's just let that sit for now," he said.

Unsure of my readiness to start dating anyone, especially someone in the dream group I attended, I agreed to sit with the idea.

My approach to life and relationships slowly changed. It's nearly impossible to remain strangers with people in a dream group, as each of you shares your nightly encounters and discusses the vulnerable intricacies of your waking life. Group dreamwork evolved into an intimate endeavor.

The idea of a new relationship gradually grew, and I warmed to the thought of asking Melanie to meet outside of the confidential container of our group. I approached Len to confirm his feelings about this topic. The conversation quickly felt like a young man coming to a woman's father to ask permission to date her. I wanted to respect the sacred nature of the group, but most of all, I didn't want to make an ass of myself. Len offered to reach out to her to ensure she was comfortable with it since she faced similar challenges. I knew that she had continued working through her ongoing separation and divorce. The news came back; she was open to a meeting! And with that, I gave her a call.

To my delight, she agreed … Melanie and I decided to meet for coffee.

Melanie, My Dream, and Moving Forward

Unexpectantly, the night before our meeting, I had a long dream of being back in Weirton, WV, my hometown:

I walk up and down Weir Avenue, where my dad's parents live. This street has an expansive view of almost all of Weirton Steel, with the myriad sounds, heat, and smoke of the mill itself. Suddenly, I see Melanie on the southern end of Weir Avenue in front of the coal tipping station, where dump trucks loaded with coal empty their contents into waiting train cars. The one thing that stands out about her is that Melanie's previously shoulder-length hair appears cut and trimmed to just below her ears. Her hair is markedly different than what I am used to seeing in our dream group. I awaken.

I didn't make much of the dream. I had a full day of clinic work in Charlottesville and planned to meet Melanie at an Exxon convenience store later in the afternoon. I felt excited and nervous driving to the store. Pulling around the corner, I anxiously scanned the parking lot and spotted Melanie standing by a telephone booth, precisely where we'd arranged to meet. My jaw dropped. Her hair had been cut just that morning in an attractive, clean, short style just below her ears. Her short hair was exactly like what I had seen in the dream!

Taken by her new hairstyle that I had now seen twice, I paid no attention to my foot, still depressing the accelerator pedal, and even less attention to the brakes! The scraping sounds of metal on metal brought me back to planet Earth as I crashed my car straight into the telephone booth next to where Melanie stood!

Like a spluttering teenager, I exited the vehicle and greeted her, professing several apologies for almost running her over. Laughter replaced all seriousness, and I told her about my dream the night before. The simple evening included a brief walk around her neighborhood, some decaf coffee, and donuts. Despite taking out a phone booth, she miraculously seemed to want to meet me again.

Our next outing occurred in a group context when Melanie and I went with our dream-analyzing compatriots to hear a samba-jazz trio perform in a bar along Charlottesville's pedestrian mall. Everyone enjoyed this short evening out. The music was stunningly unique, and the bar patrons were loud, so I had only a brief conversation with Melanie when I walked her to her car. Most of the group headed home early, but I stayed long enough to introduce myself to the band leader, Humberto Sales, an amazing flamenco guitarist classically trained in the lineage of Mario Ulloa, Elliot Fisk, and Andreas Segovia. Berto became my guitar teacher for the next eight years and introduced me to many different styles of music—in particular, flamenco, samba, bossa nova, and other Brazilian rhythms. I started allowing life to open up and present me with new experiences.

After our first date at the Exxon shop, where I put a big dent in the phone booth, Melanie and I started talking on the phone between dream group meetings. Frankly, her voice mesmerized me. It didn't matter what she said; I heard and felt something underneath her spoken words that resonated. We met a few more times for coffee, eventually leading to dinner. We talked, and we listened. Having gifted our dreams to each other in the dream group, we now listened to each other's many reasons for living. Importantly, we agreed to keep working on our internal issues.

Continuing our inner work felt crucial if anything could come of our new relationship. This was unlike any agreement I had ever made with anyone. Nor had she. Perhaps this was the first time either of us had seen so clearly that our inner worlds directly impacted our outer world experience.

Having been introduced to HeartMath and its many benefits years earlier, Melanie quickly utilized the HeartMath program when Len introduced it to the rest of the group. We now shared common bonds of HeartMath, music, Rumi, and the Tao Te Ching. A daily exchange of the previous night's dreams deepened our conversations. She continued as an administrator at the local Waldorf School, and our relationship gradually progressed. Soon, however, Melanie sensed a need for a significant change in her life and announced her decision to step down from her seven-year stint at the school.

One day, without any previous thought, a little voice in me said that Melanie needed to come to work at my pain clinic, offering HeartMath to chronic pain patients to help manage pain, anxiety, hopelessness, and depression. Melanie agreed! Several friends warned us about the pitfalls of a couple working together. Both excitement and nervousness surfaced, but we decided she would start when the Waldorf school recessed for summer break. While Melanie had some background in HeartMath, we felt that further training would benefit us both. As our first trip together, we traveled to the HeartMath Institute in California to undergo formal training in this stress management system, focusing on how to share it with my clients.

Shortly into our relationship, Melanie suggested I check out David Deida's work on male and female interpersonal relationships, focused on the inner work of tantric yoga. To my amazement, it only took me a second to agree. I would never have done something like this without outside encouragement, and while traveling to San Francisco, I attended a weekend Deida workshop for men. The workshop elicited openness, vulnerability, and honesty; sometimes, I felt out of my league. Still, I met some extraordinary people, all starting to look at and question their points of view.

Divorce, Dreams, and New Awakenings

During this time, it became apparent to Sharon and me that we should proceed with a divorce. I dreaded working with attorneys and the legal implications, but this inevitability loomed for both of us. Several times, a voice inside told me to turn around and head right back into our dysfunctional and painful relationship. I recognized this as the voice of guilt and chose not to heed its call like so many times before.

After interminable searching, I found a small house to rent in Crozet, a town halfway between Charlottesville, where our sons attended private school, and Weyers Cave, where I had my office. I continued as owner and lead physician at Balint Pain Management and an assistant professor in the UVA pain department.

Quiet, private, and unconnected to any place I had previously lived, the house became my oasis in the storms of change and divorce proceedings. After moving into the small red brick home, Melanie and her son accompanied me to the local SPCA, and I allowed two young cats to adopt me. This new but still temporary place began to feel like a natural home. Soon after moving in, I had a premonition-type dream.

I'm traveling with my younger brother on a passenger train towards Washington, DC, to find the "carnivorous" birds near the railroad track. Along with the rhythmic sounds of the wheels turning on the railroad tracks, I notice several large road signs announcing the presence of these carnivorous birds. In the dream, I have no idea why we are doing this. I awaken.

The autumn I landed in my new home, I noticed very little wildlife in the backyard, except for the occasional squirrel and the neighbors' dogs. As fall approached winter, turkey vultures started congregating and taking a rest from their daily travels on the local thermals. Soon, and very symbolically, over a hundred turkey vultures came to roost behind my new home. Staying for several months, they settled in the trees that separated my yard from a pair of railroad tracks. These birds, known to clean up dead and rotting carcasses, became my friends and companions as many of my old beliefs and rigid points of view became more accessible to see. Carnivorous birds had arrived.

I called Dr. Sam to make another appointment. He rose from his desk when I knocked on his door. We talked briefly about the previous session's MDMA experience. "Bart, opening this connection could be a massive step for you," he said. "And I like that it led Len to introduce you to HeartMath."

"Yes, the whole experience has given me a tool that I hope to use effectively," I agreed. "But it hasn't been all that profound. The experience lacks the blazing sun, symbolizing the start of an amazingly wonderful new day; instead, it seems more like turning on a small flickering night light underneath a dirty pile of socks. So, what do you have in mind?"

"We need to try a different medication—actually two medications in tandem that work slightly differently, to continue healing the hole you feel inside," Dr. Sam told me. "And we need to do it in a different setting. I know of a small, quiet cabin not too far from here. It is important to try these next medicines in a quiet, nocturnal environment. Noise and light add too much stimulation and diminish any response."

The Journey

The following week, about 30 minutes before sunset, I met Dr. Sam at a rural location with my toothbrush and some snacks. We settled into a small, rustic cabin next to a tranquil pond. No traffic noise could be heard; only bird calls and leaves rustling in the light wind. The cottage had one twin bed, a chair, and an outside outhouse.

Dr. Sam said hello and then glanced at my snacks. Half-jokingly, he said, "Gosh. Some people will eat just about anything! This brand of crackers is really dry and crumbly. Don't you ever consider that you are what you eat?" Admittedly, up to this point, my eating habits had been pretty miserable. Dr. Sam's comment planted a tiny seed.

Dr. Sam had brought his own essentials bag. He planned to sit with me until the medication wore off and then return home, leaving me to sleep there overnight. He asked me to remain at the cabin until he returned in the morning. I told him that since we had the place rented until early afternoon, I invited Melanie to come and sit with me for a few hours the following morning.

The evening's medicinal combination included a small amount of MDMA and a slightly larger helping of psilocybin mushrooms mixed in water. We talked about the dosages, and I understood they were moderately sized. Dr. Sam said the psilocybin could make the colors of the light around me highly intense and that he wouldn't speak much unless I asked him a question. I slowly gulped down the organic, woodsy, picnic-table-tasting contents of the small cup and began an inward journey, hoping to find answers.

The sun dropped below the horizon, and Dr. Sam adjusted his body into his chair in the corner of the small room. The dark paneling complemented the effortless feel of the setting as I lay back on the bed. The weather was perfect, with no humidity and a comfortable temperature. I took off my shoes and adjusted the pillow. I closed my eyes.

Over the next 20 minutes, neither Dr. Sam nor I speak as the progression toward colorful semicircular patterns fills my inner vision. Occasionally, I open my eyes and see Dr. Sam sitting contemplatively across the room. I never ask him what goes through his mind as he watches clients progress toward unimagined worlds.

The patterns in my mind start at a distance and get more extensive as the colors converge like tiles on the floor. At times, the sides of the sequences become rounded and fold back on themselves, giving the colors a three-dimensional feel. The figure of a gray alien peeks out from around a wall of color and winks. A thought says he is inviting me to go beyond the colors, but I have no idea how to do this. I have never experienced anything like this, but seeing the gray alien stretches right beyond my edge of comfort.

I opened my eyes back in the cabin and on the bed, noting some nausea, and asked for a drink of water. I looked at Dr. Sam and said, "I saw cool colors and patterns, but I feel like I need more than some recreational trip." Dr. Sam nodded and prepared another concoction of mushrooms. Not eager to revisit the earthy taste, I drank it and reclined, hoping to avoid more nausea.

So much for hope, as a mild wave of nausea settles in my stomach. Without warning, I am overcome with grief and sadness over my failed marriage. As I am outwardly crying, Sharon comes to mind. I see her face, sobbing, reddened, and in pain. Then, her image as a young woman right after we married presents itself. I let this grief thoroughly wash over me again and again. I feel despair from my head down to my toes as it completely penetrates and surrounds me. I have never felt such anguish and sorrow.

Suddenly, I see my body floating, almost lifeless, in a literal pool of grief and sadness. This pool becomes a sphere of transparent blue, and towards the middle of the sphere, there is a very bright pinpoint light. I realize I am just watching all of this. I am not in the body anymore.

My attention shifts to another brightness. I know instantly that it is Melanie's soul/spirit. She has a slight greenish tint to her light, and soon, it is the brightest thing of which I am aware. I find this overwhelmingly attractive, and I realize that within this pinpoint of light lies the totality of the universe, which is represented by the nature of her soul. I next see Sharon's light, which has a slight pink tint. Melanie's and Sharon's souls reside near each other and me. It is good to have all of us together. I see the lights of my grandparents go by as if waving hello on their way through the cosmos. Looking for my children, I see Tyler first (his light has a slightly bluish tint) and then Christopher, slightly reddish-tinted.

I then realize I can no longer see my light. Where is it? I know I must have one as well. I look to where my abdomen used to be and remember no longer being in an earthly body. An extremely bright singularity known as "Bart" opens the darkness. For some reason, I am reluctant to take on this name. I experienced this bright pinpoint of white light and understood that, at least in daily life, it is known as "Bart." I know I have close connections with the other singularities and souls surrounding me—bonds I rarely feel in waking life.

Suddenly, the entirety of creation reveals itself to me on a grand scale, as if I have been shown the whole plan. The "One Eye of God" watches over this infinite existence. On the one hand, I know this representation as a general blueprint of creation with the infinitely small center singularity containing everything imaginable and unimaginable. I also see this plan as a personal map of each of the named souls in existence.

Each soul exists as a primary singular soul, and surrounding this soul are concentric spheres of various colors. Each larger sphere surrounds the inner spheres, pointing toward the singularity. Every sphere is encompassed by an infinite number of larger spheres extending toward infinity. I thought of an analogy of a ball within a ball within a ball, extending outward and inward infinitely. These represent different dimensions, densities, or aspects of creation. For instance, the earthly sphere in which we reside is slightly brown.

The sphere of ego encompasses fear, guilt, happiness, and all other emotions. I realize that my exclusive attention on any one of these spheres blocks me from communicating with other spheres.

Everyone is known throughout the universe by a particular name, and our name defines and is symbolized by the most interior sphere and pinpoint of light. Our earthly sphere is merely a shadow of the spheres above and the imagination of those below. The spheres represent all of the dimensions of which scientists can ever dream.

I look towards infinity and again see the watchful "Eye of God." There is a sensation of being one with everything, and everything is connected. All at once, I am that "Bart" singularity, infinitely entwined with all and God. I see that I have free will to realize that bond or to block it.

Contained in each pinpoint of light is the entirety of creation. Each sphere interacts with and touches the other, like the intersecting waves of a few pebbles simultaneously dropped into an otherwise still pond. Written books are mere vestiges of a greater sphere above the writer. The imaginations of paints and media draw upon the hand of the artist and channel themselves into works of beauty.

The dimensions are endless, only waiting to be given names or assigned a symbol as we open and acknowledge their existence. Death in this earthly sphere is merely a transition in attention to other spheres. We go to wherever we are open to going at the time.

To be shown this on such a grand and infinite scale is overwhelming and profound. To feel and witness the presence of God is humbling and reassuring.

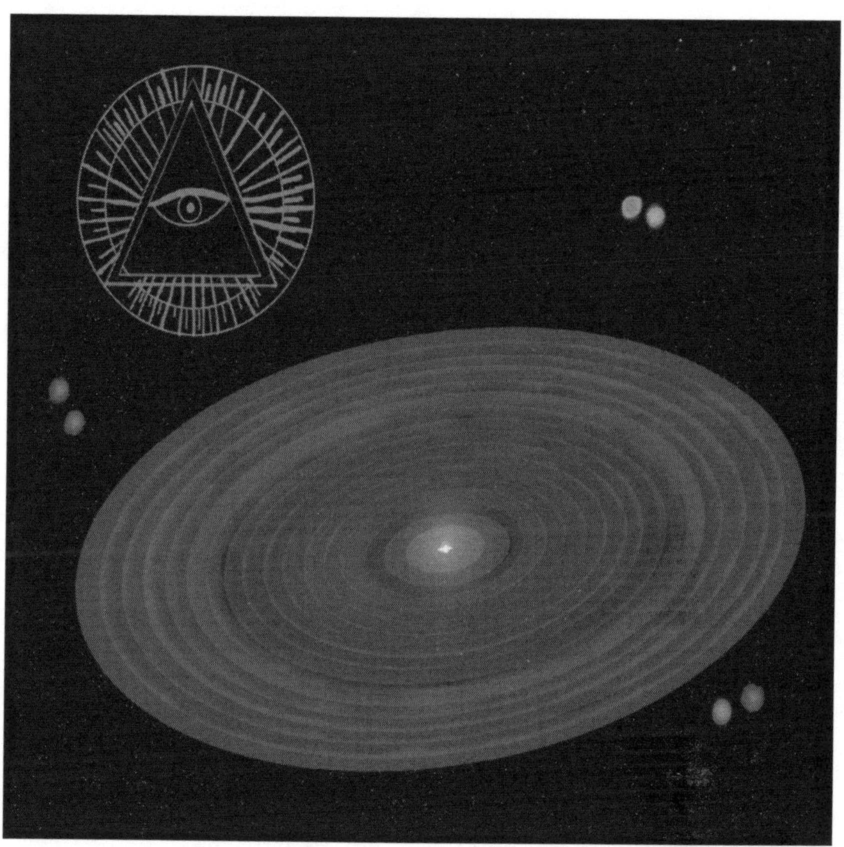

Figure 13 A representation of what I saw during my MDMA and mushroom journey.

Back to Ordinary Reality

As the journey ended, I opened my eyes, and the small cabin came into focus. A few times, I traveled back to the realm of the spheres, but I eventually decided to land here on Earth, lest I take one step too far. Dr. Sam and I went outside and sat quietly on a bench under the stars. I knew in my bones that everything I saw on this plane was merely a shadow of its true nature. Three hours had passed since my last dose, and I sat in amazement and wonder. I told Dr. Sam of my adventures, but I am not sure he understood. He did comment on the transpersonal nature of my ramblings. Before this evening, I had considered these earthly forms the only reality. The images I brought back from the journey challenged everything I knew. But just what to make of all this? Spheres, gray aliens inviting me to take that next step, singularities, souls, and unimagined connections between Melanie and Sharon were just a few.

Quietness soon came upon me, as I had talked more on this occasion than usual. Dr. Sam felt comfortable heading home. I saw him briefly in the morning when he offered me the residual mushrooms he had left. I declined, but I felt a bit of misgiving in that perhaps I had missed some other key to my being. I did need to process some of this experience before I jumped off the next cliff.

Melanie arrived around noon and brought us lunch. The light tint of green in her soul kept appearing to me as I looked into her eyes and tried to convey parts of the journey.

Initially, I only told Dr. Sam, Len, and Melanie about my adventure. I felt too vulnerable to tell anyone else, including the other members of our dream group.

Just what reality, if any, had I tapped into during that evening? While I relived some aspects of the sphere experience, a more far-reaching and unfamiliar wonder still filled me when I allowed it. I questioned if I had made up the "One Eye of God" and other figures to match some previously unconscious ideas.

I had never before thought about an afterlife, let alone the possibility of a pre-life or even reincarnation. Do we have to make up concepts such as a pre-life and an after-life to call this earthly presence life? Perhaps we have the whole idea of life screwed up. I thought of myself as existing in three dimensions, not the multi-dimensional spheres that implicate almost a continuous background to my interactions with others. The possibility that this reality was a mere shadow of a higher sphere resonated with me. This provided an answer to my initial question to Len concerning an emptiness in my life. It also brought a degree of lightness to my world. It might mean that the shadows of trees we see here on earth have, in some way, their own relative life separate, yet inextricable, from the tree and sun that seemed to create them. And what should I make of the infinite connection I had experienced between myself and everything?

Most definitely, there was something else here. I insisted that there had to be something else, and I received an answer that encompassed God to infinity through disembodiment, singularities, and the spheres. How could I comprehend and apply this to my daily life? As I got home, I glanced at the turkey vultures, waved, and headed into the house.

I had some thinking to do. And therein lay the problem.

CHAPTER 8
ONWARD WITH ECKHART

The experience of the spheres came and went like a bird call heard from afar, only an echo surfacing as a memory from time to time. I was unsure of how much of this was believable. It made sense that this earthly plane consisted of only one of many possible alternate universes, with its trees, houses, doctors, and dented phone booths. But out of all of it, what made inexhaustible sense?

Part of my mind said, "*Yes, it is interesting, but be careful. Believing this as the unchanging truth of existence might start a new religion in your head.*"

The last thing I wanted was another concept to worship.

Some of the images from my MDMA/mushroom journey felt familiar; I entertained an interest in medieval drawings starting in high school. Not to mention the "One Eye of God" that appears on every American dollar that comes through my hands. After my neck surgery, I discovered alchemy, an ancient branch of natural philosophy. I visited several websites documenting alchemical symbols, ideas, drawings, and stories. Picking up a copy of *The Emerald Tablet* by Dennis William Hauck[1], I delved into learning about the age-old process of turning base metals into gold. I didn't take the alchemical transformation as a literal accomplishment of turning lead into gold but rather as an internal

---

[1] Dennis William Hauck, *The Emerald Tablet: Alchemy for Personal Transformation* (New York: Penguin, 1999).

process of realizing one's true nature, exchanging old, worn-out beliefs about myself and existence for ideas more reflective of the sense of Oneness I experienced in the spheres journey.

I bought a few alchemical prints colorized by Adam McLean[2] and hung them on the walls of my rental home. I tried reading books on the subject, but the dogmatic language annoyed me. Continuing this exploration, I briefly subscribed to a Rosicrucian organization but found the information disappointingly intellectual and not experiential. I decided the yearly subscription cost outweighed the few speckles of gold dust mined from the Rosicrucian concepts. However, one dream did have a solid alchemical flavor during this time.

In the dream, I realize that the old king and queen are dead. I then go to a large ceremony to crown the new King Gregory, a young man with curly hair. The celebration for the new incoming King soon becomes sad as it is revealed that Gregory is also dying. I don't know why he is dying in the dream, but I find myself crying at the thought that the king and queen are dead, and now their successor is dying. I awaken.

The image of the king, queen, and their successor all dying symbolized for me a time of transition; the royal lineage was ending. But what "royal family" ruled my life up to this point? As much as I wanted to ignore it, I knew the answer. I was ruled by fear and defensiveness, both royal decrees proclaiming to preserve my sense of certainty and being right. Until this time,

---

[2] Adam McLean is a Scottish writer and artist whose main interest is in ancient alchemical texts.

my life's overarching theme and source of guidance had been fear. This lineage had to end.

As I began stepping out from under the burden and shadow of fear, Melanie and I continued building our relationship, as the divorce decrees ending our first marriages proceeded to the desk of the district judge who would sign off on them. Four attorneys and two years later, I received the official signed divorce decree while on the ski slopes of Winter Park, Colorado. My friends encouraged me to celebrate, but I didn't. A sadness lingered around the relationship's dissolution, but I refused to deal with it openly. The divorce process gave me plenty of chances to play the blame game, including my attorney's inability to negotiate with the judge in charge of our mediation, who thought all men were scum and whatever the wife said was the truth.

Uncertain about where our new relationship would head, Melanie and I faced painful situations as our respective families reacted to our divorces. She and I spent many hours on the phone, as we still lived in different cities and could only welcome the occasional night together. I had the following dream during one of our first nights in my rental home.

I wake up in the dream to find Melanie and I are in the same bed. We are in the small bedroom in the rental house. Something mysterious is occurring, and I throw back all of my covers. At first, I don't notice anything, but then I see black bands encircling my ankles. The black bands on both ankles rapidly become tiny wings that flap a few times. This is cool! I realize my body has elevated toward the ceiling of the bedroom. I see Melanie waking in the bed below me as I touch the ceiling. With no dialogue, she reaches up and holds my hand. She then grabs my arms. I pull her next to me. Amazingly, we both hover

near the ceiling. Suddenly, the scene changes, and we find ourselves in outer space with the blue globe of the Earth below us. I note that a spacecraft now surrounds us. As the craft moves further out beyond the orbit of Jupiter, the room inside the spacecraft slowly gets smaller. Either that or Melanie and I get bigger! We soon occupy the entirety of the ship's interior, and things feel rather cramped. Remarkably, we find ourselves free of the craft floating out in space. Frankly, I can't tell if we have bodies or not! But the exhilaration of this moment is tremendous! I then awaken.

This dream and the previous one about the royal family occurred very close to each other. My old ways of thinking and seeing my beliefs (represented by the old king and even the new king, Gregory) were changing. As the spacecraft dream illustrated, the confining aspects of those limited viewpoints slowly revealed themselves. Something called me toward a more expanded view of myself and life. I was glad that Melanie had decided to join me on this trip!

The Dream Retreat

Len announced to the dream group an upcoming weekend workshop with Robert Moss, an Australian author of books on dreams and shamanism. The whole group decided to attend. Melanie and I chose to stay together at a bed and breakfast, and the weekend was the perfect time to share the news of our fledgling relationship with our dream buddies. From what I remember, a few smiles and mostly silence accompanied our announcement.

The retreat ran from Friday to Sunday morning. Robert Moss led us on an adventurous exploration of our dream worlds using techniques similar to active imagination. In a group with diverse backgrounds and perspectives, we mused about our earthly existence and what might lie beyond it. Still not entirely convinced of the value of my sphere journey just two weeks before, I listened intently to folks' descriptions of their spiritual experiences. Saturday evening, the following dream arrived.

I walk up to a vaguely familiar old stone church. The large wooden double doors are in a typical medieval arched style. Dark and heavy, they quickly open by the hand of a short, hunched-back character. The silent invitation of the disfigured man resonates, and I accept. I know his name as Robert and follow him up the few stairs and through the arched gateway.

Melanie and I entered the retreat room on Sunday morning and found two seats.

Robert Moss began a group meditation as he had each session and then said, "Please pair off with someone new by gently touching them on the arm or shoulder."

Len and I had paired up previously, but he left the conference early. Unexpectedly, Robert Moss tapped me on the shoulder as my new partner. I smiled.

Little did I know that my dream the previous night of the hunchback named Robert had just intersected with my waking life in this exercise. I lay on the floor and gently touched Robert on the back of his left ankle.

"Begin to breathe gently, relaxing into the floor," Robert instructed the rest of the participants and me. Allow images to come to mind without any particular direction from you. Simply watch them come."

Slowly, a picture of an ancient English church and its large pair of double doors emerge. This grey stone church speaks of familiarity with its fenced courtyard and cemetery. I walk up to the arched wooden doors, and they open without my touch. The most beautiful and intense, white radiant light I have ever encountered appears inside. I bow and dissolve into the light, staying there for an untold amount of time.

At the end of the meditation, with soft tears rolling down my cheeks, I felt an inner melting of some old rigidness upon opening my eyes. I rarely, if ever, cried in public before, let alone tears of happiness. The sheer love that I experienced in my heart overwhelmed me.

"Bart, before you say anything, let me tell you of my experience," said Mr. Moss.

Still lying on the floor, I nodded as I wiped the tears from my eyes and tried to compose myself.

Robert went on, "As we started, the image of a stone building came to my mind. The doorway of this building called to me, and I turned to you, Bart, inviting you to follow. As I went inside, and through a radiant light, I saw an image I knew as Jesus. While I have had other intense encounters with other spirits, this was one of the more intense interactions with Jesus I've ever experienced."

Inwardly, I dropped to my intellectual knees and saw the remarkable parallels between Mr. Moss's and my visualizations. I told the group about my meditation experience and dream from Saturday night.

It struck me that the dream figure Robert and the workshop Robert were the same guides for me in my waking life and dream life, inviting me to approach the most potent symbol of the love I knew of at that time—Jesus. I didn't buy into the need to be saved by Jesus as presented by the Catholic Church, but I noted a brief silence inside of me when I remembered looking at the two pictures of Jesus hanging in my grandmother's dining room. Until then, I had refused to acknowledge the peace and wonder I experienced when looking at those pictures.

After this powerful experience, the rest of the workshop seemed anti-climactic. My inner naysayers, who inhabited my mind so long ago that they were impossible to evict under the current rental agreement, began discounting the inexplicable and astonishing events of the morning. But I started noticing stirrings in my body—shadows of excitement, wonder, or connectedness—suggesting there might be something of value here.

The Robert Moss weekend experience convinced me to give more credibility to the images seen while with the spheres, especially because many of the other retreat participants shared similar experiences. Even in my outward silence, the idea that Robert Moss and I had visualized very similar scenes of the church and the radiant light within stretched my rational mind beyond its self-constructed comfort zone. This blew my mind without even taking any psychedelics!

My logical, rational mind felt cramped and challenged. Not to be outmaneuvered, I started hearing thoughts like, *while other people had similar spiritual experiences, theirs were probably more valid and meaningful!* Oh, what a circular tale of lack I could tell myself sometimes!

We went home and picked up the threads of our everyday lives while trying to digest and make sense of everything that had happened. I gradually met some other people in Melanie's life, including her children, Nik and Lindsey, and Jeremy, her former husband.

Since the neck fusion and despite physical therapy, I have continued to live with severe neck pain, limited movement, spasms, and migraines. Thankfully, the arm and hand weakness and nerve pain improved, but not unexpectedly; the dysfunction never completely disappeared. One of Melanie's friends became invaluable. Leslie was an acupuncturist and started treating me with needles, similar to Dr. John's method. Acupuncture gave temporary relief, but during the short reprieve, I heard many negative thoughts warning that the pain would only return.

Eckhart and My Ego

One cloudy, grey day, I walked into Leslie's acupuncture office waiting area. The walls were color-washed in a soft ochre, a sizeable colorful reprint of Kwan-Yin hung on one wall, and an ornamental ceramic waterfall filled the room with a peaceful, gurgling sound.

Before I sat down, Leslie emerged from her private work area, a book in hand.

"Hey, Bart," she smiled, her hint of a Southern accent drawing out the word "hey" just a bit. "I have something for you that you might find interesting."

She held out the book to me, which I accepted. "What is this?" I quietly murmured.

"Eckhart Tolle's first book, *The Power of Now.*"

Leslie loved listening to and reading books by many spiritual teachers, often sharing their viewpoints while I lay on the acupuncture table imagining an ongoing encounter with a porcupine. She may have mentioned Eckhart previously, but I didn't remember.

"Thanks, I'll have a look," I replied sheepishly, unsure how I felt about this gift.

Once at home and covered in red dots from the treatment, I opened the book and read the first chapter's title, "YOU ARE NOT YOUR MIND." [3] My response was sudden, predictable, and unquestionable.

What a bunch of shit! Of course, *I am my mind! And who the hell is this guy who thinks he knows me, what I am, and what I'm not? Why would I waste my time pondering something as obviously wrong as that? All those philosophers, spiritual teachers, and religious fanatics can delve into this nonsensical, mumbo-jumbo crap that has nothing to do with the real world! I don't need to. I know what life is, how the universe was formed, who I am, and I don't need to look any further.*

The rant in my mind continued…

And what about all those artists, poets, dancers, and writers who supposedly pour their souls and soppy emotions out of their fingers and toes and into their works of so-called art and

---

[3] Eckhart Tolle, *The Power of Now: A Guide to Spiritual Enlightenment* (Novato, CA: New World Library, 1999).

creativity? These half-witted people probably ought to be institutionalized!

Besides, I'm not creative. How dare anyone else be creative?

Not to be exclusive, the tantrum added, *And the same goes for nature lovers, those pine-cone freaks!*

Wow. I stood for a few seconds—stunned at the intensity of the silent outburst. Once the tirade subsided in my head, I tossed the book onto an end table, unwilling to read or further contemplate this quackery of a subject.

Of course, looking back, this was my ego, that part of my mind constantly trying to preserve my particular, limited point of view from perceived and imagined insult and injury. I realize many people have different definitions of ego. I have found my ego to be those activities of my mind that continually judge and separate. Those five words, "You are not your mind," threatened everything I had learned and taught myself up to that point in my life. This tendency to bolt when I encountered anything that offered an unwanted or unsolicited idea played through once more. Until recently, I had never openly examined the nature of my mind and its relationship with who I thought I was. I always assumed my thoughts accurately described the concrete ways of the world and universe.

The book gathered six months of dust on a shelf until I finally dug into Eckhart's work, my introduction to examining mental activity from a new perspective. Until then, my rapid-fire thinking processes and memorizing ability were the king, the power, and the way to figure out people and the world. Of course, this immediate "I am right, and I know it" attitude comprised a considerable part of my miserable self. Without knowing any other way to be, I repeatedly used this poor excuse for analytical thinking to decipher behaviors. I didn't get very far, as everything became circular, negative, and harmful. I convinced myself that everything, including family history, genetics, myriad life conflicts, and the whole separate universe, caused my depression and anxiety. My beliefs weren't a part of the equation!

And along came this dream.

I walk outside a building, and suddenly, coming from my right is the comic book character The Flash. He is transported in a floating chair and surrounded by several other people. I don't recognize anyone else, but I immediately remember and relate to The Flash, who is identifiable by his bright red superhero costume with the electric yellow lightning bolt in the center of his chest. He was one of the DC comic book characters I read stories about as a young boy. I eagerly welcome him but notice that his typically tight-fitting suit is too big—sagging and dripping off him like an ice cream cone on a hot summer's day. He looks old, worn, and tired. Apparently, The Flash is a mere shadow of his former greatness.

I tell him I need to talk to him about everything I have been doing. He says that while he knows all about me already, he would like to hear it from me directly. For a moment, it feels good to see him again. But then The Flash says he has to go before I can speak further. Getting into some sort of ship, he walks up to the control panel, preparing to fly off. I beg him not to leave but know he will go anyway. I start crying. Upon awakening, tears overcome me.

I immediately recognized how my "flash" intellect asked to be reexamined as part of my identity.

I pondered this dream as I immersed myself in Eckhart's work. The combination opened a new door—maybe I could experience a self that was less dependent on judgment and fear. A portal opened to a possible way of living without constantly referencing past insults and slights. I saw this as an invitation to look at the parts of my mind that demanded a fearful future based on previous events. My habitual ways of interacting with myself and others made less sense daily. I also pondered why I needed to tell The Flash anything, as he was already aware of it.

It then occurred to me that no one could magically look at my negativity and fear and make them disappear for me. I had to be the one to honestly look at what lay behind my misgivings, anger, and lack of connectedness. I needed to sit with that part of my ego that continually said I should be miserable. Could my consciousness contain more than just compulsive thinking? While I appreciated my intellect and all it gifted me, it had become an oppressive prison, and part of me looked forward to getting out.

Discovering the Pain-Body

Despite my initial tantrum, *The Power of Now i*ntroduced me to concepts that cracked my dungeon of suffering. The most potent of these concepts was the "pain-body." Eckhart describes this in part as a negative energy field that occupies our bodies and minds that can be dormant or active and may be expressed as emotions such as fear, depression, or anger. It didn't quite resonate with me that the pain-body replicated some energy from the collective experience of humanity. But I quickly caught on to the cyclical drama that temporarily controlled me and my thoughts when I got triggered and then spread this negativity to those around me. Eckhart explained that some pain-bodies continually react—almost 100% of the time—and others' pain-bodies present themselves every few weeks. I read that section of the book several times, and eventually, I got on board with the notion of watching for my pain-body when it arose.

This brought me to a turning point in realizing my part in the generation of my own suffering.

The idea of pain-bodies made me think of my relationship with Sharon, and I remembered the first time I had experienced her pain-body while dating. About three weeks into our new relationship, medical school responsibilities caused me to run about 20 minutes late, picking Sharon up at her house for dinner. While I apologized, I noticed a slight change in her eyes as she started expressing emotional pain at my tardiness. This took me by surprise, as my hospital duties were responsible for my delay. At the time, a blazing warning sign shot through my mind when Sharon's anger and paranoia arose, but I quickly downplayed and ignored the situation. Her pain-body had flared only briefly and wasn't around long enough to activate mine.

The first time I clearly saw and felt my own pain-body was one evening as I sat at my computer playing a game after a long day at work. My pager's familiar and annoying buzz signaled a call from the local hospital. Like an ice pick thrust into my temple, the sound blasted my ears, and I felt a gnawing, clawing sensation in my chest. Having learned in dream workshops to pay attention to visual images, it took on the shape of a giant crab with claws, and as it grew, I felt the clawing gain a significant hold over me. After the feeling grew for several seconds, I heard thoughts describing this hospital page in a way demanding that I rise and express anger.

“What the hell do they want now?” I exclaimed as I shook my head and pounded my fist.

I ascertained that this might be the very thing Eckhart meant by the pain-body. I could see that my pain-body had taken control. After a few seconds of pause, I angrily answered the hospital call to discover they had mistakenly paged the wrong doctor. The pain-body told me that I needed to be pissed for the rest of the evening.

I witnessed firsthand the emergence and takeover of the pain-body, complete with all the emotions, susceptibilities, and thought patterns it employs to maintain power over me. Eckhart’s writing on the pain-body prepared me well enough that I took a deep breath, sat back, and took a moment to observe it rather than becoming entranced, which I would have done before. This was another huge accomplishment.

Contrary to my earlier doubts, I began reading and rereading several chapters of *The Power of Now* weekly. One afternoon, immersed in Eckhart’s suggestion to review a recent pain-body situation, I recalled past pain-body possessions in detail, noticing even earlier and more subtle physical or mental signals of its approach. During previous pain-body attacks, I had focused so quickly on my negative thoughts that I totally ignored any bodily phenomena associated with them.

This idea of looking at and sensing the pain-body takeover from a distance was new. It took months of halfhearted practice and vigilance (meaning many pain-body attacks) before I learned to spot the arising of this negativity, not lash out because of it, and instead keep it a much more tolerable and manageable experience. Eckhart's book introduced me to a different way of looking at myself in my mind, and it was … intriguing, awesome, and slowly changing my daily life profoundly.

Feeling a LOT more open-minded about this fellow and his extraordinary ideas, I picked up his other book, *A New Earth*, and listened to several of his recorded DVDs.

Eckhart in Person

Melanie and I hopped in the car one weekend and traveled to New York City to attend his talks in person at the Beacon Theatre. In his earlier recordings, Eckhart exhibited some verbal peculiarities, including a sharp, random clicking sound. A few other people I knew couldn't tolerate these traits, but these idiosyncrasies mattered little to me as I related to the message underneath his words and sentences. When I listened to him, I felt a current of stillness.

I listened to Eckhart's DVDs during many drives to see Melanie at her home in Charlottesville. One evening, traveling east on Interstate 64, I came to the crest of Afton Mountain, greeted by the splendor of the full moon, and instantly, the thoughts in my mind went completely quiet. I was still awake, alert, present, and in control, but there weren't any thoughts, comments, or other conversations in my head. Thoughts and words had been there for as long as I could remember, and to have them suddenly quiet was quite remarkable.

I continued to drive, and upon arriving at Melanie's home, I asked if we could sit quietly, as I wanted to experience this for a bit longer. After a few hours, the mind chatter picked up again, and I was sad that the quietness didn't last longer than it did. My mind rambled about how the silence giving way to inane banter meant I wasn't as evolved as I thought. Talk about contradictory thinking! I soon passed this off as another experience, wishing it had stayed, yearning for more serenity, and simultaneously hearing the voices celebrating that the stillness was finally over and done! A small taste of a state that might never return.

Melanie and I then traveled to Hawaii for a five-day conference that Eckhart hosted in Maui. The retreat was quite a marvelous experience—not only to be in the company of Eckhart but to be in a beautiful hotel on a pristine beach. Quite unexpectedly, Eckhart announced that he would break all of his protocols and sit with each of us briefly after our last group session.

Eckhart and I held each other's hands in silence while his staff organized and facilitated his meetings with other people. I fully appreciated the kindness and warmth in his touch as I sat across a table with him for a few precious minutes.

"Thanks so much for this time to sit with you, Eckhart," I said. "This retreat has been wonderful."

"It's a pleasure to meet you, Bart. I can often sense the silence in others, and I feel that in you."

I blushed a little but managed to get out the following sentence, "And I appreciate all the pointers you give us, Eckhart." With this, I felt underlying happiness, and I knew that all of the pointers in Eckhart's talks and books were shining the light towards this joy.

"Eckhart," I asked, "could you sign a note for a friend who could not make this trip? Her name is Elke."

"I would be happy to do that," he said. "Dearest Elke, many blessings to you. Love, Eckhart."

With the biggest smile, I stood up, shook his hand one more time, bowed slightly, and stepped away with a keepsake that I would present to Elke back in Charlottesville on our return to the mainland. We got to sit with the author of *The Power of Now* himself, and we also managed to fit in some scuba diving in the nurturing ocean waters around Maui!

The Player Piano

Soon after returning from this beautiful vacation retreat, I settled into a routine that included running my office, paying bills, teaching young anesthesiologists interested in pain management, and regular physical therapy and acupuncture for my chronic neck pain. I listened to Eckhart on CDs while driving to each of my commitments, and gradually, I sensed the underlying silence that pervaded everything, including my seemingly irrational thoughts and actions.

I also had the following brief dream.

I am in a living room. I don't recognize the space as mine, but an ancient player piano sits along one wall. I don't recall the tune currently on cue, but I notice the piano has several keys missing, and the scroll mechanism doesn't appear to be working correctly. The song starts, but numerous notes are misplayed, and the tuning needs quite an adjustment. I awaken.

When I woke up in the morning, I immediately saw that my mind, specifically the egoic part, was constantly playing the same old tunes. And I listened to them and acted on those thoughts no matter how ridiculous the ideas were, such as accusing happy people of stealing happiness from me. The dream asked me to stop the constant automatic playing of this player piano and see what I had been doing from a slightly different angle.

Figure 14. That old player piano playing the same old tunes

Surgery in Germany

Five years after my first neck surgery, my neck hadn't improved despite physical therapy, acupuncture, and a marked reduction in physical activities. Melanie and I had gone scuba diving many times since we'd met, but even in the weightlessness of the underwater world, my neck screamed in revolt with extension or flexion. I even visited a pain management colleague in Pennsylvania to burn small nerves in the arthritic joints above and below the cervical fusion. This helped knock the pain to a six rather than an eight on a scale of 0 to 10. But nothing helped at the end of a long clinic and procedural day at the hospital, where I constantly bent forward, working and operating on my patients. On Tuesdays, I headed to the hospital, and by 8 AM, I was placing needles into the painful areas of my patients by carefully watching live X-rays. To help protect me from the constant irradiation, I wore a 20-pound leaded apron around my neck for eight hours straight. Because my neck did not bend forward normally, I had to exaggerate my lower back and thoracic spine curves to reach over the patient lying sedated on the operating room table.

Further MRIs of my neck showed progressive and worrying deterioration in the cervical discs above my previous fusion. While these changes didn't pinch my nerves or spinal cord, the damage and modifications caused frequent migraine headaches, constant neck spasms, pain, and significant sleep disturbance.

Eventually, I had no possibilities but to resign to further surgery. I often saw patients with fusions at one or two spine levels who then wound up with significant degenerative changes at the levels above or below the previous surgery. This domino effect didn't happen to everyone, but it had certainly happened to me.

The only option here in the States was further fusion, but I learned that several progressive neurosurgeons in Germany used artificial discs to repair this type of degeneration. Critically, these artificial discs allowed for motion in that area of the spine, whereas further fusion definitely restricted movement.

After discussing it a bit with Melanie, I chose to go to Stenum, Germany, just outside Bremen, and allow the neurosurgeon, Dr. Ritter-lang, to remove the degenerative discs and replace them with artificial ones. We began planning. My son Tyler asked to come with us, and the whole stay in Germany would take about a month. There was one week before the surgery to prepare and three weeks post-surgery to recover.

To finance the trip to Germany for the spinal surgery, I refinanced the rural property I had received in the divorce from Sharon. The timing couldn't have been better, and soon after the new mortgage loan was approved, Melanie, Tyler, and I headed off to Germany for an adventure in medical tourism. What amazed me the most about the trip was that I somehow knew exactly what to do at every step without having long discussions of the pros and cons. Aside from some fleeting catastrophic thoughts about being stuck in Germany in a foreign intensive care unit, I carried calmness and sureness about the whole process. For the first time in my life, I experienced peacefulness during what could have been a stressful month.

The staff at Stenum Hospital took care of me beyond my expectations. As part of the pre-operative workup, they took some new cervical X-rays, along with the obligatory pre-operative blood work and EKG.

"Dr. Balint, come over here. I want you to see this," said the X-ray technician in excellent English.

"Just getting my shirt back on. What is it?" I exclaimed, a little nervous about the answer I would receive. A few steps later, I stood next to Karin, the technician, and we both stared at my neck X-rays on the display panel.

"Did you know three screws holding down the plate above your cervical fusion were broken?" she said.

"What do you mean broken?" I asked. "No one ever mentioned that, not even my previous neurosurgeon, who must have taken dozens of X-rays of my neck over the past five years."

Karin and I looked at the pictures again, and sure enough, when we looked at the plate and screws in a slightly angled shot, I saw that three screws had sheared off.

I was floored! "My goodness. These screws are broken! The plate must have been moving around all this time. No wonder I felt pain when I swallowed or cleared my throat."

The continued dysfunction in my neck finally made sense after seeing these broken bits of metal floating around on the X-rays!

The surgery went well, and except for the obnoxious roommate the staff inadvertently paired me with after surgery, I had a fantastic experience. My mind tried to make me out as my roommate's victim as I heard, *Did I have to come all this way and undergo a major surgery just to be paired with the American asshole from hell?*

Quite calmly, I asked the nurses if I could be placed in a different room. Immediately, they procured me an alternative room down the hall, and their verbal response was quite telling. "While your roommate has acted like a jerk, we were surprised it took you this long to request your own private room!"

Once I recovered enough to drink and eat on my own, I left the hospital, and Mel, Tyler, and I stayed in a prearranged hotel in Bremen. Stenum Hospital sent a massage therapist to our room many days to assist my musculature in adjusting to the newly installed artificial discs (they added about 3/8 in. to my height). For the first four or five days, I ventured out of the hotel on a limited basis as my neck muscles again recovered from being cut in half. But after that, we adventurously explored the city and had fun wandering around town, listening to local street musicians, and trying out some famed local bratwursts.

Marveling at the old-quarter buildings lining the narrow streets, which had survived the war in the 1940s, I started seeing large, colorful posters attached to lampposts announcing a political rally later that week. I figured the person named on the sign was just a local politician. Honestly, I didn't know or research German political parties or personalities. Curiosity overtook me, and as we saw the next poster, I stopped a young man and woman passing us.

In my best American English and ignorant attitude, I fumbled, "Sir, just who is this Angela Merkel that all these signs point to? And just what is the big deal about this to deserve so many signs?" This unconscious desire to be obnoxious demanded that the stranger know I came from America.

I felt embarrassed and humiliated as he shouted his answer, "What do you mean, just who is that?" acting disgusted while carrying a marked German accent. "That is our German chancellor, Angela Merkel!" The fellow also muttered a few "Dummkopfs!" in there.

Judging by his facial expression and the shrinking feeling I felt inside, I immediately deduced that I had deeply offended this man. I apologized and made an excuse to return to the hotel and rest. Perhaps the whole surgical process or the more immediate pain medicines had taken a toll on me. My mind had blanked on Angela Merkel. Of course, somewhere back in those dark recesses, I knew who she was, and it thrilled me at the prospect of seeing her in person. After all, she had been the German chancellor since 2005.

The rally brought nice weather to Bremen, so Tyler, Melanie, and I wandered over to the main square. Protestors on the right side of the venue struggled to outshout supporters who mostly stood in front of the stage and towards the left. I had never seen, nor heard live, the head of state of any country, so this was a bonus, although I had no clue or interest in the political stances of anyone in Germany.

Heading back home to the United States, the recommended dose of pain medications helped ease the discomfort of traveling. Halfway across the Atlantic, an announcement by a flight attendant asked for a doctor's assistance as a passenger had a life-threatening medical condition. The influence of narcotics precluded me from helping manage this woman's medical emergency. Besides, I had left my medical license at home. It would have been quite the joke trying to convince the airline staff that I was a doctor, as I couldn't even say "doctor" without drooling and nodding off mid-sentence.

Links between Inner and Outer

After this second surgery, I took some extra recovery time before returning to the office, refusing to make the same boneheaded mistake I had the first time by sucking up the pain and resuming work too soon. Once back at the office, I reduced my work hours and the number of patients on my daily schedule. Being the boss made that kind of decision much easier to implement. Thankfully, I was learning to ignore the self-critical remarks that I was a wimp for having the surgery at all.

Over the coming days, I cautiously moved my neck backward, forward, and side to side. Pleased to see some increases in mobility, I started looking up at the stars for 10 minutes rather than the usual 30 seconds. But quite a bit of the pain persisted. Physically, I was not back to who I had been before the two neck surgeries, regardless of how many acupuncture needles poked me along different meridians. At this time, I discovered a form of deep tissue massage called Rolfing, which helped quite a bit. Some chronic mid-back spasms and tightness also started to ease with this modality. I remember my first Rolfing session and my gratitude when I walked to my car without constant spasms and tightness. Of course, this was temporary, but well worth it.

Until now, I hadn't entirely correlated my long-running hostile narrative and the problems with my neck. I kept my physical issues separate from my previous five years of introspection. Admittedly, my explosive nighttime dreaming commenced after my first neck surgery, but only now were inklings of links seen between the two.

This dream occurred soon after we came home from Germany.

I am in an indoor, sizeable office environment, perhaps with a few windows and a door or two. I notice a sign on the wall announcing that this indoor space was a "Pain Clinic." I don't recognize it as my office, partly because the walls are more

colorful than my actual office walls. And the colors are very vivid. I then see a large snake-like creature. It is at least ten feet long and three feet around. I don't see any legs. The eyes are black, and as it opens its mouth, I notice sharp white teeth, skinny green lips, and bumpy skin that is also a shade of green. The snake starts turning itself inside out. It doesn't eat its tail as an ouroboros would, but the snake's intestinal tract is slowly turned out, such that the reddish inside of its intestinal tract is now on the outside. His green skin is no longer visible, as the skin is now on the inside of what I see. This did not appear painful, and the snake is not in any discomfort—such a strange sight. I am inquisitive, unafraid, and not threatened. Again, I notice the "Pain Clinic" sign. I awaken.

When I awoke, I again saw the "Pain Clinic" sign in my mind. The snake's action of turning inside out also burned into my memory. Then it hit me: *What is inner is outer, and what is outer is inner.* I remembered some alchemical writings around this, expressing an inner and outer alchemical process.

Do I know what is internal and what is external? I asked myself.

Could my inner pain mirror my outer pain? Was it perhaps true that internal suffering may be related to external bodily suffering? Reading and listening to Eckhart shook up a lot of rigid beliefs, including, "I know exactly what is inner and what is outer." Did buried pain and repressed trauma give rise to my neck pain? Could I view all these things differently? The miraculous actions of the snake pushed me to another edge of what I thought I knew.

CHAPTER 9
THE JUNGLE WITHIN

The vast emptiness within me propelled my search for more meaning in life. I heard that this void needs fixing before you ever feel complete and truly close to anyone. You've got to keep searching; never give up the search.

So far, I'd exhausted numerous possible solutions to fill the gaping hole inside me. Each was a temporary Band-Aid: professional and academic achievements, material possessions, food, alcohol, sports performance, numerous hobbies, and my roles as husband and father. I dared not sit with the emptiness that remained. Instead, I kept pushing it aside with streams of thought or activity, even so-called spiritual hullabaloo. I tried to avoid the void in any way I could.

I pressed onward, taking hold of the next rung of the ladder that led me a bit higher than my previous perspective, providing a bit more altitude between me and the problems that felt deadening. Thankfully, dreams continued to provide guidance, sometimes suggesting my next endeavor.

I am in a tropical jungle. Grunting sounds and the rustlings of wild animals fill my ears. Focusing on the luscious green vegetation surrounding my path, I see many different types of rainforest plants, vines, and trees filling the landscape. The green leafy vines wrap around my legs, and I am soon entirely enveloped by the plants, wondrously becoming one with them.

Soon after, several dream group members shared about meeting a shaman, Don Ernesto, who took people to Peru for ceremonial healing work using Amazonian plant medicines in their natural setting. The dream mentioned above immediately came to mind. Once again, a light switch flipped on inside. Could the dream be leading me into the Amazon? What a significant step for me to consider! With Melanie's encouragement, I took it all as a nudge to start work with this Peruvian shaman and the plant medicine ayahuasca.

Figure 15 Becoming One with the Jungle

My inner critic had plenty to say about this idea. How does a conservative, allopathic physician, raised a Catholic from steel town, Weirton, West Virginia, choose to do ritual work with a shaman? This is ridiculous! What are this guy's credentials? Who the hell is he? It's one thing to work with a trained psychologist using mind-altering medicines; still, another to throw my lot in with someone whose medicine bag consists of homemade plant concoctions, wooden flutes, fans made of bird feathers, and spiritual songs.

But maybe THIS is what will fill the emptiness, a softer voice suggested.

Maybe I'll wind up attaining enlightenment … another voice considered. Yes, I wondered about this notion of enlightenment as I continued reading books by numerous spiritual teachers.

Just this one last tool before you'll know yourself fully, someone in my head said cajolingly. Don't miss out on the one opportunity to make yourself whole!

Round and round went the conversation.

While I still operated from the defensive position that everyone took something from me, causing my unhappiness, a vague awareness of my own circular thinking surfaced. A mistrustful and suspicious attitude still ruled my world, but more cracks in this protective wall showed up with each dream I explored and each contemplation of spiritual writings. Nonetheless, I craved experiences beyond these two avenues.

My First Encounter with Ayahuasca

Luckily, I didn't have to go to the rainforests for my first experience with Don Ernesto. He also held ceremonies here in the States. Against all internal naysayers, I attended my first ayahuasca ceremony. Ernesto's liaison, Stuart, provided details in preparation for the event: what to bring, what to leave at home, and, most specifically, what to eat and drink in the two weeks before the ceremony.

My inward response to his instructions was predictable.

What? No caffeine, no dairy, no red meat, no sugar, no chocolate, no processed foods, no salt, and more? No sex? Limit or eliminate media exposure? What am I heading into, a monastery? The next thing I expect they'll say is to begin daily self-flagellation!

I nodded, feigning calmness as if in total agreement, as Stuart delivered the rigorous instructions. As if detecting the rebellion within me, Stuart said, “All these food, drink, and activity restrictions are highly recommended to optimize your ceremony experience. Certain foods can cause more discomfort, so it’s advisable to stick to the bland diet for the duration.”

Wait a minute … MORE discomfort? a worried voice asked. Again, I simply nodded.

In the end, I faithfully—though not without protest—followed the limited, restricted diet and activities until the day of the ceremony.

“If you have white pants and a shirt, bring those to wear during the ceremony,” Stuart told us. “You’ll want an outdoor folding chair, a pillow, a blanket or mat to set on the ground beneath you, and a blanket to cover you if you feel chilled. Also, please bring a container to use as a purge bucket—a pitcher or something like that. Please bring a water bottle, but remember to sip water, not guzzle it before and during the ceremony. What goes down tends to come back up. This reminds me that you should begin a water fast the morning of.”

Why the hell is purging a requirement on this path of enlightenment? I thought with a bit of dread.

Melanie and I decided to proceed with this new avenue of adventure. Soon, we drove through the tranquil countryside with our friend William to a secluded property several hours away from my home in Virginia. When we arrived, the farm felt like a retreat center, blanketed with green grass, surrounded by woods, and very peaceful. The weather was sunny. Despite the beautiful backdrop, my guard remained resolutely up as we walked toward one of the main buildings with our duffel bags and backpacks.

William explained, "I picked a small wooden flute for us to give Ernesto. It's customary for new attendees to offer him a gift. Bart and Mel, come with me to introduce you to the master."

"Thanks, William," I said as uncomfortable thoughts filled my mind. What if Don Ernesto doesn't like the flute? I wondered. What happens if I back the heck out of this crazy event at the last second? Can I get my money back?

William escorted me and my doubts to a small building, where Ernesto received new participants and seasoned ayahuasca devotees. I followed Melanie as she entered the small, nondescript structure, and my doubts instantly gave way to nervousness and excitement. I was, however, stunned to find that Don Ernesto was a young man with Mediterranean features—dark brown hair tied back in a short ponytail, blue eyes, and olive skin tone, in his late twenties, wearing jeans and a casual shirt. Wait a minute, was he even Peruvian?

An air of formality filled the small room. The seasoned participants bowed to him, hands in prayer pose over their hearts. I felt awkward about this; clearly, he occupied a pedestal in their eyes. My first exposure to an old-world healer felt strange and uncomfortable, not being big on adulation. Yet I wanted to be polite, since this man held my life in his hands for the next 24 hours.

"Don Ernesto, I would like you to meet Melanie and Bart. They are participating in tonight's ceremony for the first time," said William.

“Greetings. Welcome. Have you ever worked with this type of ceremony before?” Ernesto asked, looking directly at Mel and me.

“No, we haven’t,” I replied, handing Ernesto the flute wrapped in plain-colored cloth.

A short but touching tune came from the flute as Ernesto tried it out. “Perfect!” he exclaimed. “I was looking for something just like this!”

A few other nervous and quickly forgotten words escaped my lips, and then William indicated we should join the others outside.

Someone led us to a communal building outfitted with bunk beds with snoring space for eight people, our post-event accommodations. We set down our overnight bags, changed into ceremonial whites, gathered our props for the evening, and walked to an open grassy field with a fire pit that marked the center of the ceremony circle. William pointed to the space beside him, inviting us to set up our ground cloths and chairs. I haphazardly arranged my low-to-the-ground beach chair, pillows, and an extra blanket, preparing for a six-hour journey inward while sitting silently and upright. I also brought some water to sip, a washcloth to wipe my face, and a half-gallon Tupperware pitcher with a lid for that moment of purging many people experience with ayahuasca.

Now barefoot and wearing an unembellished, brown, kaftan-style cotton tunic, Ernesto sat serenely on a ceremonial Peruvian blanket with a bland facial expression. He arranged everything for the evening on the colorful cloth in front of his seat. This included several very non-sacred-looking 2-liter Coke bottles filled with a reddish-brown liquid that needed intermittent shaking. I assumed these bottles contained the ayahuasca I would come to know as "Mamacita," the mother vine. As everyone settled into their spots, some walked up to Ernesto's altar and placed objects there—a crystal, a feather, a small toy, jewelry, or a photograph of a loved one. Don Ernesto blessed these items, whether a personal talisman or a participant's precious object or picture. As twenty-five of us soon-to-be supersensible travelers sat in the ceremony circle, Ernesto briefly explained the evening's events.

"This is an internal process. There is no talking, no disturbing your neighbor, and NO outbursts. You can get up to go to the bathroom but immediately return to your seat, resuming your journey. To make sure no one wanders off, there are three sitters present who are not partaking in ayahuasca," he continued. Three people stood up and nodded to us all.

"Last of all," he reminded us, "If fear or overwhelm surfaces, and you feel you cannot handle it, remember that you always have your breath. Remember to breathe. Life is so simple. All you have to do is breathe."

"And now we begin."

To open the ceremony, Ernesto blessed the north, south, east, and west by taking large mouthfuls of Agua de Florida and spraying them out in each direction. Agua de Florida is a concoction of grain alcohol blended with scents of an orange flower blossom, clove, cinnamon, rose, and bergamot. Next, he blessed all participants with this holy water and said a few words to purify Mamacita. I learned afterward that the ayahuasca we were about to drink is a mixture of two indigenous plants found in the Amazon basin of South America. The mixture of ayahuasca vine and chacruna shrub has been used by indigenous peoples of South America for centuries as a spiritual medication.

I sensed profound anticipation as each of us stood in turn to receive our blessing and ayahuasca. Starting with the participant on Ernesto's left and proceeding in a clockwise direction, silently, we walked up and kneeled near the left front of his blanket. Ernesto intuitively chose which ayahuasca mixture and how much of the concoction to give each participant and carefully poured it into a small metal shot glass. As my turn arrived, Ernesto held out the container to me and met my gaze, saying softly, "Salud. To your health." After respectfully bowing my head, as I had seen others do before me, I took the container and tried to swallow the entire glass of medicine. The extraordinarily thick and nasty steak sauce tasted of chunky organic bitterness. As I didn't know what to expect, I quickly downed the drink, returned the glass to Ernesto, and walked back to my seat in the circle. Admittedly, it tasted awful.

What the hell did I do? I asked myself silently. Can I even get back to my seat without upchucking?

I took a small sip of water to rinse my mouth, heeding the advice of others not to drink much as the water tended to sit in the stomach, awaiting that instance of purging. Some people had minimal outward reaction, while a few others displayed violent conniptions at both the thought of drinking the concoction and actually doing so.

If it tastes that bad, why are they here?

As my allotment of this "medicina" (as Ernesto sometimes referred to ayahuasca) sat like a brick in my stomach, he repeated the stipulation of no talking during this personal inward journey and remaining upright for its entirety. Comforted by these rules of conduct, I silently demanded that my internal process advance, undisrupted by participants talking unnecessarily. With everyone served and back in their seats, Ernesto looked at us and fell silent. He then reached for his cup and very casually downed his dosage of Mamacita. I wondered how he could even lead a ceremony like this when under ayahuasca's influence. I learned later that his dosage helped guide him in providing us with avenues of healing.

Oh, boy! I thought with a slight nervousness throughout my body. Here we go!

Framed by the setting sun, Ernesto began singing and playing the sacred "icaros" (songs and instrumental music), hallmarks of traditional ayahuasca ceremonies. Designed to gradually open the ceremony participants, each icaro allowed us to examine our conscious and unconscious inner worlds. Some of these songs felt gentle, soothing, and loving, relaxing me beyond anything I had previously felt. Others felt sharp, like an aggressive psychic blade that seemed to split me straight down the middle of my mind. These reminded me of uncontrollable earthquakes.

At first, I saw visual images slowly rotating, gradually expanding to greens, blues, oranges, and reds. Each musical piece magnified full-fledged, fearful visual and visceral responses, most of which I would not have acknowledged before that evening. The graphic visual patterns became an ever-increasing rotary of colors, quickly spinning and then slowing, following the lead of the icaros.

Something dreadful is going to happen to me tonight, I heard myself say in my head. Why did I allow myself to end up here? They will find me dead tomorrow; my slumped, lifeless body is in this chair.

Fear slashed through my thoughts and achingly pulsed throughout my abdomen. I clung desperately, trying to maintain control and some sense of conscious stability, but a feeling of impending doom pursued me in the background. A battle raged—a war that eventually played out over several ceremonies, showing me again and again how I depended on thought and reason to try to rule my little world. Each battle alternated between "Yes, I am worthy" and "NO! YOU are NOT worthy of love." At this point, the voice demanding that I face up to my unworthiness was far louder.

While inwardly I experienced turmoil, I opened my eyes long enough to notice a comfortable coolness settling over the field as the sun retired and darkness engulfed the still-intact ceremony circle. As my inner visual show proceeded, my consciousness floated in and out of Ernesto's icaros and healing songs. The shadows projected by the centerfire grew more prominent onto the trees surrounding the circle, perhaps reflecting the inner shadows lurking behind any positive affirmations to which I clung. Unbeknownst to me, Melanie became quite fearful and overwhelmed, her whole body shaking with hyperventilation. Ernesto sensed this and quickly arose and stood before her. I heard him remind her to focus on her breath, and then he gently blew puffs of tobacco smoke onto the crown of her head. This settled her, and her breathing calmed while her body still trembled. I couldn't identify anyone except for Melanie, as no lights shone on this moonless night except for the fading flickers of a dying campfire.

Soon, Ernesto called for anyone who desired an additional dose to come up. I don't believe I did that evening or at any subsequent ceremony. As he completed the round of second dosages, I closed my eyes, clueless about what lurked in the next drama of my inner landscape.

Suddenly, my body disappeared from my awareness, and thoughts alone presided in a universe with millions of stars. This seemed very familiar, and at first, pleasure and curiosity prevailed. It then felt as if I had somehow accelerated to an unknown destination. A very discrete line in space appeared, with one side containing the stars and the other wholly blank and devoid of anything. Breaking through the silence, an intense, deep voice reverberating throughout the universe inquired,

"Are you ready to give up consciousness and return to The One?"

My mind completely stopped for several seconds.

What the fuck did I just hear? I said to myself.

I heard the phrase again, only this time, the voice reverberated with a louder and more demanding tone.

"ARE YOU ready to give up consciousness and return to The One?"

I heard and understood the question this time. For a split second, I wondered if I should return to The One. I felt a slight pull towards the void, and then I stopped.

Wait a minute. No one ever told me that I had to give up consciousness!!! I said with strong defiance in my voice.

And with that, I suddenly felt overwhelming fear, doubt, and confusion. I symbolically stood between form, meaning everything I knew, and Oneness for just a split second, and then I panicked. I didn't rise from my seat, but I struggled to mentally run as far and fast as possible from that question and the apparent boundary. I strained to open my eyes and prove that I still lived in this world. Thoughts told me I was so deeply immersed in this transcendent experience that I might never return to my life as I'd known it. I fought to suppress the fear that arose and strove to understand the confusion that came over me like a tidal wave covering a sea-level tropical island.

And run, I did. I quickly gathered my wits and returned to earth in such a rush that I effectively ended my participation in the ceremony; opening my eyes and remembering to focus on breathing accomplished this. Shame shrouded the premature termination of my participation, but I noted a sense of relief in coming back from my brush with what I considered oblivion. I continued sitting with the group but didn't let myself go back into the visions and expanded consciousness I had felt just minutes before.

On the Verge

Thankfully, Don Ernesto officially ended the ceremony a while later, blessing and wishing us well. By that point, I could get up, move around, talk with others, and get a piece of delicious watermelon, further grounding me onto this Earth. I bantered with other participants, and soon, Melanie and I retired to our assigned bunks. The underlying fear that came up for me that evening didn't quiet for quite some time, and I was unable to fully face the terror and confusion each time I heard that question about returning to the One. Eventually, I climbed down from my top bunk, tapped Melanie on the shoulder, and asked if I could lie beside her. It's embarrassing to report this because asking for support or comfort from others felt weak and shameful. Still in our ceremonial whites, we lay there, dozing off and on until morning.

I didn't tell anyone about my experience until the following day when I briefly spoke with Ernesto about what I saw and heard. He replied, "Oh! You were on the verge of meeting God." After that exclamation, I had no idea what else to ask or even say. On top of that, I felt humiliated for even approaching the shaman to ask or say anything.

As we packed up our belongings and vacated the bunkhouse, William said, "Let's break our fast together by getting some eggs at a Waffle House on the way home. Another carload of participants wants to join us as well."

"All right, I'm up for that. Did I hear someone say we must continue the dietary restrictions and abstain from intimacy for a while longer, William?" I asked, hoping to be corrected.

He grinned. "Yup. But, at least we can now use salt, which helps to blunt Mamacita's effects since she hates salt. Semi-sweet fruits like berries are okay, but avoid sugary fruits like bananas and grapes."

Really?!? I moaned internally as I longed for my daily breakfast bowl of a banana on Cheerios with milk supersaturated with refined sugar. And no dairy yet, either, I sullenly reminded myself.

"All the rest of the dietary stipulations apply for two more weeks, and we abstain from sex during that time." He smiled and then sighed as if also resigning to the guidelines.

A Tug-of-War with Mamacita

A community of acquaintances and friends formed around the periodic ceremonies in the US. We supported each other and offered gentle reminders of both the love and unspoken turmoil we all carried within.

Preparation and post-ceremony guidelines were consistent from event to event. But each journey varied through its progression and presentations, totally unpredictable. A few ceremonies were blissful; I felt like pure light and wished to extend this light to the entire universe. These were the ceremonies in which I remained unmoving in my chair for six to eight hours, which wasn't some feat of newfound willpower but a total absence of any need to move, adjust, wiggle, squirm, or wish the ceremony would end. Six to eight hours passed, and I hadn't moved other than breathing.

Typically, however, I constantly readjusted and squirmed, sometimes concocting an excuse to walk to the bathroom to stretch and cool off. Occasionally, I faced the inescapable urge to purge, the least exciting ceremony moment. Becoming aware of a lead ball in my stomach area, I tried my best to ignore the growing demand to let it all come up. As often as it arose, the noxious feeling always won over my attempts to ignore it. Many claimed purging symbolized a sacred letting go of some negative narrative, but frankly, I hated it, physically and emotionally. And I didn't like purging in front of the others in our group—it dredged up thoughts and feelings of defeat, discomposure, and further unworthiness. And yes, during several ceremonies, I wished the icaros would stop, hoping the influence of Mamacita would quickly fade.

Many parts of this healing tradition agitated me—not only the icaros Ernesto performed but also the fractal visual patterns I saw in my mind's eye. The patterns evoked panic. I felt that God awaited just behind and through these patterns, ready to annihilate me. Yes, ceremonies weren't solely about seeing love and bliss in everything. They uncovered the many layers of guilt and trepidation that caused me so much suffering. A part of me hoped for a quick end to this work.

Fortunately, these ceremonies also provided light in my darkness, giving me the strength to keep looking and watching. Ernesto often commented that inner work only began in the ceremony circle; the most essential part happened when we all returned to our everyday lives. He urged us to watch for what he called tendencies—our habits and conditioned behaviors. Sage advice.

The Jungle Calls

Melanie and I continued working with Don Ernesto off and on for several years. He offered ceremonies in different US locations, but also in Spain and—most intriguingly to Melanie and me—in the Amazonian jungles of Peru. We learned that he stewarded a 500-acre parcel of sacred land, El Santuario, along the banks of a major branch of the Amazon River. A couple of our friends attended these ten-day journeys called "dietas." One meaning of dieta involves a specific diet one follows when using ayahuasca under the direction of a shaman. A second meaning of dieta is a sacred contract between the spirits of the plants—in this case, ayahuasca and chacruna—and the participant working with the plant medicine.

Considering going to Peru stretched me. Ingesting a psychedelic under the guidance of a shaman in a foreign country, in the middle of a rainforest retreat inaccessible to vehicles and with no cell phone connection, was a huge leap outside my comfort zone. While doing a stateside ceremony for six to eight hours, I knew my comfortable bed awaited me the next day. Our friends painted a different picture while describing these silent retreats in the heart of the Amazon jungle, primarily secluded from other participants. While they detailed their adventures and travel arrangements, they also expressed gratitude for the watchful care they received while there.

Then, I had the following dream.

I walk into a jungle valley with Ernesto, and a waterfall appears out of nowhere directly in front of us. With Ernesto by my side the whole way, the waterfall surrounds me as I ascend, going higher and higher up the mountain, effortlessly rising in opposition to the prevailing downward movement of the water. Reaching the top, we look out over the entire countryside filled with jungles, mountains, and rivers, along with the ocean in the distance—a totally different perspective from where we started. We had defied gravity.

Some say Mamacita's spirit can present herself in a dream, inviting someone to join her in a dieta. This happened to me in my dream. The cleansing waters of the falls enveloped and transported me to an elevated perspective far above my usual ground-based point of view. After waking up from this dream, I knew in my heart that I needed to face my fears about traveling to Peru, as the dream strongly encouraged me to join Don Ernesto in the Amazon jungle.

After all I'd been through with Ernesto, I trusted him, to be sure. But taking ayahuasca in Peru felt different, far outside my internal safe haven. I asked myself, Should I do this? Could I trust this process in a foreign country with a different language, a distinctive culture, and a completely contrasting environment?

After a few meetings with my friends who had been to Peru and after the dream I mentioned above, I opened up to going to South America. Open to just twenty participants per retreat, we inquired about the availability of two positions. Two spots remained, so Mel and I sent in a deposit. In response, we received detailed instructions on payment and helpful hints on when to arrive in Peru before the retreat.

With passports updated and our trip fees paid, Melanie and I brushed up on our rusty Spanish with a few Rosetta Stone CDs. One of Melanie's unique strengths is the ability to pick up on another language in a tenth of the time it takes for me to learn even a few simple, useful phrases such as, "Dondé los baños?!"

Ernesto told us to bring a small gift to pass out to each of his helpers after the dieta finished. He suggested that his Peruvian helpers loved pop-American t-shirts, so Mel and I picked up more than a dozen with quintessentially Americana motifs. With plane tickets in hand—as well as a tightly knotted area in my midsection that was pretending to be my belly—we headed off to Peru.

An Exciting New World

The two-segment trip, stopping in Panama midway, thrilled me. We spent our first night in Miraflores, a small seaside district in the Lima province, and the next day, we returned to Jorge Chavez International Airport to board our flight to Pucallpa, our next destination before the jungle. A warm and clear day greeted us as our plane flew north with the most incredible view—the snowcapped Andes Mountains out the windows on our right and the Pacific Ocean on our left. The spectacular Andes mesmerized me. Here I sat, reliving a grade-school geography lesson on the continuous mountain chain that extended from northern Canada to the tip of South America. Soon, the plane turned eastward, and the jungle, with its maze of rivers below, exploded into view out of my tiny airplane window as the sun dipped below the horizon.

Suddenly, the plane shook from the thunder and lightning of a towering, ominous thunderhead that filled the sky as we slowly descended. Every little bump while riding in an airplane always brought up my trepidation of crashing in a ball of fire, and this was no different; I closed my eyes, and my hands white-knuckled the armrests, hoping for it all to pass. The flashes of lightning and torrential rain quieted, and a few silent prayers later, the lights of Pucallpa came into view.

We pulled into the terminal, and a sigh of relief signaled relaxation of both my body and mind. I hugged Melanie quickly, and she returned a reassuring smile as we exited the plane and headed to find our baggage. Several porters asked if we needed assistance as I scoped out potential taxis.

"They have regular cars here that can fit all of our luggage," I murmured to myself as another persistent thought came and went. "And many people speak excellent English."

We stayed that night at a well-run, attractive local establishment called Los Gavilanes Hotel. The receptionist carefully explained several of the hotel's policies.

“Please sign here and take a few complimentary sample bottles of soap and shampoo. Your room is #3, and your towels should all be ready. Please visit the attached restaurant if you are hungry. Don Ernesto instructed everyone to gather at the downstairs meeting room at 3 p.m. on Wednesday. And feel free to connect to our internet,” she added.

After a refreshing night in a comfortable air-conditioned room, Melanie and I awoke for breakfast at the hotel restaurant and started meeting other ceremony participants. Sticking to our prescribed diet, simple fried huevos and arroz filled our plates. We spent several days getting to know the other adventurers—exploring the city, visiting colorful, lively, open-air markets, dining on tasty Peruvian dishes, and chewing legal freshly dried coca leaves. Frankly, the coca leaves affected me little because the freshness, wonder, and excitement of this entirely new environment dominated many of my senses.

Four or more motorcycle taxis vied for position at each intersection in the alarmingly narrow, two-lane roadways. Moto-taxis are basically rickshaws pulled by motorcycles. With room for up to three passengers, we learned to always agree on the fare before hiring the driver and vehicle. Otherwise, outrageous demand for an exorbitant payment might surprise you at the destination. You never knew what cargo the next motorized taxi carried—huge banana bunches, freshly butchered animals, chickens on the laps of children, building supplies, or sacks of rice.

The indigenous Shipibo-Conibo living in this area of Peru displayed heartwarming friendliness. They exhibited and sold their artwork and needlecrafts outside our hotel on the sidewalks. While we enjoyed meeting them and admired their amazing work, we were on a retreat and unable to purchase anything until after our ten days in the jungle. We assured them we'd come back.

The night before the official retreat started, we enjoyed our last full meal for the next ten days—a local standard called chicken chaufa, a fried rice dish with chicken, carrots, peas, and onions. Every forkful suddenly represented a new appreciation for plentiful, savory meals as we turned our eyes towards the seasoned dieta veterans telling stories of the jungle. It surprised me to feel so relaxed and comfortable in this small, welcoming city.

Soon after our meal, Ernesto called us all together in a small room in the hotel to announce the itinerary for the next morning. Filled with ordinary chairs and a conference table, the clean room looked out onto the small swimming pool surrounded by green leafy plants.

In Spanish, Don Ernesto thanked a waiter for the additional water glasses on each table and then proceeded to address us in fluent English. All of the participants for this particular retreat came from the United States.

"Beautiful day today. I trust all of your flights and connections went smoothly," he started. We all nodded. "Two people arrive tomorrow in the early morning. After they get here, we meet in front of the hotel with the belongings you wish to take to the jungle. Taxis then take us to a small village along the river, where dugout canoes await to transport us to El Santuario."

These specifics were new to Mel and me. While we had talked with friends prior to coming here, time hadn't permitted us to discuss every last detail. Neither Melanie nor I had known to ask some of these logistical questions. Part of my process involved starting to trust that everything worked out as it should.

Ernesto continued, "If you have a bag or two unnecessary for the jungle, you can leave it here with the hotel staff."

That was great news, as we had an extra bag with clean clothes for the trip home.

Someone asked, "Don Ernesto, how were you ever interested and called to this type of work?"

I hadn't quite thought of Ernesto's actions as work, but I figured that was a fair assumption.

"I grew up in western Spain," he started. "Ordinary schooling, but somewhere in my middle teens, I noticed an interest in shamanism. Dreams confirmed this, and the plants led me to this region of Peru, where I studied under a few different master shamans. My intense journey consisted of trials, isolation, study, and ceremonies."

His description of his calling and training impressed me, but I hadn't known he came from Spain. His devotion to the plant spirits ruled his inner life and actions, which reassured me.

Into the Jungle

The following day, we took a bumpy, three-hour taxi ride from Pucallpa to a tiny town, Nuevo San Juan, the last outpost, before heading into the jungle and El Santuario. The town was nestled on the banks of the Ucayali River, one of the Amazon's major tributaries. Our group drank water at a local open-air diner, and Ernesto left us to make final arrangements.

We lugged our backpacks down to a graveled bank along the river. A few children played there as I tried ever so carefully not to get my shoes wet. Local men waited for us with two primitive dugout canoes. One man took our packs and arranged them neatly in one canoe while we clambered aboard and arranged ourselves two by two for the next part of the journey. The canoes seemed slightly overloaded as the water line rose to just barely below the boat's edge. Nevertheless, I felt impressed at the planning and orderliness, as the two canoes accommodated all 20 adventurers, our backpacks, some bags of food and supplies, and a few of Ernesto's staff. We all took turns bailing water from the canoes' bellies along the way.

I felt a calming presence as the cool mid-morning weather, smooth, clear water, and occasional birds welcomed us to the Amazon. I saw many unfamiliar species of birds, bats, monkeys, trees, and underbrush as the sparse buildings and homes gradually gave way to a luscious green landscape and total seclusion. Occasionally, we encountered similar wooden dugout canoes occupied by local tribesmen and women, gracefully plying the waters in the opposite direction and carrying their precious cargos of indigenous woods and fruits to market. I looked around, taking it all in, feeling a profound curiosity and wonder—I couldn't believe my life had led me here. I took breaths in and out. Laughingly, I hoped to catch a glimpse of crocodiles and piranhas.

We arrived at the disembarking site, and four of Ernesto's crew awaited to help steady the canoes, offload pack after pack, and direct us to the safest spot to step ashore on the muddy bank. We all needed some help with our gear as we climbed up a steep, slick riverbank, hoping not to accidentally drop anything into the water. Slinging all of our belongings for the next ten days over our shoulders, a single-file line formed for an arduous two-mile trek along a dirt path heading into the unknown.

I hope to hell someone knows where we are going, I thought. Why didn't I bring my GPS?

Along the way, Ernesto pointed out local flora. "Look over here, everyone. This is the ayahuasca vine, as it grows naturally in the jungle. And here is some commonly known Cat's Claw, which is very medicinal in its own right."

The jungle interested me, but the growing discomfort of my backpack greatly distressed me. The temperature climbed, and the unrelenting humidity distracted me. After many strap adjustments, we arrived at Ernesto's land, El Santuario, and he introduced his friendly staff, all from the Shipibo tribe. They greeted us with broad, welcoming smiles as we gathered at a small structure with wooden beams, a thatched roof, and benches and tables.

Goodness, we are finally here, I thought silently. I couldn't have gone on much further! Damn! Flying insects already trying to bite me! I continued, followed by several hand slaps on my neck. Jesus! I would never have guessed this place was so hidden!

Handed a container of water, I eagerly gulped it down, continuously wiping the sweat from my brow.

Ernesto gave an overview of the retreat and announced that our first ceremony began in a few hours. Oh, shit, I forgot this happened on day one.

Our silence began immediately, so I gave Melanie one last hug and kiss before a guide escorted us to our tambos (tom'-bohs), the solitary structures we would call home for the next ten days.

Surprise and slight disbelief overcame me as Pablo, one of Ernesto's crew, walked me past the maloka—the sizeable thatched-roof structure where all ceremonies occurred. The rustic building blended in with the surrounding environment.

Trodding along in my hiking boots on the dirt paths along the lazy flowing rivulet of clear freshwater to our right, I thought, Man, this jungle vegetation and the voracious insects would swallow the maloka and all other wooden buildings in a few weeks if not for the constant tending by folks like Pablo who care for this land. I learned that Pablo and his colleagues came to El Santuario weeks before the first group of dieta participants each season, armed with machetes to literally hack the way for us all.

Pablo escorted me through the dense green jungle, past towering trees filled with bird calls I never imagined, to my isolated tambo—a structure without any walls or doors, just a fibrous leaf roof covering a bare wooden platform. Even on a slight rise, I couldn't see any signs of other humans because of the prolific trees and foliage. As I took in all the things my tambo didn't have, I noticed what it did have—a small handcrafted wooden table, a single wooden chair, and an unsupportive 2-inch mattress surrounded by a mosquito net on a crude, wooden bed frame. A two-gallon plastic bucket and a five-gallon water jug sat on the wooden deck.

Figure 16 My secluded Peruvian tambo in the Amazon

"Is it safe out here so isolated?" I asked Pablo.

Through a pronounced Peruvian accent, Pablo reassured me. "No worry, señor. Dos guardia walking all night. No worry. Is good. You safe. No worry, serpientes, no worry pantera. Pantera cry. You hear first."

He warned, "Wear shoes. Siempre [Always]. Serpientes pequeñas at night. Cuidado." Then he added, giving me a reassuring smile, "Ceremonia a las cinco en punto. I come back before."

He then pointed toward a wooden structure surrounded by a thatched screen on three sides and said, "Baño. Hit with stick, move bugs." Pablo hit the side of the wooden structure that acted as a seat. Several flying insects emerged as quickly as they could.

Ah, I thought, *my deluxe, semi-private toilet!*

"Thank you, Pablo."

Figure 17 My Private Toilet Facilities in the Amazon

Glancing downward, I noticed a long, orderly line of jungle ants marching toward a recently deceased mouse on the ground outside my tambo. Thirty minutes later, the mouse carcass and the ants had disappeared as if never even there.

Perhaps Mamacita called me to the jungle to help dissolve my inward tangle of thoughts and beliefs as if they were never there. Just like these ants!

Taking a quick view of the surrounding trees and brush, I smiled. *How am I ever going to make it ten days living without any type of enclosure?* I thought as I ran through a mental picture of torrential rain getting everything in my tambo soaked.

Melanie and I had brought along hammocks with mosquito netting. I hung my hammock, then unpacked my candle and matches, handheld water purifying bag, writing tablet, sketchbook, and pen, and reached into the bag to dig out the white ceremonial clothing. The eco-friendly bug repellant available to us consisted of rubbing the leaves of a local jungle plant called guayusa (why'-you-suh) on our bodies to ward off the little pests. You couldn't use any toothpaste (we brought baking soda), underarm deodorant, shampoo, shaving cream, body wash, essential oils, or perfumes. Paying gratitude to the jungle meant leaving most comforts of modern life at home. Imagine how ripe we all smelled by the end of the retreat!

My Dieta Experience

Isolated from the others in our group, I immersed into the aliveness of the Amazon. I spent my days and nights just a few feet above the plants and animals that called this place home. The constant humidity caused leather accessories, like one person's favorite leather ball cap, to quickly sprout mold. Ziploc freezer bags with large moisture-absorbing packets kept our clothes dry until we took them out to wear them. A pair of rubber boots protected our feet each time the rain came. There is a reason it's called a rainforest.

We practiced total silence unless visited by Ernesto or his staff (except for playing an instrument in our tambo), and we fasted—

eating one small meal each day of half a boiled plantain with either plain rice, hominy, or couscous.

Damn! I heard in my head. *I could have been happy with just about anything except a damn plantain!*

I enjoyed the solitude with nothing to do except for an occasional walk and my inner conversation. Every day, Pablo brought a pan around mid-morning and scooped out a dark tea into a hollowed-out coconut shell. Usually made from bobinsana (bow'-bin-sah-nah), he occasionally served tea from the chuchuhuasi (choo-choo-wah'-see) plant. On the sixth day of the dieta, I found a small piece of river fish on my plate beside the standard carbohydrate fare. It's hands down better than any fried fish I ate during Friday fasts growing up under Catholic dogma.

We also received 12 or more guayusa leaves each morning with instructions to cut up the leaves, soak them in river water, and use them for daily bathing. With anxiety and fear-reducing effects, the leaves helped us adjust to jungle living.

Beginning that evening and continuing over the next ten days, we sat through five ayahuasca ceremonies, with rest days for integration between the first, second, and third ceremonies. As dawn on the seventh day came, I prepared myself for another day of rest and reflection. Then Don Ernesto announced, "Along with the traditional ayahuasca ceremonies, many dietas include the partaking of Yawar Panga, a non-psychedelic Amazonian plant that causes intense stomach and intestinal cramping and purging. This ceremony starts in the late morning and lasts for as long as it takes you to drink about three gallons of river water." As I listened in shell-shocked disbelief, I realized this day was not a day of rest. It became a day of trial for me.

"The purpose is to cleanse your abdomen, gallbladder, and intestines," he continued.

What the hell... I thought to myself. *Not once have I ever heard about this!*

We gathered in our usual ceremony circle in the maloka, and Ernesto's helpers placed a large three-gallon bucket full of river water beside each of us, along with our purge buckets. Ernesto motioned for each to come up and receive Yawar Panga, which had little, if any, flavor.

I sat back down and started drinking the water by dipping my cup into my bottomless bucket.

How the hell am I ever going to get through this? I asked myself. Dread and a pang of sudden nausea came over me.

Soon, intense abdominal spasms and subsequent vomiting ensued. Frankly, I didn't want to take another drink. I couldn't put up with this for another round.

"Once you get towards the bottom of your water bucket, let Pablo know. He will judge whether you are finished or not," came the word from Ernesto.

Drink after drink, it seemed that endlessly I refilled my cup. I tried to pace how much water I thought I could ingest. Each sip brought nausea. With continuous waves of spasms, repeated vomiting came upon me. After two hours of sitting in the maloka during the mid-day heat, I glanced around, noticing that my cycle paralleled those of my fellow adventurers. At least I didn't appear worse off than anyone else!

I finally had only an inch of water at the bottom of my bucket, and I motioned to Pablo. He looked and said I was finished. And was I finished? Tired, aching, crampy, and sweaty, I couldn't even muster a smile or a single thought of congratulations. Shaking my head, I rose from my seat and very slowly and defeatedly shuffled off to my bunk.

I spent the remainder of that day puking in my semi-private, hand-dug, hole-in-the-ground toilet. Three hours passed before the stomach spasms slowed, making way for intestinal diarrhea instead of vomiting. I really couldn't say which was the least fun—hardly a day of rest.

I did sleep soundly that night and awoke at 4 AM to a handbell that signaled the start of other ceremonies. This time, the bell announced the beginning of a puja (a blessing ritual) led by Ernesto. I didn't mind pujas, as I enjoyed the chanting, but I didn't appreciate having my sleep interrupted for one. Half asleep, I plopped down on a log in front of the altar. Only thoughts of my terribly uncomfortable mattress and closing my eyes came through my mind. It seemed like an eternity while Ernesto led us through the usual chanting sequence.

That afternoon, we started the fourth ayahuasca ceremony earlier than any of the others. Hot and humid, thunderclouds roamed the sky, looking for a convenient spot to dump rain. So far, only light showers had occurred on this trip. The dirt paths never got as muddy as I thought they would, and my things in the tambo stayed relatively dry.

Jungle ceremonies and US ceremonies were incomparable. Drinking the medicine in the plants' native environment bumped up the intensity several notches. Sitting with the jungle plants and animals, the myriad sights and sounds were marvelous to behold, especially at dusk and dawn. It occurred to me at one point that the great Brazilian songwriters received musical inspiration and their complex rhythms while sitting in the jungle listening to the singing of the monkeys, panthers, birds, crickets, other insects, and frogs. Truly symphonic.

I realized that everyone I met and every sound I heard in Peru was like a doorway, an invitation, into my own heart.

Nighttime brought a different atmosphere to jungle life. Certain birds vocalized only at night, announcing dryness or the coming of rain with distinct calls. Unafraid of local animals, I was alarmed when luminescent insects at least three inches long flew around and in my tambo. I couldn't see each insect, but the fluorescent patches brought images of formidable creatures to my mind. The sounds didn't diminish at night either. They seemed even louder as darkness approached, probably because that was when I prayed for silence.

What Mamacita Taught Me

The most important lesson I received from the ceremonies was that the plants could open and expand my point of view, clarify issues, and help me look at the dreams that I brought. However, I still had to do all the actual work while *not* under the influence of plant medicine. It was solely my job to look at the beliefs I had made and sworn by as the truth. To expect Mamacita or someone else—a guru, spiritual teacher, psychologist, etc.—to do the work for me meant that I believed myself too dumb or inferior to do it independently. Expecting the plant medicinas to bring me bliss and enlightenment on their own was saying that I must depend on some outside magical force to help me remember the joy that I always am.

From my perspective, many participants fervently prayed to the plants to remove all their fears, worries, and anxieties. They repeatedly brought the same issues to the table, ceremony after ceremony, hoping Mamacita would dissolve past trauma. I found that the Mother Vine brought me to each lesson, sometimes painful, sometimes ecstatic, and left me to complete my homework post-ceremony. Very early on, the plants taught me that any bliss, joy, peace, or absence of thought I experienced during a ceremony was mine to access at any time, even without the aid of plant medicines. Indeed, if I am joy itself, only my beliefs block the remembrance of my relationship with Oneness.

Mamacita helped me with dreamwork:

I am near a woman with mechanical arms that extend in a circular pattern as if she had them wrapped around a large tree. I don't know her from waking life. In the dream, she falls to the ground, trying to clap her arms together in some futile attempt to accomplish something. To my mind, this appears quite a pathetic gesture.

During a ceremony, this same dream figure caught my eye as her mechanical arms extended in front of her, almost zombie-like. I stood watching her as the robotic arms morphed into real flesh-and-bone arms. Without saying a word, she wrapped those arms around me in a warm and loving embrace that I rarely allowed myself to receive in waking life. I then realized I had been giving family and friends robotic, perfunctory hugs laden with guilt and underlying anger. My embraces were mechanical in every sense of the word. Seeing this tendency so clearly gave me the possible course of action: continue offering lifeless hugs or allow this habit to dissolve.

Mamacita also relentlessly reminded me that I always had an alternative recourse in my responses to life.

Sitting in my tambo one late afternoon between ceremonies, a dark, black cloud the size of a basketball slowly lifted out of my head.

I watch the black cloud slowly rise, and soon, it starts cursing me, saying, "How could you give me up? How could you let me go despite all the years I protected you and cared for you?" A long curse-filled tirade follows, and then silence settles over me as the black cloud slowly fades away.

Shouldn't I feel lighter now that the cloud is gone? I certainly don't. I wonder if it simply relocated and now inhabits someone else's energy field. This line of thought amused me. Imagine me, previously a hard-core rationalist, wondering about intangible black clouds moving from person to person!

Thoughts continued: *Ahhhh, this cloud represents my victimhood and my boneheaded commitment to continually stuffing my emotions down deep inside no matter what pain I feel, like neck pain.*

As if hearing an echo of the black cloud's perspective, it screamed at me, ***"Meet anger with anger! Combat hatred with hatred!!! No other options exist. None!***" The cloud departed, but it took me a while to discover that I indeed had a choice in how I see and respond to everything, and I could choose paths that led to less pain and suffering.

In another ceremony, one particular icaro that Don Ernesto sang battled me at my core. This icaro shook loose every sensation that I identified as "Bart," as if a planetary calamity tore apart every square inch of land and ocean from the inside out.

After this happened, it felt like an expansion occurred between my atoms and molecules with each note of the mystical song.

The finished product had no gravity at all to hold it together. Earth no longer existed; only individual pieces floated randomly through space. Bart, as I knew him, no longer existed, no matter how much I tried to hold my point of view together. It was painful and terrifying.

Ernesto sang so intensely that I couldn't tolerate looking at him when I tried to open my eyes. His exaggerated mouth movements revealed every tooth in his mouth as he verbalized the words. He displayed a distorted mouth opening and closing as if he violently chewed food. With Spanish lyrics, I couldn't catch the literal meaning of this icaros. Intense fear vibrated throughout my body. How I wished the damn song would end. I knew symbolically that the icaro and Mother Vine had devoured Bart.

I breathed a sigh of relief when the seemingly relentless icaro ended. I took a breath, and a small tear fell from my eye.

For a brief time during this ceremony experience, I noted that I was watching everything, including everything I thought and did. It was as if I was observing everything on a movie screen.

When the ceremony finished, I returned to my tambo. The inner quiet I felt inside remained, and at times, I ***was*** that peace looking outward through this body and into this world.

This is what it's like to be enlightened, were the words I heard.

Integrating the Experience

After the last ceremony, the vow of silence ended. Rather than talk about the intensity of our ten days in the jungle or swap stories of ceremonies, we enjoyed deepening our relationships by sharing stories of where we lived and how we were called to the jungle. Mamacita met each of us at our depths, leading us through unique and life-changing experiences.

The following day, we dined on a feast worthy of kings and queens: fried eggs, potatoes, and salt! While it was one of the best breakfasts I had ever been served, I couldn't eat much, as my stomach had shrunk from our one-meal-a-day fast. As in the Stateside ceremonies, ingesting salt officially ended our ten-day fast.

I gathered my things in my pack, looked around my deluxe jungle facility, and, though tired, felt joy in my bones as I walked the two miles back to the river. The same dugout river canoes met us at the riverbank, safely transporting us downriver to begin our trek home from a fantastic experience. Disembarking in the small town, I chatted with Melanie and a few others as we rode in the taxis back to Pucallpa.

Scheduled to fly to Lima the following day, Melanie and I booked a hotel room, showered, changed clothes, and rested on a comfortable bed in air-conditioned privacy. We felt welcome and safe there. Still, slightly in a daze from our jungle adventure, we spent one night in Miraflores, near Lima, after our Pucallpa-Lima segment. The Peruvian dish of Pollo a la Brasa tickled our olfactory senses, wafting out of the grocery store a block away.

Due to a booking error, Mel and I sat apart on the Panama-Washington, DC leg of our flight home. A wonderful human being, José, from Panama, sat next to me. Quickly becoming friends, we eventually visited him in Panama on our next trip to South America. José even came to our wedding several years later.

Who is this guy, this new and different Bart, who befriends a total stranger, a foreigner to boot, while sitting next to him on a plane? I wondered.

When we arrived home, it felt like my body had returned to the US, but my brain and heart remained in Peru, lingering there for a few more weeks. I had felt a sense of integration, even homecoming, sitting in isolation with the jungle for ten days. I also sensed a letting go, an expansion, and almost transparency while there. The trip opened up something new in me, not the least being a realization of a completely different way to hug my friends and family if I wanted to do so.

My harmful thoughts and habits didn't vanish overnight, but a small part of me opened more to change. My anger, jealousy, and attitude that others always tried to take something from me persisted, but something softened in that hard-core external armor that I called Bart.

CHAPTER 10
RETREAT INTO THE CATHEDRAL OF INTELLECT

Back from our first ten-day retreat in the Peruvian Amazon, Melanie and I jumped into seeing patients at my office. My stint in the jungle gave me a new appreciation for the concept of personal readiness. Not everyone is ready to dive into their inner world to pursue an angelfish. Indeed, not everyone can spend ten days fasting in a silent ceremonial retreat! To do so requires some willingness to change and to view things differently, and one cannot force change.

My nurse practitioner and I referred many patients to Melanie for heart-focused stress management coaching and dreamwork to better handle their physical, emotional, and mental pain. We watched as many refused to pursue this inner work, attending only one meeting with her and never rescheduling. I considered making HeartMath a compulsory part of their treatment, but I knew it wouldn't work. I knew personally how fear leads to great resistance to change. Also, the other physicians who worked with me mostly ignored the fact that we now offered these two alternative modalities to patients, so making it mandatory was futile. Instead, Mel, my nurse practitioner, and I continued working with those adventurous few, those ready to examine their lives from a different angle.

My mystical experiences during journeys and ceremonies provided expanded points of view for my ever-changing concepts of the universe. I mostly kept these to myself. My childhood traumas and their associated beliefs (e.g., everyone is trying to take something from me) still held me in their grip, but I now looked at my views in a more engaging and "spiritual" way. I occasionally illustrated a point in conversation by using a quote from a teacher, such as Eckhart's "You are not your mind." Unfortunately, I mostly tried using my newfound spiritual or more intuitive knowledge to pretend once more that I stood superior over others. I still lacked a realized embodiment of many emotions and kept trying to use my intellect as a way to avoid deeper connections with people.

Many of the same negative thoughts and beliefs hid behind a new character—the "advanced" Bart. Who wouldn't consider themselves enlightened after all of my recent mystical experiences? Plus, I had intermittent periods of functioning as the witnessing observer of everything. Something just watched everything I did throughout the day, and it seemed I was that something. This brought a slight feeling of accomplishment.

I saw that lurking behind each thought of advancement came a voice.

*HA! **ME**, and NOT **YOU**!*

A bit of superiority snuck in through the back door.

One fundamental and lasting change, however, regarded how the dream of the woman with mechanical arms taught me a new way to hug.

"So, how was your trip to Peru?" asked Raul, waving from across the room as Melanie and I went to our first post-Peru dream group. Melanie moved forward and gave Raul a big hug.

"Everything I heard and saw twinkles in my memory," she said, extending her hug for a few extra seconds.

I also came over and wrapped my arms around Raul. I squeezed but chose not to lift him off the floor.

"Where did that come from, Bart?!?" Raul exclaimed. "That hug was different from any other hug you've given me!" He studied me quizzically.

I thanked him and gave a brief background recital of the woman with the mechanical arms. Of course, I still only hugged a chosen few in this way, but it was different, warm, and heartfelt. With this hug, I could at least imagine an expanded expression of genuine care for others.

Outside of my dream group friendships, I occasionally met a friend or two for lunch.

A friend my age had been recently diagnosed with Parkinson's disease, often characterized by progressive, uncontrollable tremors. I learned of his diagnosis, which worried me, from another friend. He'd always been a vibrant and sporty type who loved traveling, and I knew Parkinson's could take that away from someone quickly. I wanted to see him and asked if he'd like to meet.

"Hello there, Steve. So good to see you! What's it been, almost six months since we last met for lunch?" I said as we shook hands and smiled at each other when entering our favorite local pizza restaurant. The waitress led us to a table in the middle of the floor. After light-hearted bantering about tales of our recent pasts, Steve finally brought up his diagnosis.

"Bart, I must say, this diagnosis sucks. While right now, the tremors are controllable, I worry."

"I feel for you, Steve," I said, noticing helplessness as I considered how I would react if such a future stared me in the face.

"And do you know what I am worried about most?" Steve said softly with tears in his eyes. "I'll miss being able to play guitar."

An avid guitar player, Steve and his theatrical partner performed in a duet at local bars and theaters, playing and singing original songs. I knew that not being able to play would devastate him, and it would devastate me. I never knew what to say in these situations, so I watched my newfound spiritual intellectualism take over.

With no explanation, a very straight face, and no emotion, I coldly responded, "Well, we will all have to stop playing guitar sometime."

Steve's face dropped about a foot; at first, I didn't even realize why. A puzzled look came to my face for a second before I realized the incredibly callous sentence that had just silenced the entire room. Steve stood and gathered his few belongings with minimal conversation.

"You might know that intellectually, Bart, but it came across as arrogant, uncaring, and just plain stupid!" Steve said as he slammed the door to the restaurant on his way out. My body stiffened inside, and all emotions were stifled. Our food untouched, I quickly paid the check and somberly drove home.

My hugs had gotten warmer, but I still didn't know how to comfort someone in emotional pain.

I recognized that this "arrogant, uncaring, and stupid" intellectual knowing was one of the tendencies Don Ernesto had suggested I watch out for in my daily life. Showing off my intellectual superiority over others, I used my mental prowess to showcase my elevated status—even hijacking other teachers' phrases to accomplish it. Previously, my pronouncements of authority drew on historical or medical facts. Now, they also included spirituality. A part of my mind justified my superior spiritual intellectualism, insisting that the other person deal with their reactions. It wasn't **my** problem that others were so sensitive to **my** truth.

I often wonder what my friendships would be like if I hadn't said things like this.

A definite feeling of loss and regret followed, but I knew I couldn't change the past. I attempted to apologize to Steve, but my message went unanswered.

Reluctant to Experience the Body

As part of treatment for my ongoing neck pain, I went to a therapist who specialized in Thai massage. Each time Mel and I walked up the stairs to her massage studio on the second floor of an office building in Charlottesville, hesitation and warning came through my thoughts.

Just look at all these references to Thai healing practices, I heard as I gazed at all the Buddhist spiritual books and a small Buddhist shrine on her shelf.

Am I required to believe all of this Buddhist-based dogma?

"Hello, Mel and Bart," Louise, the bodyworker, said. "Who's turn is it to go first today?" The heating pads warmed in the oven as she prepared them for the massage table.

"I will go first," I responded, heading into the dressing area to remove my street clothes. Climbing onto the warmed padded massage table, I covered up with a freshly laundered sheet.

Like clockwork, Louise asked, "So, what's your body saying to you today?"

And each time, I answered by rolling my eyes and silently shrugging my shoulders. "Same old stuff going on, just like last month."

Even though I was continuing to read Eckhart and exploring my pain-body, I wasn't convinced that the physical body stored old traumas or even that the body communicated anything of importance other than pain.

While I'd heard about negative energies settling into the body from friends who followed Sufi teachings, looking for these debilitating energies made no sense to me. I certainly didn't want to start looking for them within myself. As I mentioned, readiness is critical.

I still let my fear of change unconsciously dictate what I would or would not look at. Just like my pain patients, I only traversed my inner world as far as fear allowed. So, instead of examining the crippling energies that I kept locked up in my body—like any anger hiding behind my neck pain and chronic migraines—I ignored these physical clues and looked solely at my still, ever-powerful, dominating thoughts and beliefs. My recent experiences left me feeling expanded and less defined by this prison of a body. So why would I ever want to reconnect to a bodily sensation again—as it had only brought me pain and suffering? I didn't want to rekindle the representations in my body that arose along with feelings like anger, sadness, disappointment, hurt, and the like. I had blocked them for good reason as a child. Why would it suddenly be better now as an adult? It felt like regression, not advancement or evolution. I still believed that ignoring or denying their existence served to eradicate them.

Intellectual Worship

After visiting the jungle, I developed a penchant for sitting in silence at times. One evening, I found myself on the couch when a vision came:

The aching along the sides of my forehead parallels the distant thunderclouds that appear outside the front room window. These clouds announce the arrival of lightning, while the bodily pain points toward a storm brewing in my head. I realize that my headache starts in my temples and gradually spreads to the back of my head and onto my crown. A thought occurs: "Oh, my temples on the side of my skull are my temples of worship. I worship thought!" I gaze at this thought with quiet curiosity as the night sky illuminates between claps of thunder. Almost immediately, an image of a colossal medieval stone cathedral appears on my head; this enormous structure sits there like some oppressive, gaudy hat. I feel its weight compressing and twisting my neck—a sense of struggling to keep it straight and upright mixed in with the chronic neck pain itself.

Figure 18 Cathedral of the Intellect

I realized I'd been worshipping my intellect. It alone had become my god and my savior. No wonder my headaches continued relentlessly before AND after my neck surgeries! It was my sanctuary—no matter how uncomfortable, debilitating, or deadening. I'd been addicted to the safety of my intellect.

Holy shit, I thought. *I've had all these headaches and two major neck surgeries. I painstakingly built and now carry around this cathedral of intellect on the top of my head; it's been that way for years!* A silence washed through my mind.

Reminding me of my previous dream of the Flash character, who now wore a baggy suit that no longer fit, I thought, *I'm slowly emerging from this cathedral's cold and dreary confines that dictate the uninterrupted importance of my mind. Flash's ill-fitting suit and the picture of the massive cathedral where I have confined myself are further invitations to keep looking at what I believe has made me.*

I also saw how a part of my mind could take just about anything, even spirituality, and twist it into another bastion behind which I could hide—just another retreat into the cathedral of the mind.

Paying a little more attention to what thoughts came through my head, I noticed that silence surrounded all thoughts every time. Even in chaos, silence and peace permeated everything.

The Vultures

Following our first Peru dieta, we participated in several ceremonies with Don Ernesto in the United States. All involved the usual pre- and post-ceremonial fasting, outdoor folding chairs, and the standard purge bucket. One ceremony consisted of the following:

I find myself lying on my back on the ground. Looking outward from the inside of my skull, my perception is now located at the pineal gland, just about at the brain's center. I see every skull bone, facial muscle, and the skin that covers it all, as if looking at a primarily translucent, 3-D model of my head, but from the very middle of the brain, peering outward.

At least five vultures land near me and walk up to my 3-D figure. Fearless at this point, I just watch. The vultures start picking my facial skin apart, each bite grabbing and tearing at my skin and muscles. And yet, remarkably, I feel no fear or pain. Drops of blood well up with each bite. I looked around my skull, seeing each bone again from the middle of the head, not from the outside. The vultures bite and pull at my eyes, ripping and cleaning out the eye sockets themselves. Yet, I still could see. My "sight" is not dependent on my eyes.

Then the scavengers take small bites from my mouth, pulling apart my lips and tongue with which I believe I speak to the world. No pain, no fear still. I continue watching, gradually noticing more openness within.

Suddenly, the carrion eaters transform into angelic figures, softly lit and shimmering with transparent features. Their faces fill with compassion as they work. These divine beings aren't biting and ripping; they ever so gently touch a part of my head. Each touch of grace brings a more profound understanding that the earthly body of this man named Bart might not be as solid and real as I think. Peace pours through me. These angelic figures lovingly rekindle a spark in me, the spark of remembrance that I am not simply limited to this flesh and bones. They show me the transparency of the body. A profound stillness surrounds my beliefs about what my physical perceptions mean.

Figure 19 Scavengers

This sense of not being exclusively flesh and bones persisted for some time after this journey. And since that time, recalling the angelic vultures has brought peace and comfort.

A Course in Miracles and Challenging Internal Dogmas

In *The Power of Now*, Eckhart refers several times to another book called *A Course in Miracles* (ACIM). A little voice in my mind suggested that if Eckhart quoted from this book so much, I must at least look into it. Published in the mid-1970s, ACIM was a completely different kind of book than any others that I had read. I learned that Helen Schucman began writing ACIM after having the book's ideas channeled through her in the mid-1960s. The concept of channeling didn't resonate much, but the published works helped me explore my religious upbringing. Many questions about Catholicism plagued me as a child and teenager. I always sensed a reverence for something higher than me, but I couldn't accept many of the concepts presented in the Bible. As a result of my religious schooling, I imagined a jealous, murderous, erratic, yet somehow all-loving God who eventually decided, based on some arbitrary rules (also known as the last judgment), whether I got to enter heaven. My thoughts and deeds during this life comprised the sole basis of God's final decision as to whether I was worthy. Regardless of all the penance and sacrifice I might endure during my lifetime, if God condemned me with a snap of his fingers, I would end up in hell. I didn't speak openly with anyone concerning my conclusions, but an internal, unconscious dogma made a home in my mind. This internalized ideology presented itself as some version of this phrase:

"If I experience joy, God will allow me to feel it for a split second, and then He will obliterate me."

Hardly a comforting thought to have just before falling off to sleep!

ACIM completely turned Biblical teachings upside down by introducing me to the idea that God created me perfectly and that God himself does not judge. The real issue was how ruthlessly I judged myself and others. Eventually, I started to feel how tiring all this self-judgment and judgment toward others had been throughout my life.

ACIM kept inviting me to view this concept of judgment differently. The purposeful use of Christian terms helped me address my questions about Christian dogma. Sometimes, you must work with an old paradigm from a different angle to inspire change.

When I first started reading ACIM and its notion of true sight, I had this dream:

During a dream sequence, an ordinary coffee cup appears, not too big and lacking outstanding marks or coloration, perhaps like the one I use every day. I sense something different in how I see this particular cup, but I don't know why. I see a delicate white shimmer on the cup, perhaps some crystalline coating. Then, a catalog of thousands of items appears in my hands. Anything I could ever want is there— household items, furniture, cars, and even the clouds in the sky. There is also a list of all thoughts and emotions, including anger, fear, boredom, joy, contentment, and others. I open another page, and there in the catalog is a picture of the same cup I just placed on my desk. Below the description of this cup is a statement bracketed by several asterisks.

The information is this: ***Everything in this catalog, without fail, EVERYTHING, is made of cocaine. NO EXCEPTIONS. ***

Hmmmmm … All of these items, in fact, all articles and all forms, are manufactured with cocaine, ***I thought. A feeling of curiosity comes over me, and then I awaken.***

As I woke, I recalled that cocaine is a chemical extracted from the South American coca leaf. Indigenous groups have used coca leaves for thousands of years for medicinal purposes and as an energy boost. In the last 150 years, Western medicine discovered that cocaine solutions served well as excellent topical anesthetics, especially for eye surgery. While coca leaves are non-addictive, cocaine is highly addictive.

Just like using cocaine in eye surgeries, any thought, belief, object, or emotion can be used to numb and superficially anesthetize my true seeing of who I actually am. Even the act of searching for who I am can numb me to the truth.

I felt that I found another piece of the puzzle I had worked on for years.

While ACIM suggested that perhaps my chronic judging would end someday, the more significant revelation was ***how much I judged everything now***. My judgments continually revolved around some unexamined theme, such as "Boy, I wish this rain would stop," which comes just minutes after saying, "Boy, we sure do need rain."

Before this point, I thought everyone and everything else did all the judging; I wore blinders regarding all the criticism I handed out!

Once I began looking for it, I caught myself judging this and that all day, and it didn't matter what. Most concerned other people, work, the government, and world events. Excelling at judging inwardly regarding my thoughts and actions, I also criticized my body for being weak, frail, and unreliable. I could go on and on about being too short, fat, bald, and clumsy. The list of faults never ended.

ACIM continued helping me explore beliefs about salvation (aka going to heaven). In my upbringing, just being born into this world made me a sinner. I could only win salvation by believing the right things, suffering through the proper repentance, and paying a vague and ever-changing price. I never accepted church teachings claiming that someone had to be crucified and murdered for me to be saved.

I always asked*, How does murder achieve love?*

ACIM asked if all of this could be seen in an alternative way. I started hearing, *Did I possibly crucify myself every time I responded with fear instead of love?* The short answer, *Yes,* immediately popped into my head. Many interactions with attorneys and tax authorities reeked of mistrust and scarcity. My chronic apprehension surfaced with each political news report. Just entering my office brought angst and dread of another day with difficult staff or patients with complex presentations. At times, it felt as if the fear in my body strung me up for a painful death. I didn't literally see this as a crucifixion, but rather the denial and obstruction of knowing my true self. With each new understanding, a little more space opened within me.

Another issue I had with the Church concerned the unshakeable specialness of Jesus, whom I sometimes resented with a passion. The Church repeatedly taught that God had only one Son, and I, the flawed, sinful human, was most assuredly not that Son. These teachings brought up hateful feelings in me. Why was Jesus that Son and not I? I was a lowly peon, doomed to the whims of a maniac in heaven.

Thankfully, I was open to the teachings of ACIM, which promoted that while Jesus may have been more experienced in spirituality than I, Jesus was a brother and fellow traveler, not a deity ruling over everyone and demanding worship. As I took in these words, comfort washed over me. These writings resonated with my personal encounters with Jesus in dreams and meditations.

As part of my reading of ACIM, I joined a local study group. After a short period, I thought I knew more than anyone else, and I was not hesitant to let everyone know.

"Does anyone else have any comments on what we just read?" asked Sonia, the local ACIM study group leader.

"Yes," I responded. "Everyone is looking at this in the wrong way. And let me tell you how you are doing that."

With disapproving looks from several study group members, I grew silent, realizing I had said something that might be true but didn't need to be said right now.

The leader boldly told me, "You know, Bart. You are not as enlightened as you think."

These types of discordant interactions followed me around for many years. Because of them, I stopped going to organized ACIM study groups, and several friends dropped me off their contact lists. But I reasoned my way past all that because it felt good to have some knowledge others didn't have. I felt safer, I guess, in a world that had successfully stolen my happiness. The cathedral of intellect remained secure and protected and had a very willing occupant—me.

What Is Truth?

About this time, my friend Lewis introduced me to a somewhat irreverent spiritual author.

"Hey, Bart, glad I got to speak to you. Have you ever read Jed McKenna's books on spiritual enlightenment?" asked Lewis.

"No, I haven't," I responded. "Who is he?"

"Well, Jed's a bit of an enigma and stays out of the public eye, but he wrote a few books on some of his experiences working with others using a process he calls 'spiritual autolysis.' McKenna asks us to examine all our beliefs until we narrow them down to only what is true in the end," Lewis explained. "I downloaded a copy of his first book, and here it is on a CD."

"That sounds interesting, Lewis. I'll take a look and let you know what I find!"

After Lewis's invitation, I took the CD, opened the files, and started reading. About six months later, Lewis attended another ceremony with Mel and me, and by then, she and I had both read Jed's trilogy on spiritual enlightenment.

"Hey, Lewis, that's quite the series of writings you gave us," I said.

"Glad to hear it! Did anything he said to shake up your world a bit?" Lewis queried with a knowing grin.

"Not much," I chuckled, continuing, "only driving home the idea that everything, without exclusion, that I believe or can conceive of is not truth. Only that. Nothing huge." We all laughed. "But, when I read how each person dismantled their thoughts and belief constructs using the spiritual autolysis process, it surprised me that they didn't implode."

"Julie nearly did," Melanie interjected, referring to one of Jed's students in the book. "She was blown away and lost when her world crumbled."

"That's true …" Lewis nodded in agreement. "It's a tough pill to swallow that this thing we've all been seeking, which we refer to as truth, is unknowable; it's indescribable, unchanging, and unperceivable. And this truth is truly who we are. We may experience ourselves as spheres, light beings, and souls, but in the end, all these are only mystical experiences and not the truth of who we are."

Silence. We stared at one another, absorbing those words.

I added, "My whole life was one continual attempt to prove that my experiences, thoughts, and beliefs were real. And now, someone tells me everything is false or, at best, only briefly relatively true. Then there is this thing-non-thing that we call truth that cannot even be described. How can something be true that can only be written about in false words?"

Silence again. This time, smiles spread across our faces, remembering the ludicrous nature of the spiritual search for truth.

Excited to discuss Jed's work, I rambled on, "And it was affirming when he emphasized many times that each of us can watch ourselves. Mamacita got me started doing that, and Jed encouraged me to do it as often as I can remember—when on the computer, brushing my teeth, talking with people, even when simply thinking."

"What about the time he got entangled in a police chase, Bart, and he used that to demonstrate how we can step in and out of our costume?" Melanie prompted.

"Oh, yeah, he illustrated how it's possible to gradually see the illusory nature of my identity as me. I see more clearly now that this role I live out as Bart—the doctor, ex-husband, partner, friend, and father—is only a costume. I can wear it, remove it, and put it back on as I choose. That's big." I smiled. "I sense that I can be much more than the limited costume I wore all those years, and it can completely change from moment to moment. That feels so freeing!"

Exploring the unknowable truth added a different angle from which I examined my life. How did this truth relate to daily occurrences—not only my dreams, but in active imagination or ceremonies? Did this mean that all these unique and coveted happenings that I thought held major significance were simply mere life experiences, as significant or insignificant as taking a breath or blinking my eye? I wanted them to mean something essential, yet I simultaneously recognized the trap of demanding that.

I watched for references to truth in ACIM as I continued reading. How did truth and ACIM fit together? As even ACIM pointed out, all perceptions, words, and even concepts, such as Jesus and the Holy Spirit, are eventually untrue. Everything has, at best, a relative degree of truth that only points in the direction of truth, or so the concept goes. All beliefs and points of view can lead one way this second and in a completely different direction in another. In other words, perception and awareness aren't the truth, as they can change. Jed and ACIM both stated that truth is beyond consciousness and all perception. And even then, perhaps I have said too much, for truth and God are beyond any understanding I pretend to have about them.

This left me shell-shocked.

As I reflected on these things, my first ayahuasca ceremony came to mind when a voice asked, "Are you ready to give up consciousness and return to the One?" In other words, "Are you ready to give up all you have thought of and believed of yourself and your life, along with what you consider being conscious, aware, or enlightenment, to return to truth?" How do I even return to the truth? In what direction? And besides, what should I wear? I began to see the circular nature of such mental somersaults. I started calling those endless mind cycles rabbit holes.

Back to South America

As Melanie and I grew closer, she decided to move in with me in the Shenandoah Valley countryside. In addition to the love emanating between us, we enjoyed similar activities, including skiing, target shooting, scuba diving, and traveling. We shared an interest in and promised to continue observing our minds to shed light on our conditioned tendencies or repetitive reactions. We watched for our pain-bodies, doing our best to discuss them with one other. However, despite everything we shared, I never convinced her to golf with friends and me regularly! And she had quite a fluid, natural golf swing.

I talked with my sons Chris and Tyler about our experiences with Don Ernesto, and a tiny seed of interest seemed to take root. Agreeing to sponsor both of them, I sent them the contact information to register for a ceremony. They both signed up for the next available sitting.

Mamacita brought up images provoking fear for both Chris and Tyler in these first ceremonies. I hoped that with Don Ernesto and Mamacita's help, they could sit with this fear, no matter what arrived in their mind's eye. Tyler vowed never to do another ceremony as the fear overwhelmed him. However, Chris seemed to have a good relationship with Mamacita and requested that if we ever returned to Peru, to please take him along.

For several months, Melanie and I discussed taking another trip to the Amazon. Things went back and forth until another friend, Ella, started talking about it, too. At Ella's house for a casual get-together, the conversation came around to our adventures in Peru.

"Ella, I could be wrong, but you *have* been to Peru with Don Ernesto, haven't you?" I asked.

"Yes, I have, and while I struggled with the ceremonies, I loved being there amongst the plants and the gentle Shipibo people. Mamacita has helped open up quite a bit for me, and as I speak these words, my heart leaps."

"Did you go anywhere else while you were there?" Melanie questioned.

"Just around Lima and the suburb, Miraflores," Ella stated. "You two stayed in Miraflores on your last visit?"

"Yes," Melanie smiled and nodded. "We stayed at the El Condado with a grocery store across the street selling the most wonderful Peruvian foods."

"Hallelujah!" she replied. "The Peruvian chicken is mouth-watering and excellent, especially after fasting for ten days! I hear there is a Peruvian restaurant in Harrisonburg. Perhaps we should go there sometime."

I exclaimed excitedly as my taste buds, seemingly with a mind of their own, immediately conjured up the exquisite taste and texture of that roasted chicken and fried yucca.

The conversation continued, and in the end, we all decided to sign up for the next Peruvian retreat with Don Ernesto. We also planned to see some local Peruvian sights while visiting this time. We told Chris about the proposed trip, and he said he could adjust his work schedule for as long as we wanted to stay.

I also contacted José, the Panamanian fellow Mel and I met on the plane back from Peru. He was most excited as we told him our plans to fly into Panama City and happily said yes when we asked him to tour the local sights with us for a few days. The entire trip came together smoothly, and a month later, Mel, Chris, and I headed to Panama.

Seeing José and the Sights

I love sitting in a window seat while flying; visiting Panama City was a fantastic experience. As the pilot lined up for the runway, we could simultaneously see the Atlantic and Pacific oceans, their respective waves lapping against narrow beaches abutting the jungle greenery. José stood waiting for us at the terminal in his small economy car. Our luggage wouldn't all fit, so we stowed everything we didn't need at the airport. Moderate temperature and stifling humidity greeted us as we traveled from the airport to José's apartment.

"So great to see you, José! How have you been?" I asked during delightful observations of the buildings and bustling city streets in Panama City.

"I am good and excited to announce my retirement from the canal authority," he replied in a very animated voice. "As you know, I have worked as a canal customs official for many years, and I've grown tired of taking small boats out to the transiting cargo ships needing to declare their cargo. Climbing up those rope ladders in a choppy sea intimidates me, not to mention the tension generated by ship captains who don't want their cargo closely scrutinized! A part of my job that amazes me is that I often charge the captain of larger cargo ships a transit fee of nearly half a million dollars to transport their cargo through the canal." He was thrilled to have Mel, Chris, and me stay with him and his roommate for the next few days.

"Any chance we could visit the canal tomorrow, José?" asked Chris.

"But of course!" José returned. "Let's first take your things to my apartment, and then we will dine on one of the offshore islands."

I knew little about Panama except for the usual history class lessons on the Panama Canal, so I wasn't sure what to expect. I was amazed by the tropical climate, intermittent rain showers, high humidity, and cosmopolitan feel rivaling almost any American city. Palm trees and other luscious tropical vegetation surrounded José's apartment on a quiet residential street. After parking, one flight of stairs led us to our friend's apartment in his home country.

The next day, José took us to his workplace along the canal and told us more details about his job and the upcoming canal enlargement. Visiting several locks along the way, it amazed me how these big ships fit into a canal barely a few feet wider than themselves. Several days later, after getting a first-hand view of the canal and the city, we said goodbye to José and his roommate. Everything progressed like clockwork as we collected the bags from airport lockers and boarded our flight. José promised to visit us in the US the next time he came to visit his family.

As we flew over South America, I kept track of our position relative to the Earth's equator. Recalling a world globe I studied as a schoolboy, I could see where Panama ended and Colombia began. Soon, only the Pacific Ocean was visible as we left the Atlantic far behind. Fog rolled in from the ocean, obscuring our view, so a short nap was in order. I woke just in time to catch a glimpse of the now-familiar sights of Lima from 30,000 feet. As we descended towards the airport, I noticed another plane perpendicularly cruising towards us from our right. The plane almost appeared to be heading straight towards us, but with plenty of time to spare, it ascended, and we passed directly below its contrail.

We checked our backpacks at the airport to do some sightseeing before going to the jungle, a convenient feature to which I had quickly become accustomed. Since Mel and I had visited just a year before, we knew how to get a taxi and headed off with Chris to Miraflores for the night. We walked around this section of the city and ended up window shopping at the Aztec market filled with blankets, paintings, and endless reminders of Peru. We returned to the airport the next day and boarded a flight to Cusco, our stopping-off point for the Sacred Valley and Machu Picchu.

Our descent into Cusco provided magnificent views of the coastal desert and the Andes Mountains. I was thankful for the pilots' skills as the approach into Cusco took us through a narrow mountain pass with a final landing at about 11,000 feet elevation. Our next steps worked well—one more taxi, hotel negotiations, and a call to the local travel agency I had hired to take us around the area for several days. Unfortunately, altitude sickness quickly overtook Melanie. Chris and I had headaches, but Melanie suffered horribly from nausea, a massive migraine, extreme fatigue, and overall malaise. We heard that coca tea helped alleviate these symptoms, so we boiled leaves in some water, and Chris and I immediately experienced the healing effects of the coca plant. It took Mel a few days to recover, and she only felt better after we descended into the Sacred Valley and Machu Picchu at 8,000 feet.

Our local tour guide met Chris, Melanie, and me in front of our small hotel and led us to a bus full of tourists that transported us to the train bound for Machu Picchu. Along the way, our bus was targeted by the local *policia* for a traffic stop. After about 20 minutes of negotiations, the bus continued along its way only after our tour guide opened up her purse and paid a bribe—business as usual. The full splendor of Machu Picchu unfolded in all its glory as we climbed a slight rise out of the train station at the bottom of the mountain. Nestled in the green mountains in a secluded area, this ancient town of crafted rock, terraces, and vistas was a marvel to behold as I imagined a thousand people scattered throughout the gardens and buildings living their lives. I saw why this area was so sacred to the locals who had lived here for generations.

When we returned to Cusco later in the day, Melanie's fatigue and joint aches lingered. We drank more coca tea and headed toward more local sights. And all this time, we stuck to the diet as Don Ernesto suggested—essentially the same for all single ceremonies and retreats. Restrictions included no sugar, minimal meat except for chicken and fish, and reduced salt. Unfortunately, foods to avoid included the local delicacy of Peruvian guinea pigs.

Back to Lima, with the Cusco/Sacred Valley/Machu Picchu adventure forever seared into our hearts, we hopped on a quick connecting flight to Pucallpa. The Andes and the Pacific Ocean were no less majestic, and we somehow missed the usual afternoon thunderstorm when approaching the Amazon. It almost felt like we had just left this small Amazonian town yesterday as the familiar sights and sounds of Pucallpa flooded our senses. Traveling along the same route to and from the little airport to Los Gavilanes Hotel, it amused us that the road construction seen on our last visit continued, just like at home along route I-95. It would be a few days before we met up with Don Ernesto, so we asked the front desk clerk if any of Ernesto's party had checked in as yet.

"Yes, señor. There are a few people here. I think they just went up to the restaurant. Oh, and this part of your group is from Spain. And don't forget—you can check a bag or two here at the hotel if you don't want to carry everything into the jungle!"

Was she commenting on the size of my luggage? Jeez, it's not like I brought my La-Z-Boy recliner, I said silently with disgust. Then I continued, *All right, I perhaps brought too much, as usual—but do I have to get so sensitive about it?*

Mel nudged me and giggled, correctly interpreting the look on my face as embarrassment mixed with self-criticism.

With our luggage stowed in our small, comfortable room, we headed for the restaurant. Walking through an archway, we spotted half a dozen participants and learned they came from Spain, where they attended ceremonies under Don Ernesto's watchful care. So very interesting! Most of them spoke English quite fluently, and between their free-flowing conversation, Melanie's rudimentary Spanish, and my shrugs, we all got along well. How marvelous to be part of this group.

More and more of our fellow adventurers arrived in the following days. Half of the participants were folks we knew from United States ceremonies, and the other half hailed from Europe. In Pucallpa, we walked through the open-air markets with wide eyes as taxidermy crocodiles overwhelmed the tables and walls on which they were displayed. Rows of herbs and spices hung from metal hooks or overflowed from metal storage barrels, tall baskets, or burlap bags, including dried coca leaves, vegetables, and animal parts, ready for the next buyer.

Then, we finally met with Don Ernesto for our last night in civilization. Don Ernesto gave the same talk from the previous year, only this time, he said it once in English and then again in Spanish so that everyone in the group understood. Except for perhaps Chris, everyone there had been to the jungle before. We learned that one person, Herb, was already at El Santuario finishing his first retreat and would stay with our group for ten additional days. All told, at the end of our time in the jungle, he would be there for about 22 days! I tried not to imagine the smell of his clothes at the end of his jungle time.

Back to El Santuario

While I didn't remember every bump along the rough dirt roads to Nuevo San Juan—the tiny village where we again climbed into dugout canoes, I wondered how these taxi drivers maintained their cars with potholes and uneven roads like these. I got an answer—the taxi we drove this time sported a sizable crack in the windshield, where someone's head probably collided with it after hitting a huge pothole or dodging an animal, bicyclist, or pedestrian.

Finally, at the Nuevo San Juan marina, a carefully graded riverbank covered in gravel, I experienced a returning, a familiarity, and a kinship with the gently flowing water.

We boarded the dugout canoes two by two, and a few conscripted folks bailed water when needed. Chris and I had sat together many times on a boat—sailing to numerous dive sites miles from land during our trips to the Great Barrier Reef and across the Caribbean Sea, though never before on a boat this small or primitive. We immersed ourselves in the sights and sounds of the river's cacophonous animal life.

"What do you really know about this guy, Ernesto?" Chris asked with perhaps slight worry as the canoes pushed off from shore.

I glanced in Chris's direction, putting my hand in the cool, clear water. "As far as his background, I only know as much as what he told us last night at the group gathering. But I know I have a certain trust and confidence that Ernesto and Mamacita will watch over us. Besides, his younger sister, Via, is here. He adores her and would never put her in harm's way."

Several idyllic hours later, the boats arrived at the small, steep bank of El Santuario, beyond which the sights and sounds of civilization faded. For the next ten days, I called this home. I recognized several of Ernesto's crew, and a couple yelled "Hola!" to Melanie, remembering her from the last time. They helped us with our packs and belongings as we started the several-mile hike through the dense rainforest. Slightly better prepared than last year, my pack seemed lighter and less burdensome. This time, I had even brought my guitar. I couldn't wait to play during downtime between ceremonies. I sweated in the late morning heat and humidity but didn't wilt. Occasionally, I glanced around for Mel and Chris, each walking along as if in a dream, their gazes floating from a plant to a little creature, then up into the canopy to track a bird call or monkey's cry. But everyone's eyes quickly returned to the ground to watch for the many roots that could trip us up.

We finally arrived at the rustic buildings and meeting area, and Don Ernesto began: "Now that we are all here, let me introduce you to one more participant, Herb. Herb attended the last dieta and now will be part of your group. He will be doing the same five ceremonies but has one advantage: he won't need to repeat the Yawar Panga intestinal purging ceremony on Thursday. Participants should only do that once a year at most."

I quickly calculated, '*How soon would I have to return here to avoid the dreadful Yawar Panga?*' Then I laughed at myself. *I haven't done this year's retreat yet, and I am already thinking about another.*

Gosh, another rabbit hole of endless thought right here in the jungle! I noticed my love for exploring rabbit holes was offset by the dread of knowing there was no answer. *Have I always demanded such certainty and predictability in my life?* I thought.

After being shown my tambo, I realized my newly assigned wooden platform with a thatched roof was even more secluded than the first time. As I was not on the main path, I rarely saw anyone but Ernesto and his staff at my tambo. Such seclusion. Melanie and Christopher's tambos weren't too far apart, positioned along the creek, in prime position to catch a slightly cooler breeze. I gave each of them one final hug, trusting they would be shown what they needed to experience. Of course, I felt a bit protective of Chris, as I had promised his mom that he would return alive. But I realized that even a simple instruction on hanging his hammock was not what Chris needed. He needed to proceed through all of this by himself—for himself.

This dieta progressed similarly to last year's, but with more rain, mud, and mildew. Having been called to infuse his shamanic work with even more Hindu flavor, Don Ernesto offered a daily, hour-long, pre-dawn puja before the Hindu *lingam* (a sacred object representing Shiva) for those who wanted to participate. Due to the camaraderie in participation, I liked to chant, but I couldn't see it as a way to become more spiritually advanced.

With several different preparations of ayahuasca at his side during our ceremonies, Don Ernesto tried a few different ones on us all. The texture of one he served me tasted particularly disgusting, with an enhanced, nasty wooden chunkiness, and I experienced relentless nausea with several dosages. This particular ayahuasca formulation hit me with a psychic harshness that overshadowed any brief period of joy with a dark intensity notable by an absence of any colorful visual patterns.

Unlike my first ayahuasca retreat, I had loose stools soon after arriving in the jungle. So now I purged from both ends, with vomiting and diarrhea. I carefully filtered my drinking water but wondered if the slightly different ayahuasca mixture was contributing to my loose bowels. I repeatedly visited the *baños* and quickly re-ingrained the habit of hitting the sides of the wooden box with a hole in the top (aka my toilet seat), an imperative to startle any insects, spiders, or snakes lurking beneath my tender behind! I sensed that the local frogs, monkeys, and birds still remembered me from my last trip; their songs felt comforting as I sat in ceremonies and on my own. Once more, they all played together in sound and time, welcoming all brave enough to come this way.

One afternoon, between ceremonies and being free of medications, I pulled out my pen and paper, writing down whatever came to mind. It began with the expected sequence—a thought crossed my mind, the pen settling on the paper, my hand moving, and then the appearance of a written word as the pen glided from one side to another. Suddenly, everything flipped. My thoughts didn't initiate any of this; the paper did! The ink wasn't coming from the pen—it came from the paper. The notebook expressed its consciousness by writing to me on the blank sheet. The words appeared as the paper brought them to this world. The pen and my hand merely followed the guidance of the ink. And last of all, the word appeared in my mind!

Cause and effect reversed for a short time.

I previously believed my thoughts precipitated my hand's movements, causing words to eventually appear on a piece of paper. But the opposite happened, as the paper initiated the writing.

Do I see cause and effect backward? I asked myself. *I had just clearly witnessed something defying what I believed. I was utterly amazed at this experience. Wait, didn't I read in ACIM that just because we strongly believe in our version of cause and effect doesn't mean it is true?*

Remembering Jed McKenna's writing, I watched myself get into a thinking match with cause and effect. At first, it almost felt like insanity creeping into the picture. Gradually, each question my mind threw out met a response of silence.

What will everyone else think if I say that cause and effect may not be what we believe it is? The question hung there. Eventually, I felt the futility of asking endless unanswerable questions.

Once I had experienced the reversal of cause and effect, my intellectual mind immediately jumped back into the view that all my current purported suffering directly resulted from the heat, humidity, and meager daily rations.

The next ceremony started simply enough.

A few colorful visual patterns and an enhancement of bodily perturbations. It feels as if long-forgotten subconscious ideas try to escape from every sweating pore on my skin. An intense tingling pain predominates from my feet up into my head. Then, through the darkness, thoughts of overwhelming fear and guilt swirl around me. Because I've always had such a strong belief in my complete worthlessness, I feel sure that reuniting with God one day requires extreme sacrifice on my part. These thoughts spark an intense affirmation that my friends must crucify me on the land where I live back in Virginia. This is the only way to qualify for salvation. Am I going insane? I plan the whole event in my mind, and in almost every way, it parallels the writings and understandings of the Church on the unmitigated requirement of the crucifixion of Jesus. No questions, ifs, ands, or buts allowed, as this unconditionally must occur.

In the midst of the ceremony, my thoughts focused so intensely on my crucifixion that I saw no other option. The slightest chance of returning to God demanded that I sacrifice my physicality in this most dramatic of ways. The entire scene was very dark and foreboding from start to finish. Melanie later told me how manic I appeared at that point in the retreat. The one rational thought that intervened was that our local county commissioners would undoubtedly frown upon such an act, as it probably violated some county code. Part of my mind demanded my physical crucifixion, and another held out hope that county ordinances and following the letter of the law would keep me grounded.

With this, I saw and experienced how my anger and disappointment toward others always started with anger, guilt, and shame toward myself. I had read about the projection of my guilt onto others as described in ACIM. Now, I have experienced the process myself firsthand. I avoided experiencing this self-directed anger, accountability, and shame as long as I pointed outward; now, I felt the full force of this self-loathing as I withdrew all the barbs I aimed at others. Why shouldn't I be strung up?

My exploration into self-crucifixion exemplified the extreme swings I cycled through, a pendulum of *I am worthy, and I am not worthy* circular thinking. I recognized this insane, repetitive cogitation and so-called rationalization as futile. These mental loops resembled the unresolvable thoughts that led me to exasperation the day I declared to Len, "There must be something else here." Projecting my sin and guilt onto someone else temporarily alleviated the pain and turmoil I experienced. Until the guilt, shame, and anger boomeranged back at me …

That night after the ceremony, I had a very short dream.

I am standing in a nondescript place. There is no apparent reference to time, place, or why I am even there. An unfamiliar woman walks up to me. She hands me a piece of paper with some writing. Usually, I can't read what is written on paper during dreams, but this paper is different. I clearly see the words, "Would you just stop and look at this place?"

When I woke, I continued seeing the paper and the words as clearly as in the dream. While it seemed to me I had seen this same dream years before, this time, the words on the paper meant so much more to me. This simple question related to Jed

McKenna's suggestion of watching everything I do and ACIM's writings about looking at my beliefs. But as no exact directions surfaced, I harnessed patience and told myself that a process for "stopping and looking at this place" would reveal itself. Instead of demanding the answers immediately, I trusted life a bit more to show me the way.

It took a while for an answer to come, but I continued to keep the thought in my mind as I pondered other aspects of my life while in solitude in my tambo. Although I had left the US, ventured to Peru, and experienced profound insights into many of my thinking processes, my neck and head pain hadn't improved. I still really enjoyed my patients and work at the hospital, but the daily grind, especially working in a heavy X-ray apron, was taking a severe toll on me. I had reduced my overall hours and the number of procedures I performed, but the back and neck pain were still unbearable.

Towards the end of this second dieta experience in the jungle, it came to me—I just needed to retire. Get out of medicine, sell my practice, and stop torturing myself every day with one more attempt to cover up what I was going through physically.

Despite our vow of silence, I took a rest period to walk to Melanie's tambo and let her know what I had decided. Her eyebrows raised, surprised to see me come down the path.

"Melanie, something just came to me …" I started.

"We need to be silent," she said hushingly. "Can't this wait?"

"I need to stop. I need to stop working. I need to stop practicing medicine. When we get home, I'll tell the office I will be there only one more month." We stared at one another. Silence returned. Her face seemed to express confusion and relief.

With Melanie still in mild shock, I walked off to my tambo, knowing this decision felt right. A vague feeling about retirement convinced me that stopping was precisely what I needed to do to slow the continual damage to my neck and thoracic spine. Gradually, a sense of ease slowly and delicately incorporated into my being like a breath of fresh air.

After the last ceremony, the final afternoon with the group became a few hours of celebration. I pulled out my guitar, and several others played some of their favorite songs. A man from Spain sang Flamenco-style lyrics when I played typical Flamenco chords and rhythms. Open and comfortable with one another, we all walked a short distance to a known mud hole along the river bank with the finest, silkiest mud available for bathing and exfoliating; a perfect post-dieta spa experience in the middle of the Peruvian Amazon.

My mental and physical burdens seemed much lighter on the hike out of El Santuario. Perhaps it was the slight elation I allowed myself, knowing that Melanie and my son Chris had survived the grueling dieta. Maybe Chris had found an opening to seeing things differently and with more illumination. Herb, the fellow now with twenty-two straight days of fasting and ceremony, struggled to carry his belongings. I felt so good to know I could carry his pack and my own without any problem.

"I got your back … pack, Herb," I said without hesitation and with a slight chuckle.

"Thanks, Bart," he replied. "But I need to do this on my own. Don't worry. I will make it to the river canoes before they leave!"

We nodded, and I strolled ahead with a bit of a spring in my step that I hadn't displayed for a while. *And just how long will this last, you moron?* I heard a voice in my mind say.

A bird call and leaves rustling brought me back to the jungle. I said my goodbyes as I knew my path was changing, step by step. Meeting up with Mel and Chris, we handed off our packs to Ernesto's helpers. We then settled into our seats before gently pushing away from shore as if by the hand of Mamacita herself.

The rhythmic rustling of the trees along the river bank whispered, *While you may dream that you are in a place without the green of my vines and trees, the coolness of the river, or the sounds of my animals, know that we are never far from your heart and your awareness.*

The connection to this beauty deepened in my heart.

"So, Mel, what are you taking away from your two Amazon dieta experiences?" I asked as I stuffed my stinky, smelly clothes in a suitcase, preparing for our flight out of Pucallpa.

"Hmmmmmmmm," she mused. "That's a tough one to answer. Amazing. Incredibly challenging and exhaustingly miraculous. Each dieta differed. Mamacita and her plant buddies like bobinsana did so much beautiful work with me these past two years. My heart space feels open more often. I can sit with complicated emotions and physical prickliness without escaping, repressing, or denying them. I find more tenderness for myself and others. Mamacita keeps showing me how vast my mind is. I never knew green leaves could transform into sacred geometric patterns. I would never have believed I could live in an open-air hut, at the mercy of anacondas, panthers, tarantulas, and colorful tiny venomous frogs, AND not be terrified. Of course, I'm also clear that it's up to me to keep finding the ways I keep my old patterns in place."

She sighed, and her eyes watered. "And being in the jungle reminds me of my connection to Southeast Asian rainforests where I spent about six precious years of my youth." She looked away for a while, seeing something or someone beyond us. "Something is so familiar about this land and these people ..." her voice trailed off.

Leaving the Jungle Together

As we traveled back to civilization, I wondered what we might have been running from as we separated ourselves from nature's offerings centuries ago. I felt thankful that some people devoted themselves to keeping this natural connection alive. Gratitude toward Don Ernesto filled me for his courage to offer all these mind-expanding experiences to folks like me.

Heading back to Lima, we stayed a few more days once again in seaside Miraflores. Comfortable in this part of the city, we couldn't wait to devour some of the local Peruvian Pollo a la Brasa roasted daily at the grocery store across the street from our hotel.

The following day, Mel, Chris, and I headed off to a nearby laundromat, with our bags of odoriferous clothes from our ten-day Amazon stay stiffly walking behind us. I began filling one washer with clothes as Mel did the same in another.

I turned to Chris; "Hey, Chris, hand me your sweatshirt to go into this load."

He didn't budge. There it was: the familiar tendency of his to balk at requests or demands made by authority figures.

"Chris, that sweatshirt reeks!" I insisted. "You can't subject someone else on a plane to that stench for our flights home. There is no way I will sit beside you and that stinky sweatshirt for hours on end. Come on, give it over." And there was my tendency to push and be the parent—who, of course, is always right, right?

Still no gesture of compliance. He glared at me.

Other patrons, whether they understood English or not, sensed the tension between us and gave us a wide berth as this played out.

Then, as if some last bit of pain-body residue fell away from Chris's persona, he shrugged, pulled his arms out of the sleeves of his stinky hoodie, and handed it to me with a gentle smile.

I smiled back, feeling my pain-body back down too. "Thanks, Chris."

Three pairs of hands quickly folded and packed our freshly laundered clothing for the walk back to Hotel El Condado. We dropped it all off in our quarters and headed to the large, modern grocery store about half a block away.

"Can't wait to eat some Peruvian chicken!" I exclaimed.

"And fried yucca! I can't get enough of it," Mel chimed in.

We wandered through the aisles of ready-made entrees and side dishes, practically consuming each selection with our eyes. Then, we paid at the checkout and carried the mouth-watering food back to our hotel.

And the feast began. "Chris, it's so fun to share this Peruvian food with you and in Peru, not at some restaurant in Virginia," I said.

While we hadn't said much, Chris's 22nd birthday occurred in Peru, while we were out in the far reaches of the jungle.

He nodded, biting into a humongous ear of corn—corn as thick as a rolling pin and with extra-large kernels to boot.

I continued, "Any reflections you'd like to share about your dieta experience, Chris? We'd love to hear."

He paused from snarfing down his meal. "Well, even though I completed some ceremonies with Don Ernesto in the US, this retreat differed from anything I've done before. While a rite of passage, I still had many questions about why I traveled to the middle of the Peruvian Amazon. Yet something inside me demanded that I experience this. How did we know we would be okay out here in the jungle? So many unknowns!"

Sipping his lime-flavored Jarritos soda, he continued, "This ten-day dieta changed me, unlike any single ceremony. I arrived holding onto many fears and had to face them. It felt like I was coming apart. I probably would've been diagnosed as having a mental breakdown back home. But the jungle and Don Ernesto's staff treated me lovingly. Don Ernesto made it clear I had support to stop and end the dieta early or continue doing all five ceremonies. That Don Ernesto instructed his staff to take me to the river to cool me off physically and emotionally during a couple of ceremonies were gifts to me. It allowed me to learn how to deal with terror differently. It helped me examine my fears internally rather than assume they all originated outside me."

"I was so amazed by your humility and courage, Chris," Melanie said softly.

"Yes, Chris, you could've ended early, yet you decided to continue meeting whatever kept coming up for you," I agreed. "That takes strength of character and a willingness to face hidden parts of yourself."

"It feels as if Mamacita told me, 'Chris, it's time to start waking up.'"

We finished the meal in silence, and I withdrew into my head. I wondered how I would "look at this place," as I had already been asked to do in several dreams. Then I realized, *Wow. By seeing the cathedral of the intellect, I* ***am*** *starting to look at this place.*

After that, silence. At that point, I didn't know what else to think about, and as usual, some thoughts suggested jumping back into something negative.

Once more, I heard the remote echo in my mind, repeatedly questioning my recent decision to stop practicing medicine*; how pathetic you are to even think about giving up your career, business, and livelihood. So what if you are in physical pain? Just suck it up, as you've always done!* After all, medicine was my profession, a large part of what I did and who I was for 35 years.

What was it that I told patient after patient when surgery had finished and it was time to move?

Oh, I told each and every one of them, "Don't worry. Don't be afraid. You are only waking up."

Was I speaking to them or to myself?

The negative voices ranted, but now I could watch them arise and then proceed back into the silence.

CHAPTER 11
INQUIRY

Arriving back in the US, I knew I had to retire; no lists of pros and cons ever surfaced in my mind because it was already made up.

"Amy, can you come into my office for a bit?" I asked my office manager of 14 years.

"So, how was your trip, Dr. Balint?" she asked curiously.

"We had a wonderful time in Panama and Peru!" I exclaimed. "Surprisingly, it felt like a homecoming when we finally stepped out of our dugout canoes in the Amazon wilderness. Half of our retreat group came from Spain. It was terrific to be there and also good to be home."

"Melanie and I purchased some small gifts reminiscent of Peru, Amy. Could you hand them out to our employees for me?"

Amy nodded, smiling, and took the bag of gifts.

"Oh, I almost forgot," I said, with a playful grin, since there was no way I could have forgotten what I was about to tell her. "My neck was unbearably miserable the whole time there, especially on the flights to and from Peru and when sleeping on my thin mattress on planks of wood. I know that continuing work just makes it worse. I've decided that I need to retire for my physical and mental health."

"Well, someday we will all retire," said Amy. "You're just joking, right?" She stared at me, anxiously silent, as she awaited my answer. I gazed back at her, also silent.

"You're not kidding, are you?" Her body went tense. And, uncertain whether she wanted an answer, she asked softly, "When do you think you might do this?"

"I'll be here one more month seeing patients, but will continue fulfilling my administrative and payroll responsibilities into the foreseeable future," I answered, as Amy steadied herself with her left hand gripping the edge of her desk.

"One m-m-month....," stammered Amy, looking a bit pale. "What are we going to do?"

"Don't worry. Everyone's jobs will be fine, and the office continues as usual," I said. "Things will work out. I'll print a small flyer for my patients and referring doctors announcing my retirement."

As I left her desk, she looked stunned.

After telling Amy, who needed to be the first to know, I informed the physician and the nurse practitioner who worked for me. While everyone knew of my ongoing neck issues, nobody had expected me to stop so soon, at age 55. Melanie and I also discussed her continuing role in the practice, including coaching interested patients in HeartMath.

"It won't be the same without you here, Bart. I completely support your decision to step away. It's fun working with you. But I also completely get it. How can I help?" Mel had a tender look on her face. We hugged, and she left my office.

And so, I completed the first steps toward retiring as a chronic pain management physician and entrepreneur.

Continuing Forward with Jed and Scott

Jed McKenna's books further induced me to look at and potentially change my perspective. The idea he presented about only truth being true sank in very profoundly. While ACIM spoke a similar message, something really clicked reading Jed's writings. My convictions point to relative truth, but nothing I believed was consummate truth. All my thoughts, beliefs, and anything I ever learned could be questioned. I felt a sense of the truth throughout everything.

I realized I'd made a solid 180-degree flip away from how I'd viewed life before my neck injury.

The only certainty I had believed in until that karate match revolved around cerebral understanding. I'd known exactly who I was and who everyone else was. I felt confident that I knew anesthesiology inside and out and many other subjects as well. Analytical and conceptual knowledge had been truth to me. I'd worshiped cognitive mastery as the only true path one should take.

But like the degenerative vertebrae in my neck, my cathedral of intellect had begun to crumble. I'd realized that truth isn't anything I can think of or imagine in some form. Even my felt sense of truth is only a pointer toward truth.

Jed started a blog where ordinary folks like me could submit questions about spiritual matters and chat with fellow readers and Jed himself. Many followers tried to poke holes in Jed's statement that only truth is true; it made for interesting reading.

Many posts quoted other teachers and sources to support their thinking and questions. I began seeing that I now trusted my own experience more than I trusted teachings from others (even Jed's) or supposed facts in a book or article. I asked myself how I would describe my understanding or knowledge of an author's ideas in my own words. This illustrated my move away from concrete, knowable information and toward leaning on my moment-to-moment experience.

Soon, I found myself writing to Jed directly.

"Jed, I found the last person's comments interesting, but I wanted to hear how ACIM affected that person internally. Personally, whenever I read a few lines of ACIM, I sense a quietness inside my head where my mind might be, and I notice a silence outside of my head, sitting slightly back and to the side."

"Bart," Jed wrote back, cutting right to the chase, "I recommend you check out Scott Kiloby on YouTube, specifically his videos on the 'unfindable inquiry.' These may help you bring all of this together."

"Thanks for the recommendation, Jed. I will look him up."

Jed described in one of his books that he intuitively knew where people needed to head to help dissolve their rigidly held beliefs. My impression was that Jed sensed something in my description of the two apparently separate places of silence, one inside and one outside of my head, which told him I might find some help in Kiloby's work. I jumped on Jed's recommendation and opened up YouTube.

Occasionally, I read or watch something, and it immediately lands. This happened with Jed's statement concerning truth and Scott Kiloby's YouTube video on the unfindable inquiry.[4] The

---

[4] Scott Kiloby, Unfindable Inquiry, https://www.youtube.com/watch?v=eNwAVOYVMac&t=3s

unfindable inquiry made sense to me within minutes of tuning into Scott's channel. He suggested that we interpret and interact with our world through thoughts, mental images, emotions, bodily perceptions, and awareness. We unconsciously weld or Velcro together an idea, a mental picture, a feeling, and a physical sensation to manufacture our perception of ourselves and the world around us.

After listening to one video, I played with this form of inquiry on my own. An example follows.

I see an object on my desk. In my mind, I hear the word *cup*, and I fleetingly see the letters C-U-P in my mind's eye. A confirmatory feeling says, *Yes. This object is a cup.* My mind adds, '*cup of coffee.*' I notice that I have fused the word "cup," the phrase "cup of coffee," the mental picture of the cup, and the affirmative physical sensation. These separate parts and descriptive terms now seem to occur as a unit—a cup of coffee. Supposedly, this composite tells me exactly what that object on my desk is.

I don't question it. I take it as a fundamental, unshakable idea.

With my eyes open, I see the cup. I close my eyes, and an image of a cup of coffee appears in my mind's eye.

One might ask, "Is that picture of a cup you see in your mind the same cup on your desk?"

Pondering this a second, I thought, *No. That picture, in my mind, is just a picture. It isn't the actual cup.* It occurred to me

---

that the pictures I see in my mind are not the actual objects to which the images refer.

It never occurred to me before that what I see in my mind's eye is NOT what I see in the physical world.

Ah," I thought, *"I've just dismantled a few stones from my cathedral of the intellect! All this time, I've taken my thoughts (and the unconscious feelings, mental images, and sensibilities associated with them) as tyrannously true. Maybe that's not so...*

This realization left me feeling deeply quiet.

I closed my eyes again and continued studying my imagination of the cup along with the letters C-U-P floating out in front of my mind's eye. I also heard the word "cup" as a spoken word. Scott explained that some people hear their thoughts more than see them as words or phrases. I both hear and see them at different times.

I then heard my mind tell me what the purpose or meaning of this object, "cup of coffee," was. *It is to drink, enjoy, and refresh.* I noticed a feeling in my body that I quickly labeled pleasant, followed by a slight smile.

And underneath this simple cup, my mind uncovers more and more meaning. How amazing.

While I had heard thoughts and seen images in my mind for over 50 years, it never occurred to me that I repeatedly glued together these separate experiences, brewing my own mental cups of coffee!

We all assign and bond labels, purposes, meanings, a past, and a future to every object around us, whether it is a cup, a smell, a picture, a person, a skin sensation, etc.

Another layer of thought arose. *Oh, that cup is empty! And I shouldn't have drunk it, as I know it will keep me up tonight! You stupid you, Bart*! Quickly following this thought, I felt stirrings in my body, particularly in the temples and lower abdomen, that I promptly identified as irritation.

Wow, a few seconds ago, drinking a cup of coffee was enjoyable, and now its significance is unpleasant. My mind is SO fickle!

I learned that with inquiry, I could start anywhere in this scenario and look at all the associations I put together related to the simple cup on my desk. This challenged my I-have-it-all-figured-out mind to consider and actively view each little belief I held as absolute and unquestionable from various angles instead of from my standard, default viewpoint.

I followed Scott's instructions regarding how to determine what I believed at any moment. When someone asks you how you're feeling, you may reflexively answer, "I'm fine," yet inside, your gut clenches as if to say, "I'm anything BUT fine right now." The mind gave an inauthentic answer, and the body gave a different answer by clenching. We can consult our physical sensations and emotions to get to the bottom of what's true for us at any moment. Or we can ignore them as I had for so long. I began to learn through inquiry to check in with my body for any constriction, contraction, or tenseness in response to words or a mental image. Instead of only buying into the words my mind came up with, I began consulting the body for guidance.

I continued exploring this cup of coffee scene, and the most significant charge in my body came with the thought, *You stupid you, Bart*! At Kiloby's suggestion, I wondered just what this object "Bart" was and how that name was now associated with being "stupid." Could I find which part of "Bart" bore the stupid label? Remember, the premise of this inquiry process is that, eventually, what you've deemed as real and solid is unfindable.

Kiloby also mentioned that with each labeled object, we tend to attach another label to indicate whether that object or sensation is "me" or "not me." I had never heard that labeling as an overt, conscious thought, as it occurred automatically and unconsciously. The coffee cup's invisible label of "not me" obviously distinguished it from me. I also saw that any bodily kinesthesia related to "me" meant that the sensation was irrefutably a part of me.

This illustrated that I had a significant role in constructing the scenario of Bart versus the universe.

Listening to Kiloby's videos, I closed my eyes and tuned into what came through my awareness. At Scott's instruction, I focused on what went through my mind. I saw a mental image of my head and forearms and immediately noticed a bodily sensation/feeling that seemed to confirm this separate human being named Bart.

OK. Then I saw the letters in the word Bart, *B-A-R-T.*

Are those letters B-A-R-T, me, the guy called Bart?

I looked at the letters, first as a complete word and then one letter at a time; each time I looked, I checked for some reaction in my body to answer the question. "*Am I 'B'? Am I 'A'? Maybe it's 'R' that defines me?*"

"Is there a feeling in the body that indicates that yes, one or more of those letters is, in fact, Bart?" I asked myself. Everything was quiet in the body.

"No, they are just letters in my mind," I answered.

As soon as I said that, I noticed a sensation in my belly. I paused, giving attention to my belly area.

"Is this sensation me, the one named Bart?" I waited and sensed.

The belly sensation remained the same for a bit and then faded.

"No, it isn't. It's just a sensation in my stomach," I answered to myself.

The movement in the belly quickly faded, and my body remained quiet.

A few seconds later, the word "stupid" popped into my awareness. I heard a vocalization of the word, as well as being able to see the letters. I also noticed a physical sensation in my arms and chest that my mind labeled "stupid." Again, I looked at each of these details, all seemingly attached to form a concept of "Bart, the stupid one." With each, I could see that the different parts were ultimately unrelated. I couldn't find anything that unquestionably meant "stupid," and I couldn't find stupid in my mental image of Bart.

This was a brief self-led session, but what happened amazed me. A slight space began to take hold between the images, words, and feelings I had previously taken as fact, as if the mental mortar holding them together partially dissolved. Following these different associations, I watched as each gradually fell apart.

Is it possible all these elements of my experience are connected ONLY because I say so or believe so? Is this the case with everything I believe?

Realizing that I constructed my world by mortaring together mental pictures, words, stories, and bodily sensations—AND that I put them together while trying to define myself—astounded me.

From Inquiry to Insight

I discovered another thing in the next few days: you never know how many hidden connections remain.

"Hey, Bart!" Melanie called from the bottom of the stairs leading to the second floor of our home.

My body tensed, and I felt that sensation I had labeled "stupid."

Hmmmmm, I never noticed that before. Why would a feeling I automatically labeled "stupid" be coming up now? I thought. As I walked to the head of the stairs, I noticed a sense of guilt.

"Bart, you look tense or burdened somehow," Mel said. "What's up?"

"You know how I just did that short self-inquiry session where I investigated my name? I thought I was done with being attached to a sense of "me" as Bart. And then, just now, when you called out my name, I again felt that sensation I labeled 'stupid,' and that gradually changed to a feeling of guilt."

I stood there quietly, sensing what had come up. "Oh, and now I hear comments like 'What did I do wrong this time?' and 'I shouldn't be doing what I'm doing.'" I winced as I heard these internal criticisms. I realized I had heard these types of accusations many times when my parents uttered my name as a child.

"Wow, that shows us that we never know what else we will stumble onto in unraveling our beliefs," Mel smiled with understanding.

I stayed quiet, letting it all sink in. "Yes, I just get to keep meeting what shows up, leading me to the next layer of my tenaciously held convictions."

This realization was daunting. I still believed there was someplace to get to, some destination where I'd know for sure that I was DONE and enlightened. Even though I'd read Jed's works, that shot that idea down …

This inquiry proved highly practical in my social life as I ruminated over someone who irritated me. I fumed as I saw a mental snapshot of them. I then felt what I could only describe as a vibration in my body immediately recognizable as anger. Frankly, I had grown tired of the editorial repeated a million times. I wanted to start somewhere to help pause this ongoing cycle of storyline, anger, more mental reenactments, and more anger. Reasoning and talk therapy only brought me back to the same old theme about how this person caused me emotional pain and how I was justified in my anger toward them.

So, with my eyes closed, I brought up a mental impression of the person who had hurt me. Anger welled up in my chest. The word "anger" was audible and visible in my mind. So, could I find my anger in that word? Anger seemed like an authentic, independent entity. I'd only briefly investigated it before when I looked at the pain-body while reading Eckhart. I'd always tried to avoid it! Maybe trying to escape it was not the best approach, especially as I saw that inquiry invited me to move towards it and inspect it closely.

So, which letter of A-N-G-E-R contained the anger I convinced myself I felt? My mind hit a dead end. I couldn't find a separate object called "anger" in either the picture of the person I claimed angered me or in the word "anger."

Could I find anger in the sensation I felt? I labeled the feeling as anger, but when I sank into it deeply, I noticed just a feeling, an energy in my body. Not necessarily comfortable, but nothing said, "This is anger!" Soon, the feeling dissipated and dissolved. Why had I been so adamant about avoiding a simple vibration? This was SO new for me—to sit patiently with an uncomfortable sensation! And then I found that it wasn't what I thought it was after all.

To be thorough, I revisited my mental image of that particular person. Where in this person's picture was anger? No matter where I looked, I couldn't find it. Somehow, without trying to entice me away from feeling angry or getting them to apologize, the emotion had dissipated and was no longer linked to that person. The sensation I'd called anger wasn't completely gone, but it definitely loosened. An opening and relaxation throughout my body followed. I no longer felt alienated from that person; in that way, I didn't hold them at arm's length as I had with so many people all my life. The gap of separation I felt between us had markedly changed and now didn't feel so impossible.

An addiction and numbing to negative emotions still existed. It took some looking, but I eventually recognized my predisposition to self-pity, anger toward others, and depression.

A part of my mind loved these emotions and the mangled emotional bodies I left in my wake.

Through several inquiry sessions, I saw that underneath my indignation and disgust lurked a perverted love of these negative emotions. For a while, my ego convinced me that this confused and warped sense of love was all that I was worthy of feeling.

While helpful to point outward at whatever caused my anger, it was even more beneficial to catch a glimpse of the "me" who demanded I react with anger. Those glimpses helped me understand my active role in every reaction instead of remaining convinced that when I felt aggravation, it was solely because of some external insult and that I remained the powerless victim.

Like a kid taking a fresh view of the heavens with a new telescope, my mind opened to different perspectives I couldn't previously imagine. Melanie also caught the same bug and pursued inquiry. Fantastic to compare notes and have someone to share my wins and observations; I knew she felt the same.

"Bart, Jed just referred me to Scott's unfindable inquiry also!" She told me. "I checked it out. It's a different approach to questioning your beliefs from what Byron Katie offers, but very useful. With The Work that Katie developed, I keep challenging all my judgments of others and myself, and now, with this inquiry stuff, the potential is limitless!" Mel was noticeably giddy.

Melanie attended a nine-day Byron Katie School for The Work in California, and I decided to work directly with Scott. I signed up for one-on-one sessions with him to facilitate me through some further inquiry. I don't remember the specific topics I looked at, but each session left me with a sense of peace.

My stories of victimization had become so real that I needed a trained facilitator without an agenda to support me in exploring all the different components I had welded together. If I had done some of these earlier sessions by myself, I would have gotten stuck in my mythos again, going round and round. Scott helped me focus on the most prominent experiential arisings and guided me back to my body.

Melanie also worked directly with him. She focused on her relationships with her young adult children and their life trials. She realized all the labels she stuck on them and how that impacted the depth of their connection with her. The intense picture of her children's issues softened as she continued inquiry. Strong emotions and tension she'd felt navigating these challenges relaxed and let go.

Here's a transcript of a recent short inquiry session:

Me = Bart

F = Facilitator

[I close my eyes and relax.]

F: "You mentioned that you had a topic for us to inquire into today?"

Me: "Yes. I want to look at a situation that I repetitively re-live. I almost got into a physical fistfight with my father at age 16 or 17. I see the whole incident: I get irritated, disgusted, and pissed. Even after all these years, I find the incident irritating and saddening."

[I relate a brief scene (referenced in Chapter 2), which ends with me in a boxing position, ready to strike out against my father.]

Me: "I took a step toward him, fists clenched at my chest, hunched forward, and prepared to fight. I would've punched him if he had taken a step toward me. At that point, there was a second of quiet, and my father backed down. He walked away. I can still feel that situation right now."

F: "Where do you feel it?"

Me: "I feel a tightness, specifically in the pectoralis muscles in the front of the chest."

F: "Yes …"

Me: "… and immediately when I go to the tension, I see my arms slightly raised in a boxing position with fists ready to go."

F: "Yeah."

Me: "I now feel tension in my face and a sense of resolve—that I was not going to back down. That resolve seems to be right behind my slight grimace and narrowed eyelids. I sense some guilt telling me that this feeling of resolve is something I dare not feel nor ever admit to having."

F: "Can you hold that all there—gently staying with it? Watching it? Feeling it? The fists, the tension in the face … The knowing that I would not back down, even those words … Let me know if anything else comes."

[We sit quietly for a while as I meet this experience.]

Me: "I see and feel myself sitting in this chair with my eyes closed. But then I also see this figure superimposed over me, almost like a shadow figure, including the back of my head and the back of my chest with its fists raised. So, I see two images right now."

F: "Is it OK for that shadow figure to be here?"

Me: "Yeah, it's okay. It's interesting to see that. Yeah. And I just heard myself ask, 'Who are you?'"

F: "Who are you?" the facilitator repeats.

Me: "And the answer from the shadow figure is, 'Well, I thought I was you.'"

F: "Hmmmmm, yeah."

Me: "Now I hear, 'I thought I was protecting you.'"

F: "Yes … So let that land. 'I thought I was protecting you.' Feel what it is like to hear that."

[I became visibly emotional as some tears came to my eyes.]

Me: "Well, it feels very loving. It feels very gentle and honest."

[My voice now sounds tender. Again, I sit with the feeling of the shadow figure.]

F: "Take your time … Let me know when you're ready to move on."

Me: "There seems to be a whole gang of shadow figures underneath my conscious thoughts—fleeting images that tell me where I am in everyday life. This hunched, ready-to-strike figure has always been there, ready to protect me. It followed me around before and after that incident at 16. I see where this hunched figure has manifested physically in my posture."

F: "Yes. Do any of those shadow figures want to come out into this waking world for a moment so they can be recognized?"

Me: "Oh yeah, they all do. These shadow figures would love to come out from the shadows, so to speak."

F: "We welcome them to come out from the shadows. And if you hear them, would you speak with them so we can give each of them a voice as they come into the light of your awareness?"

Me: "It just occurred to me that these figures enjoy being finally recognized and revealed. The shadow figures are enjoying the light."

F: [Gentle laughter.] "That's perfect, too … for them to simply enjoy the light."

Me: "Yeah, they are basking in the openness they have never had."

F: "Can you tell them they have all the time they want?"

Me: "Yeah, and one of them said, 'OK, now that he has acknowledged us, we can be released if he wants.'"

F: [A gentle chuckle.]

Me: "So now I see the whole incident differently. In their own way, these feelings are trying to protect 'me.' Some of these shadow figures could appear quite negative, but they have always been there to protect me. I can now bring them home."

F: "How does that feel, seeing it that way?"

Me: "It feels right in the heart space. Tingling in the shoulder and neck. Relaxing. I see and hear the word 'home.'"

As in this session, thoughts, images, and bodily conventions connect in endless permutations, and underneath these memories are connections that aren't initially apparent. What do they mean? Maybe nothing. Behind it all is openness, which I had rarely allowed myself to feel before I learned this technique.

After many inquiry sessions, it occurred to me that there is nothing in the universe separate from myself called "fear" or "anger." I make them up, assemble the pieces, find the witnesses or bits of evidence or proof in my body or out in the world to corroborate my screenplay and assign them labels of my choosing. Most importantly, behind each concept of fear—of which anger and anxiety are just a few variations—I add an idea of how this fear defines and separates me from you, others, or fear itself. There is always a slightly faint snapshot of myself accompanying any of these emotions in my mind's eye, whether I insist they are good or not.

Through the association of all these individual parts, I saw how I used the Velcroing process to cover up and plaster over the joy I sensed in my earliest childhood memories. And with each coat of plaster, I tried to bury that joy further from my remembrance.

An Inquiry session served as an open space to bring up a dense, fierce emotion—such as anger towards someone or myself—and quietly experience its dissolution. It offered a chance to slow down all the thoughts and feelings around a particular subject or motif—a time of pause, offering more attentiveness and giving myself more room to allow whatever arose. This space allowed me to get quiet and listen and feel into my entire experience, no matter how rocky any circumstance felt. It gave me an opportunity to explore the world as I'd constructed it—checking out all the fragments (words, pictures, memories, future projections, emotions, and sensory input) that I stuck together and called my reality.

With inquiry, awareness of all the ignored, denied, or omitted fragments of my experience is enhanced. The simple recognition of all these parts brings a feeling of completeness, like when the shadow figures appeared in the above inquiry session. It felt expansive to allow them some room to surface in real time instead of repressing them.

Inquiry is a space where opposites can meet without any agenda; neither is the victor. Neither expecting good nor bad to triumph, I saw them both as labels attached to everything, perhaps positive on one day and negative on another. Needing another way into my suffering, I observed the many components of my fears and joys in a way that talk therapy couldn't begin to deconstruct.

Neither a fix-it nor a fix-you program, inquiry invites me to rest with what shows up and allows ample room for expression or movement. Usually, one aspect of the experience, such as the bodily feeling or the mental picture, dominates in any instant. I may want to look at this component as it says, "Follow me." An unraveling occurs quite naturally. The facilitator helps the client pursue these avenues.

I saw how I had constructed my definitions of fear and its many manifestations. I remembered all the times I worked with patients, and they burst out with exasperation and fear, "You can't possibly know my pain!" It occurred to me that I couldn't even come close to guessing all the components someone might tack onto their definition of fear or pain. I realized that everyone puts their world together piece by piece, and we can never know precisely how the other person does that. This inner work helped me empathize with those fearful outcries, an empathy I never allowed myself to feel before.

The Retreat

After practicing inquiry for a while, Melanie attended Scott's first retreat at the Kiloby Center for Recovery (from addictions) in Rancho Mirage, CA. As she had decided to train as a facilitator, the retreat offered direct instruction from Scott and some of the first trained facilitators. Once home, she shared numerous instances of dropping long-held beliefs and fixed views of complex relationships. For example, Melanie told me that she watched as the damning label of "addict," which she had assigned to a loved one for years, fell away, leaving her with deep compassion for this person instead of blame and apprehension. She witnessed another retreat participant's crippling label of "manic–depressive" dissolve as a facilitator delicately led the woman through her stories, memories, heavy emotions, and physical reactions linked to this diagnosis of mental illness. This inquiry left the woman with a glimpse of her unsullied, integrated self—a massive shift from her previously dark self-image.

Intrigued, I registered for Scott's second inquiry retreat in Palm Springs several months later. The retreat title was something like "Enlightenment …" which struck me as odd since Scott often pointed out that nothing could be enlightened in this world of form. The egoic self simply hijacked the idea of enlightenment, using it as another feather in its cap—another goal that needs mastering to gain salvation.

Before going, I had this dream.

I lie on an operating table. All I see are a few lights. Scott Kiloby stands next to the table on which I lie. It appears Scott and I are both wearing street clothes. Unafraid, I am fascinated by what is happening. Then, silently and without explanation,

Scott produces a reasonably large-diameter needle about two feet long. He places the needle through my skin, carefully advancing it to a spot deep in my body. I feel no pain as he does this. I awaken.

As I woke up, I instantly recognized similarities between this dream and my work in the operating room with patients. Under x-rays, I guided long, thin needles to precise locations in a patient's body to anesthetize, burn, or freeze nerves, which helped their chronic pain. It occurred to me that in that dream, Scott showed me how to look at specific bodily impulses using inquiry. Although I didn't know what it all meant, this dream stirred a deep curiosity.

Mel and I arrived in Palm Springs, and the retreat commenced the following morning. We walked from our hotel to the Kiloby Center as the sun began burning off the scant morning dew on desert plants along the way. On a typically chilly morning, we wore light outerwear, soon to be stuffed into our day packs as the desert temperature quickly climbed.

The Kiloby Center occupied a portion of the first level of an unobtrusive, well-kept office building. A receptionist's podium sat at the entrance, and brochure stands filled with information on addiction and other client resources lined the walls. The small lobby led to a large open area where our group gathered for conversations, inquiry demonstrations, yoga, and Q&A sessions. Along the periphery of this area were several smaller rooms where participants met individually or in smaller groups with trained facilitators to delve into personal inquiry sessions.

About 20 participants attended, along with Scott and several senior facilitators. Scott talked extensively about "bodily contractions," areas in the body where past traumas, negative beliefs, and long-denied experiences awaited reexamination and a return to wholeness. Frankly, I still didn't resonate with the idea that the body held past traumas, but I found myself listening and wondering how this correlated to my pre-retreat dream.

We each had inquiry sessions with Scott and the trained facilitators to try out different inquiry styles. During my session with him, he zeroed right in on my ongoing insecurities about writing music. He knew exactly what to ask to provoke my bodily fixations and kick my negative stories into high gear.

We also learned of Real-Time inquiry, developed by Wayne Hayden-Moreland, a form of group inquiry where participants take turns reporting their in-the-moment internal experiences. We each began learning to self-inquire by way of this process.

I enjoyed meeting a roomful of like-minded people open to looking further at their lives. I didn't strike up a conversation with any particular bodily contraction during this retreat, but I can't understate the importance of Kiloby's personal instruction concerning inquiry. I left the retreat encouraged to deepen my exploration of this work.

Visiting the deserts of Southern California reminded me of two dreams in which a woman handed me a piece of paper with the message, "Would you just stop and look at this place?!" Several things came together all at once.

I realized the similarities with ACIM's suggestions to look at what I had "made" and the inquiry techniques of watching what things I tried to stick together. In other words, I "made" things real when I associated different objects, characteristics, senses, and mental pictures/stories/words. It became clear that the “making” referred to in ACIM related to the same process as Velcroing or welding in Inquiry—aka, creating my own private version of this world.

Couched in different phraseology, syntaxes, and overall approaches, ACIM and Inquiry led to the same peace inside me. These dovetailed with each other as I utilized them in my daily life.

The paper with the words, “Would you just stop and look at this place?!” reminded me to slow down and observe what thoughts passed through my mind.

CHAPTER 12
CANCER AND THE BODILY CONTRACTION

I stopped treating patients the month after returning from Peru. I hung up the lead apron that had weighed me down for 30 years but continued my administrative role at the office. My neck, head, and thoracic spine enjoyed the partial respite from the arduous work of bending over patients on and off the operating table.

Gradually, I warmed to the idea of selling my practice outright and leaving the business of medicine altogether. After consulting an attorney, I devised a plan to sell the company to Dr. William Altright, who had worked for me for over ten years. Now, I just needed to find out if he wanted to buy.

"Good afternoon, William. I see that the patients have adjusted to my absence from the office. Everything around here going smoothly?"

"Smooth in many ways, but the patients may not be as adapted as you think," Dr. Altright replied. "Quite a few patients still ask about you. On top of that, referring doctors continue to request a consult with Dr. Balint."

Knowing that my name remained on everyone's speed dial gave me a warm glow of pride throughout my chest. I inwardly heard a voice that said, *Careful. Too much of this good feeling would be toxic.*

"William," I said, "we talked about this a while ago, and I wondered if you are still interested in buying the business."

"You're suggesting I buy Balint Pain Management, right?" replied Dr. Altright.

"Yes," I said.

Dr. Altright nodded as if to say, "Tell me more."

"Here is a preliminary proposal from my attorney to get us started. There would be some cash up front, finalization of the accounting year, and formal papers to sign to turn over the business's stock. One of my conditions is that no employees be let go for six months following this buyout except for solid reasons of insubordination. I know it's one thing for the staff to adjust to my stepping away, but it will be another when the employees find out I am selling the practice to you. The staff needs to know that their income, paycheck, and job security will be stable under your leadership."

Dr. A quickly rifled through the papers I presented him. He stopped on the one paragraph that might be a sticking point—Melanie's continued work with HeartMath for the patients.

"Bart, all this looks good, but I am sorry. I cannot continue Melanie's employment. I know how to prescribe medicines, give injections, and work with each patient's psychological needs personally. If I determine a patient will benefit from HeartMath training, I can teach them. And besides, all Melanie would continue to do would be to suck money from my pocket."

I wasn't surprised by Dr. A's speech, but I hoped he would keep her on for a few months during the transition. I knew that being fired would be a sensitive point for Melanie, but it had to happen for us to keep growing.

The day came when Dr. A and I exchanged the final documents announcing the official transfer of my business. Melanie knew her future under Dr. A's employment would end soon, but it was still a shock when she received her official notice of termination. Melanie and I simultaneously cleaned out our desks at BPMC.

"It's easy to understand that Altright is letting me go. He never agreed to do the HeartMath program with me, as you requested of everyone at the office. And he made it clear to me early on that my presence here was stealing some of his income. But his approach shocked me when he informed me of his decision. He walked into my cubicle and began speaking at his normal volume such that two or three other employees heard every word. When I realized what he wanted to discuss, I requested we move to his office and close the door. Amazing, the lack of tact and compassion! What an asshole!" Melanie said with tears on her cheeks and hostility in her voice. "Frankly, I couldn't have worked for him anyway. I recognize that. Perhaps this is a blessing, but it sure does feel shitty right now!"

"I'm sorry it worked out this way," I said, hugging her. "I tried making this different, but stuff like this reinforces why being equal business partners with him was impossible."

Personally, a sense of accomplishment filled my chest as a wave of relief appeared and then diminished, knowing this business chapter of my career had ended as smoothly as it did. Launching Balint Pain Management took a lot of persistence and hard work. I had grown such that I had added Melanie's HeartMath facilitation and dreamwork to complement the care of patients and their long-standing pain. The business had always been arranged for my quickest departure when the time came—and the time had come.

Melanie and I rented a small coffee shop near the medical office to celebrate with our staff and patients. The room hummed with conversation, hugs, and laughter. I then took the stage, with my acoustic guitar and Melanie singing. A bittersweet moment filled the space as I witnessed colleagues and patients tapping their feet gently to a Brazilian song, "Corcovado," sung in English and Portuguese. I appreciated the warmth received and given during those few hours. The staff and patients had all signed a "best of the future" card, and several gave gifts, such as a small Chilean clock I received from a patient and her husband.

Retirement and Family Struggles

And so, the two of us moved into another phase of our lives—retirement. While many changes occurred in how Melanie and I dealt with our work situations, we also encountered changes in our families' dynamics. Melanie's father died unexpectedly from complications due to an acute lung issue. Her younger brother passed away under mysterious circumstances at 50 years of age after suffering many years of schizophrenia and homelessness for long stretches at a time. Found in a highly wooded area near Great Falls, Virginia, his decomposed body and subsequent autopsy showed no signs of physical trauma. These deaths left her mother in a state of shock and depression for years as Melanie and her sister grieved.

Over several years, my mom became reclusive to the point of refusing to eat out at a restaurant during our few visits to Toronto, Ohio. Living in a low-income facility near her hometown, she stopped driving and soon gave her vehicle away. A progressive and undiagnosed weakness in her legs limited her mobility to such a degree that she required an electric scooter to get around her one-bedroom apartment. I asked her several times to at least come and visit my home in Virginia for a possible move, but she refused. Her financial difficulties grew, so I agreed to help her with unpaid credit card bills. Soon afterward, my mother had breast surgery for a benign condition and needed to be in a care facility for a short time. After being discharged to her home, her withdrawal became even more pronounced, as she refused to open her apartment door to travel twenty feet down the common hallway to collect mail. Luckily, her brother and his wife, my Uncle George and Aunt Gail, graciously transported her to doctor's appointments and picked up groceries.

I tried talking to Mom about her inner world, and except for the anger she held for most people, an unwillingness or inability presided over even a brief look at her emotions. She even refused to look at happy memories from her upbringing and relationship with her parents. Any conversations about these subjects ended in further anger and loathing.

Inner confusion roiled inside me around Mom's outward seclusion and her inability or lack of desire to walk, as well as her seemingly inward withdrawal towards an existence of depression. Lacking empathy for her, let alone compassion, I felt totally at a loss for what to say to her most of the time.

During my last visit with her, she finally asked to move in with Melanie and me, but this time, I refused, saying our home was not equipped for someone requiring full-time use of a wheelchair. I explained that I could not lift, bathe, and handle her general needs full-time. While I still feel remorse over telling her this, I thought I had no choice.

Two weeks after my last visit, massive blood clots formed in Mom's legs, traveled up into her lungs and ended her life. Perhaps her unwillingness to examine anger manifested physically as external immobility. I only felt irritation.

After divorcing my mother years prior, my father eventually stepped into a new family after becoming espoused to a sweet and playful lady he had met at a local Weirton picnic. Ironically, my brother and I had both married (and divorced) partners named Sharon; thus, my dad's new companion became the third Sharon Balint of our family. Still estranged from my dad, I opted out of their wedding, as feigning cheerfulness around my relatives seemed farcical. My paternal grandmother died from esophageal cancer during this period, but I also didn't attend her funeral. Not because of my relationship with her, but because, once again, I couldn't stomach being around relatives. The easiest thing to do called for running and holing up in the cathedral of intellect. Several relatives still mention my absence at these events, which occasionally elicits guilt.

One night, in a dream, my grandmother returned, but not quite in the way I ever expected.

I am in an open field with gently rolling hills in all directions. Suddenly, a figure runs toward me. It is my paternal grandmother, who recently passed away from esophageal cancer. Naked and engulfed in a raging fire, she runs with her arms extended in a posture similar to a crucifixion. Her skin appears charred and red, and the flames arise from every part of her body. She doesn't acknowledge me, but I am shocked to see her painful grimace as she runs past. I awaken.

Two weeks after this dream image appeared, an artist friend, Kris, invited me to visit his studio. He showed me one painting he had just completed, thinking it might interest me. The painting presented nice abstract textures and various colors, but out of the corner of my eye, I saw a two-piece creation that abruptly stopped my browsing. The painting depicted a human figure engulfed in flames with arms outstretched, just as I saw in the dream of my grandmother. The connection between this painting and my dream was so unmistakable and captivating that I immediately purchased it.

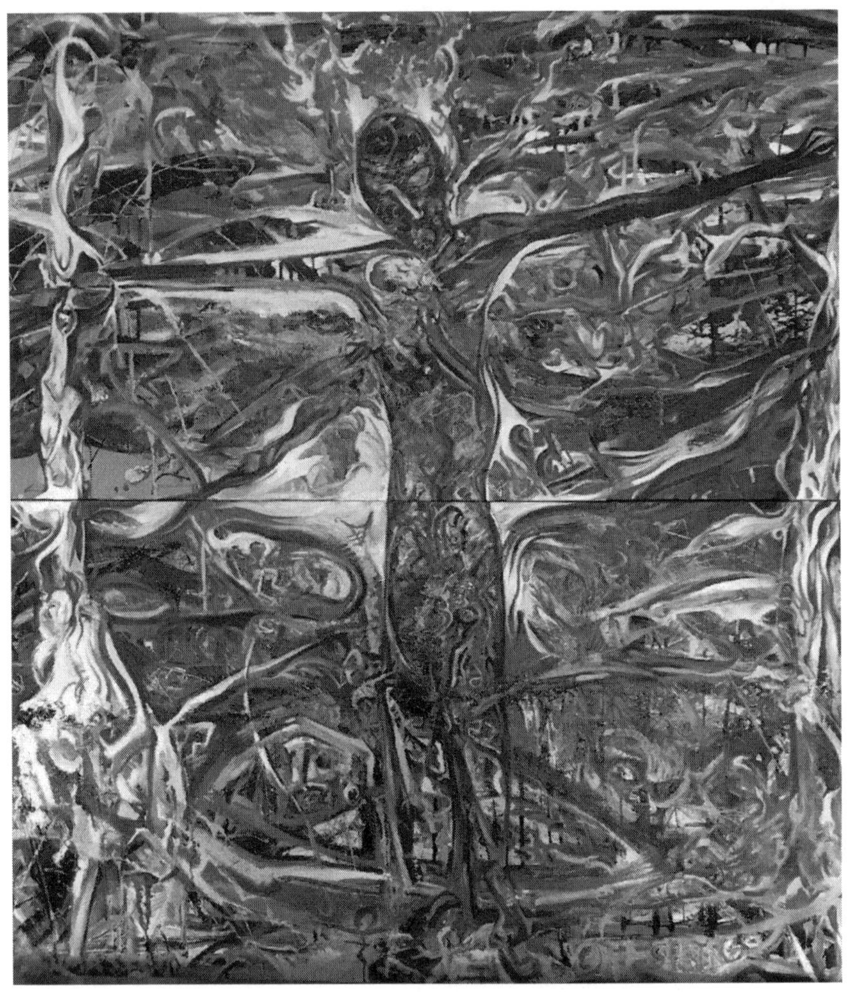

Figure 20 "Burning" by Kris Bowmaster, circa 2014 (Bowmasterart.com)

The meaning of this dream stumped me, and superficially, I thought it reflected my continual struggle with various family members.

Ten years after my father's remarriage, chronic obstructive pulmonary disease and atherosclerosis from 60 years of smoking plagued him. Eventually, he required open heart surgery, so I returned to Weirton to visit. While we never talked about my long absence, being around my father's constant criticism of everything still plagued me.

Sitting at my father and Sharon's dining table one evening, the conversation took an unusual turn. My stepmother Sharon asked, "Bart, have you ever seen your father angry? More recently, it seems anger has been getting the best of him, which worries me."

Sharon's fretting didn't surprise me, as she seemed overly anxious about many things, but it baffled me that she said his anger only now began to show after many years of marriage.

"Angry? Oh, my," I said. "My father was the angriest person I knew growing up. He often flew off in a rage, especially striking out at his children at the littlest thing. Angry? Undeniably." Not mentioning any specific incidents, an urge to spill the beans rose and quickly faded.

I noticed a slight bit of vengeance in my body as I finally talked about his wrath to her; someone in the family actually wanted to know about his anger. Until this point, no one had ever asked, including my brothers.

I looked over at my father and saw a small tear appear in the corner of his right eye.

"Strike out at my children? When did that ever happen?" he said quite innocently. I didn't take his response as an attempt to lie and cover up something, but his answer took me back a few steps.

My father continued, "I don't remember anything like that. I know at times I was irritable, but physically beating you? I don't remember."

From this, I concluded that he had blacked out every time rage overtook him. I didn't say this, nor did I press the issue. To pile one accusation upon another made no sense.

Taking advantage of this rare conversation, I boldly asked him about the discipline in his family growing up. He said his mother physically punished the kids and especially took out her frustrations on his older brother. My father then held his head in his hands, and we all sat quietly for the rest of the evening. One more unfinished topic, never to speak of again. Disappointment showed all over my face when the discussion of this sensitive topic terminated abruptly.

After my father's open-heart surgery, he stopped smoking. For me, that was positive as, for the first time in 55 years, I could be around him without a constant cloud of smoke hanging between us. Unfortunately, he soon developed leukemia and underwent mild chemotherapy for several years. Still, exhaustion followed him everywhere as his bone marrow stopped making red blood cells needed to move oxygen around his body. Between leukemia, anemia, and chronic lung disease, his activities grew more and more limited. His second wife's anxiety heightened as she perseverated about the possibility of his death.

Whether her general chronic nervousness contributed or not, Sharon, my father's second wife, passed away from an acute coronary event long before my father succumbed to leukemia. Such a brutal twist of fate, in that she had felt sure he would die before her. Watching television in bed during their usual nightly routine, she complained of chest pain and, not ten seconds later, fell forward in full cardiac arrest. While my father never wanted to talk about this either, I know it affected him tremendously.

Life with My Father, Again

After his wife's passing, my father came and lived with Melanie and me in our barn apartment for several months one winter. He helped me with projects around the farm and assisted me in putting together a woodworking shop. His preciseness brought out my best irritation as he constantly measured and re-measured boards and saw cuts.

"Dad, it's only a barn, and I'm not trying to make this shop a showpiece," I said.

His sense of symmetry and "getting things done right" frustrated me initially, but in the end, I realized that he only tried to get things lined up to make the job easier.

My father's criticisms surfaced frequently, especially when traveling together to and from his oncology appointments.

"Who the hell decided to call these hills mountains?" he exclaimed while looking at the Blue Ridge and Allegheny mountains that bordered the Shenandoah Valley.

"I don't know, Dad." I returned. *Boy, have I had enough of his lifelong criticism, and now he is critical of the valley and mountains I call home.*

"Why don't we just stop and ask someone?" I challenged with a slightly raised voice. "Let's call up the Geographical Society that names different landmarks and ask them if they know what they are doing."

My father stopped for just a second. "What?" he said.

"Yes, let's call someone to ask them how these little hills were named mountains."

Our conversations around his criticisms continued from there. He complained about the neighbors' messy yards or the colors of their houses. I just started responding to these exclamations with,

"Okay, let's stop and ask these people why they are slobs."

Eventually, after one of his disparagements, he answered his own question with, "Yes, I know! Let's stop and ask these people what the hell they are doing," adding a laugh at the end. I, too, chuckled, allowing a slight smile to emerge. Until then, I never laughed with him, no matter how funny the situation was.

For years, my father lamented, "I'll never get to drive my 1949 Ford Custom again." For the longest time, I didn't realize Ford made a car called a "Custom." Until that point, I refused to learn more about anything that might bring my dad some happiness. Eventually, I realized that his first car as a teenager had been a '49 Custom convertible, his most prized vehicle ever. I never knew how he came to own it or why he had to give it up. Something clicked inside, telling me to investigate this a little further.

Eventually, a 1951 Ford Custom convertible appeared on the local market. This '51 Custom carried the same features as a '49, except for having two chrome bullets on the front grill instead of just one. In reasonable shape, the car required new wiring, hydraulics, and engine work. After being declared roadworthy, I transported the '51 to my father's basement garage in Weirton, his hometown. Seeing the look on my father's face as I gave it to him was a pleasure I rarely allowed myself. Working on the car in the midst of his leukemia journey filled much of his time and brought him great satisfaction as he and his lifelong friend, Dale, tinkered with it several days each week.

Figure 21 George Balint, Sr., with his 1949 Ford Custom in 1957

He lived with leukemia for several years but quickly declined as the chemotherapy stopped working. Melanie and I traveled to his home in West Virginia to be with him for his last weeks. During that final visit, my father's friend Dale helped me bolt the newly re-chromed front and rear bumpers onto the Custom.

With the car finally completed, my father hauled his significantly weakened body from his bed down the stairs to the garage, where he presided over one last ceremonious inspection.

The smile in his eyes said it all.

Although it had been two years since his second wife passed, my father had never moved her clothing from their closets. Every article of her wardrobe remained exactly as it was the day she died. Her jewelry, in a wooden wall jewelry cabinet built by him, hung untouched on the wall to the right of the entrance to their bedroom. Carefully placed on the mat by the front door, her white canvas tennis shoes awaited her feet to slide into them again. My dad said the issue was that his stepdaughter couldn't move forward with sorting through and selecting some of her mom's belongings to keep and letting the others go. While unspoken, he needed to make sure his second wife's belongings would be taken by his stepdaughter before he could leave this world. The same day, we walked my dad to the basement to see the car; his stepdaughter agreed to help move her mom's things. The next day, I was with him when he passed.

Watching his death, I still felt a remoteness and distance between us. Guilt tenaciously surrounded my half of that relationship, and anger still bubbled up when thoughts of my childhood came through. With my parents' deaths, I still felt that Iron Man suit locking into place around my body, providing me protection.

Soon after, he came to me in three dreams, and each time I rejected him. As much as I found him irritating in waking life, I found him exasperating when he appeared in my dreams. And then there was a fourth dream that presented a twist.

Once again, when walking in a nondescript area, I notice my father following me. I immediately feel the old rage inside. I do not want to interact with him at all. Then I see a woman next to me.

She says, "Your father wants to ask you just one question."

I thought, What part* of 'I-don't-want-to-talk-to him' doesn't she get? *I don't want to listen to any questions!

The woman repeats, "Your father wants to ask you just one question."

I remain silent for a second and then nod in agreement.

The woman continues, "Your father wants to ask you if he did everything you asked while he was still alive. Did he do everything you requested?"

I stop walking. My mind stops. There is a deep silence that seems to last an eternity. Suddenly, a feeling starts in my legs, traveling up my torso and into my head. It is a feeling of love, appreciation, and remembrance. Immediately, my body tells me the answer is "Yes!"

"Yes. Tell him that yes, he did everything I asked him." Tears fall from my eyes while a warm feeling spreads through my throat. There is no question that, indeed, he did everything I asked.

Until that dream, I had been immovable in my loathing and hatred for him. But in the split second of silence that stopped all my thoughts, I felt my anger for my father slip away. The long-standing hatred dissolved, and I felt my body become light and free.

I could even relive those terrible, painful situations with my father when I was a child and see them from a different perspective. I didn't deny that they never happened, but I could see how those incidents and everything else that had happened to me had led precisely to this moment of forgiveness. That simple question, "Did he do everything you asked of him?" brought me a different viewpoint that changed how I understood life forever.

My Cancer Shakeup

Mel and I settled into retirement. We traveled to Hawaii, Brazil, Morocco, and a few places in the Caribbean, did several Colorado ski trips with friends, and went on a cross-country road trip with a friend in our Airstream trailer. Gradually, I decreased my physical activity as my neck continued to hurt. I developed an idea for a book, initially comparing ACIM and inquiry. Then, I realized my first book needed to be about my inner travels.

Routine. I counted on it after retiring. Sure, issues still cropped up, but primarily, things were smooth. Two buddies and I frequented our favorite pizza place, and bit by bit, I started taking home more and more of the stromboli I previously devoured in one sitting. That same stromboli progressively stretched into two meals. Overeating in an attempt to fulfill myself and feeling that fullness as fat coursed through my arteries no longer interested nor dominated me when eating out. At about the same time, Melanie decided to try a whole-food diet, and since she did most of the food prep and cooking in our home, eventually, I followed the plan, too. Unexpectedly, I started losing some weight, a nice side effect of eating more healthfully. The weight kept sloughing off. Getting close to my high school weight felt good.

Good, that is, until I saw my GP physician, Dr. Otis, during a routine yearly checkup. Regular blood work accompanied every office appointment for fifteen years. A few days after this routine visit, his front office called to schedule a follow-up as soon as possible.

“Hey, Bart, I am glad you could come back when my staff called,” said Dr. Otis, looking more serious than I had ever seen him.

What Is going on here? I thought with more than passing suspicion. *Dr. Otis never looks at me like this or speaks with all these pauses. He looks nervous.* My eyes squinted, and my head tilted as I waited.

Dr. Otis continued, “The lab just returned with your blood tests. Most of it looked okay, except that you have developed severe iron deficiency anemia, and your IgM count is through the roof. As you recall, IgM is one of the blood protein antibodies that lymphocytes produce to fight infection. With these levels, you probably have lymphoma or cancer of the lymphocytes. You will need a bone marrow biopsy to confirm this. Also, when the IgM gets too high, there is a real chance of a stroke any time.” Dr. Otis stopped speaking and looked at me, giving me a moment to digest the news.

“That doesn’t sound very good,” I said, unsure what to think and not knowing what to say. *What does all this mean? I thought I was doing so well, losing some weight and all! Fuck! And a stroke at any time?*

“Look, Bart. This is not easy news for you to receive, and I won't pretend it is. And we won't even know if this IS what's happening until the test results return. Fingers crossed. But what's also true is that we can often help folks with this diagnosis, but we must get you over to the oncologists immediately. In the meantime, you need to see the GI doctor so they can examine your stomach.”

I felt knocked to the ground by a smack in the back of the head that came out of nowhere. Subsequent tests revealed that I had a rare B-cell non-Hodgkin's lymphoma; statistically, only 50 to 60% of patients survived for five years. Upper GI and PET scans showed stage IV lymphoma characterized by high levels of IgM and iron deficiency anemia. My stomach was so riddled with lymphoma that I no longer absorbed iron.

Why me? Why now? Is this payback for something I did earlier in my life? Is this payback for something I am doing now? Has this cancer been growing in me for years? Is this God punishing me for not being a religious guy? Conversely, isn't this the lymphoma linked to that common weed killer? Aren't some people cashing in big on Roundup lawsuits?

Several jury trials ruled that a common weed killer, Roundup, might cause this type of lymphoma, and those lawsuits continued to make their way through the court system. Attorneys promised big monetary rewards if lymphoma patients could prove that exposure to Roundup caused their cancer. I considered this but decided I didn't want one more legal fight, no matter how much money my attorney could make.

I'm not an affirmation-spouting, let's-hope-for-the-best kind of guy, and the diagnosis landed like a lead weight, and most of my initial reactions came out as anger and irritation. Worst of all, probably because it was much more immediate than even impending death, came the thought, *How many times are they going to have to stick me to get an IV for each chemo treatment and office visit? My veins have never been that great for access, and I dread it every time since they often can't get blood on the first stick!* My pessimistic predictions immediately took over even though the chemotherapy wasn't scheduled for a few weeks.

Thankfully, my oncologist offered me the option of having a blood access port placed before the first round of chemotherapy. With this procedure, the surgeon inserted a sterile tube into one of the large veins of my neck. Connected to a small reservoir, it maximized blood access with a minimal number of sticks. On top of that, a prescription for topical anesthetic cream allowed me to numb the port a few hours before each medical visit. I highly recommend this to anyone facing a course of chemotherapy.

After hearing about my diagnosis, everyone began telling me what I should be doing with just about everything. Even though I had severe iron deficiency anemia, one medical professional warned me not to take supplemental iron as it would kill my liver. One person said to eat more greens; another cautioned me to avoid all pork. Do this religious ceremony, and try that healing technique. Don't ever do that, and never let "bad" thoughts come up. This well-meaning advice from family members, friends, and medical caregivers gave me a sense of overwhelming guilt because it all suggested I wasn't doing something right. Feeling angry and fearful most of the time, I woke up each morning trying to make sense of things. Most suggestions turned into guilt trips, which came out as indignation toward the other person.

Leaning on Inquiry

I woke up one morning tired of the rage I had held inside. Before lifting my head off the pillow, I thought of the inquiry work. Why was this advice pissing me off? By this time, I'd spent enough hours in inquiry to know that external events didn't necessarily dictate my perceptions and interpretations. I reminded myself that any internal reverberations served to keep me looking at my beliefs and underlying fear. However, even with this inner work and reading, I still blamed other people and circumstances for my miseries. Things had been relatively comfortable and steady for a few years, and I recognized, but almost totally refused to accept, the notion that I needed something shaken up in me.

An earthquake occurred right on schedule this time; it called itself cancer.

While most people probably dreaded a cancer diagnosis, inquiry explorations revealed a connection between my fearful, future-oriented thoughts and long-obscured bodily predilections.

Something from even deeper in my body demanded attention.

Wait. This call to go inward into the body's sensations is what Scott introduced me to during the retreat Melanie and I attended. Could bodily contractions associated with stuck energies reflect a relative possibility?

When I sat in inquiry, cancer confirmed that sensations welded to past traumas and current negative beliefs remained stored within my body. Exactly where I didn't know, but perhaps I was ready to look at releasing them.

My body said, *Pay attention to my feelings. Sense where each one starts. Follow it wherever it goes. And especially consider that the commentaries associated with it are only of your making.*

I sat and watched and felt. That severe, familiar, body-numbing contraction I felt during the physical beating at nine years old arose. Unconsciously, I had been hiding behind and building an identity around this contraction.

Many other deep sensations reflected various traumas I incurred many years ago. Feeling a lightness and a decreased opaqueness of my apparent physical boundaries accompanied the recognition of each contraction for a short time.

During my medical training, not one professor lectured on the possibility of a body-mind connection or somatic tightening. Medical school instructors ridiculed consolidations, body tension, and "psycho-somatic diseases," labeling patients who reported them insane, neurotic, or both. Their best and most scientific solution always relied on people taking more pharmaceuticals. Any hint of a relationship between our body and mind flew in the face of mainstream Western medical knowledge. Frankly, that had sat fine with me as I tried to bury these psychic knots as far as they would go; I certainly didn't want to hear that you had to look at and feel them to help reintegrate them.

Cancer brought me along in my journey by revealing how blindly I held onto traumatic stories. Experiencing the body's aches, pains, and tense spots through inquiry revealed a reliable connection between my thoughts and the physical sensations associated with them. I had previously thought emotions emerged automatically, were immutable due to my humanness, and were always precipitated by outside events. After repeated looking, I realized I kept the tensions in place as long as I attached significance to them over and over again. And when I willingly sat with these sensations and neutrally acknowledged the stories, none of these experiences held up as independently solid. Equally notable was that none of them lasted; each arrived and departed.

I gradually felt an opening and understanding of bodily held trauma, bodily condensations, and their intimate connection with my mind and the mental picture of whom I thought I was. With each realization, I traveled one more step toward the front doors out of the cathedral of intellect and back into a connection with the rest of my body.

Soon after informing some friends of my cancer diagnosis, many stopped calling or contacting me. I don't know what prompted this response from them, but it reminded me of my inability as a young man even to sit and talk with several relatives who approached the boundary of life and death. Relevant for me became the exploration of the feelings associated with my perceived abandonment by my family and friends. I felt this desertion throughout my being and blamed them for it.

So, I inquired.

Facilitator (F): "Bart, what brings you to this meeting today?"

Me: "I have several friends I haven't heard from since being diagnosed with cancer. It brings up anger and the feeling of abandonment."

F: "Can you feel that now? Can you sense a story about this?"

Me: "Yes. The feelings automatically arise when I hear this narrative again and again. I have this pit in my stomach, a drooping and sadness in my face, and a forward slouch of my shoulders—quite defeated. And then, as some attempt to build myself up, I feel anger. First in the clenched fists, then in the jaw. Everything tightens. And this sequence of my anger towards them repeats over and over."

F: "What seems to be most prominent right now?"

Me: "This movement and feeling in the face that wants to point toward some image of them and scream about their cruelty towards me."

F: “Stay with that feeling, but do you also see in your mind the picture of these people doing this? Can you see them?”

Me: “Yes. I can see them. I want to hurl something, even if it is only an insult or accusation.”

F: “Looking at their faces, what feature seems to cause the most anger?”

Me: “Their fucking smiles. I hate those smiles. And always telling some stupid joke or inappropriately laughing even when I need to sit and not joke for a few minutes.”

F: “What else comes up?”

Me: “They have had the same stupid behavior forever, ever since my childhood.”

F: “Go back to that smile. Can you sit with that for a bit?”

Me: “Yes. I see now; it is just a picture. And I see that change into a clown face, and while I don’t particularly like clowns, that change softens this feeling.”

F: “What’s present now?”

Me: “I am just sitting with that clown face. But I also notice a thought, ‘Well, I’m still angry with them for not caring even to contact me.’”

F: “How do you know they don’t care? What tells you that?”

Me: “My mind stopped there for a second, realizing I had no clue as to whether they cared or not. Perhaps briefly, a bodily sensation seemed to confirm their uncaring nature, but I realize that anything I add after that is just a made-up subplot.”

F: “Where are you now?”

Me: “The fighting posture is gone, but part of the mind still wants to tell some urban legend of abandonment. I feel that in the belly area.”

F: “Sit with that feeling in the stomach. Does it have a shape, a color, or other features?”

Me: “It seems to be dark but not totally opaque. It moves and undulates a bit. It is waiting.”

F: “Waiting for what?”

Me: “Waiting for me to sit with it and see how I have used it for many different emotions, not just abandonment. And with that, it seems to fade and is replaced by a sense of curiosity in my mind and head area. I’m slightly sad as I have always hated it, tried to ignore it, and took some medicine to make it go away. And I know I need to sit with this again.”

This stirred up curiosity about these sensations that I had ignored, thought were created at the time of the Big Bang, or denied even existing despite feeling them.

A Dance, not a Battle

The gentle approach to facilitation that Melanie learned during her inquiry training helped both of us to try and stay open to the many emotions that came up during the initial stages of my cancer treatment. These investigations brought ease to me as I proceeded through grueling treatments and adventures into the unknown.

Early in my cancer treatment, I decided I didn’t want to approach it as a battle. I had heard, read, saw, and experienced many cancer patients who described their process as a war: “He fought courageously to the end.” Or “She never gave up in her battle with cancer." These kinds of sentiments populated many obituaries and headstones. While perhaps true for them, something profoundly different described my exploration of lymphoma. My experience with inner healing over so many years demonstrated that the more I battled anything, the offending experience always reappeared, but perhaps in a different form.

This whole episode, which continues to this day, gives me ongoing opportunities to examine all my beliefs and points of view, positive or negative.

Not that I did nothing to support my body through this bout of cancer. The word "dance" came to me. Even though I don't dance that well, a dance with cancer was a fair characterization, especially since cancer appeared to be in the lead early on. I developed a Caring Bridge blog site to inform others of my process, and I named my page "Freefall with Bart."

Who knows where it will lead and how it will end if it does? And who knows what discoveries await along the path? Yes, "freefall" resonated. My openness to being with whatever arises during this part of the journey continues to unfold.

So many thoughts came to mind after receiving the diagnosis of lymphoma. Ideas of what it means to die. Thoughts of going through one medical procedure after another. Thoughts of leaving loved ones behind to deal with my affairs and sixty years of accumulation. Thoughts of their grief of me being gone. Ideas of not knowing what is next. Ruminations on punishment and the possibility of going to hell since I didn't believe what the Catholic Church or any other religion espoused.

From where did the lymphoma come? And did it relate to any previous trauma? And what, if anything, was my subconscious trying to tell me by the development of this life-ending disease? Others asked me what I thought this cancer meant. And I wondered at times what it meant about me.

The mind said, '*That IS the big question.*'

What does it mean about me? And perhaps its purpose is to keep asking, *What does this mean about ME?* until I finally see that the question is asking, *What or who is the 'me' that this question is even referring to?*

Adventures in Chemotherapy

With the oncologist's agreement, I waited one month before starting chemotherapy, attempting to raise my iron levels through an iron infusion and a diet higher in natural iron. With those small changes, my hemoglobin rose a few points toward normal.

The first day of actual intravenous treatment came quickly. Ignoring the negative naysaying doomsday thoughts became impossible. Hatred and rage arose on the short drive to the infusion center. These feelings surfaced more intensely with each subsequent visit, although perhaps I only watched them more closely. Part of my mind argued that these feelings were too real and of such profound density that they precluded any meaningful inquiry. Simply one more sentence heralded by some bodily tightness and vibration, spoken over my internal loudspeaker, which then vanished over the horizon.

This is the last thing I want to do right now! I yelled inwardly. I had never noticed the snide look modeled on my face during these inner outbursts, but my bitterness reflected in the car's mirrors and magnified with each bump in the road to the cancer center. As the treatments continued, catching these postures and gestures associated with emotional reactions became easier.

Melanie assumed more of the driving, leaving me in the passenger seat to squirm in all the discomfort. At times, I glimpsed the "me," who I thought suffered through this diagnosis and treatment—noticing a bodily outline that confined my mind in this world. There were even glimpses of watching the aware "me" around which this supposedly all revolved.

Once chemotherapy began, Mel became obsessed with sterile technique. A throwback from her days in biomedical research, she treated our kitchen as her lab bench, taking care to keep foods bacteria-free since the chemo knocked back my immune system every three weeks. She acted as a gatekeeper, vetting any visitors to ensure they were as healthy as possible before a visit. An unexpected treat for me, daily litter box cleaning fell to her, and she took up more laundry duty, often a job I did before. She offered me foot reflexology or energy work to try and keep energy centers open and running efficiently.

Each treatment visit started similarly, falling into another rhythm of sorts. A nurse took my vital signs, and multiple tubes of my blood went off for analysis. I spoke briefly with the oncologist, and after confirmation of my name and medical number on the chemo drug bags, the infusions started. Venous access was a non-issue, as all infusions dripped into the access port on the right side of my chest. I parked myself in the infusion chair for four to six hours, watching the grass grow outside the clinic windows. The discomfort of the recliner, a far cry from my beloved La-Z-Boy, reinforced my disdain for this insane scenario!

I didn't appreciate the pre-infusion Benadryl, as it only made me tired. Necessary, I was told. Unavoidable, they said. Melanie and I researched alternative treatments to help with some of chemotherapy's side effects. We found additional supplements to support my body: a liver detoxing tablet with milk thistle and other herbs; copaiba, an essential oil that showed some promise in cancer treatment; a mitochondria-supporting powder and green drink to beef up my energy; concentrated whole-food derived supplements; and more.

"Sorry, we don't allow and refuse to look at scientific articles on potential supplements. We don't want to see them, let alone consider how they might help each patient," the doctors and nutritionists barked. Only one pharmacist at the center even considered reviewing an article on milk thistle and its ability to support liver function in young children with blood cancer. He explained that he had seen many children die from chemotherapy-induced liver failure and wished he had known about this simple supplement years before.

The treatment center offered psychological support for cancer patients and their families. I applauded that as I utilized this service a couple of times, meeting with a former colleague. I remembered my previous sadness and disappointment when my dad received treatment for leukemia. This would have benefited him and his wife, but his cancer center lacked this essential support.

Infusions went smoothly, but I dreaded the oral prednisone given afterward. It brought out anxiety, depression, hyperactivity, irritability, and significant sleep disruption. I hated this. I often called it the Prednisone 500, reminiscent of a visit to the Indianapolis race track. Many folks get depressed on prednisone. I was so hyper that my speech went a mile a minute, matching the best auctioneer, and I lay awake at all hours of the night, restorative sleep a vague memory of a previous lifetime. I finally asked the doctor to reduce the dosage, and they decreased it by 20 percent, but unfortunately, most of the side effects remained. Even with prescribed sleep medications, I only managed four hours of sleep every night. The last day of prednisone demanded a mini-celebration.

At times, I caught myself playing the victim who lashed out at everyone and everything. I got angry at Melanie, the hospital pharmacists, the nurses who helped with the infusions, and even the support billing staff. Don't forget about my anger toward the insurance company! Plenty of targets circled the edges of my mind.

One of the well-documented complications of these chemo drugs came with a breakdown of the nerves in the hands and feet. Called peripheral neuropathy, this often-seen side effect can be devastating as the tips of every finger become sausages of burning numbness and tingling. Many of my pain clinic patients had encountered these side effects. Soon, I felt these symptoms myself. I could still use my fingers, but the burning was constant and annoying. *On top of cancer, now my fingers may burn for the rest of my life?!*

When I brought this distressing symptom up during a visit, multiple practitioners asked the same infuriating question. "Are you unable to put buttons through a buttonhole?" the attending physician asked. "If you can still put buttons through the hole, then you don't have peripheral neuropathy to any significant degree."

Not discounting the disability of those who cannot button shirts, this question ignored the intense pain I experienced. The demeaning question became another "witness" to or evidence of my victimhood during this phase of treatment. Fierce indignation and fear arose each time I felt ignored and pigeonholed into some category: “Well, your pain can't be that bad because you can still button a shirt.” Medical school taught that this was the gold standard of pain from peripheral neuropathy. However, now I realize how ridiculous that question is to someone who can still button buttons but has severe and unrelenting burning. The issue continued until the chemotherapy ended; since then, my nerve endings have partially recovered from the insult.

I told myself it wasn’t a battle. A more valid statement may have been, “What part of this is NOT a battle for me?”

I went to war again and again. Different things to outwardly point at, but all of them revolved around a deep inner fear. The longer I suffered and the more inquiry I applied, the more I saw that all the outward pointing deflected my attention from earnestly looking at precisely how I designed and maintained the sacrificial lamb I thought I was. What was I trying to save through each skirmish and angry episode? I saw the godforsaken part of me that asserted it was unambiguously real. The battle wasn’t due to cancer or its treatment. The struggle reflected my rigid expectations and intolerance to unpredictable and uncontrollable outcomes. But it also involved a deep devotion to seeing what “I” was all about. The world, as I constructed it, kept me steeped in suffering <u>with or without a cancer diagnosis</u>.

Several more PET scans, another GI endoscopy, many blood tests, and several years of infusions brought me to the point of the cancer being declared “indolent.” This means that the cancer is currently calm and relatively quiet. Now, I continue periodic blood checks and watch what emotions come up in me with each interaction with medical professionals. The lymphoma still waltzes throughout my body and leaves its footprints in the form of high IgM levels, but this warrants no specific pharmaceutical treatment at this time.

While the journey with cancer has been a dance, the primary battle has been with my reluctance and resistance to reconnect to my body. These neglected stagnations and accompanying narrations knew no other way to get my attention than an extreme expression called cancer.

I grappled with my growing convictions to never enter another hospital again. The medical insurance machine was a rigid institution, putting on a front of individualized care, but not much different from a meat grinder. I argued with God for putting me in this position. Ultimately, I recognized this agony as a brutal campaign to deny my true self. Oh, how attached I had become to the old, intelligent, but fearful identity I had constructed.

I kept asking myself, *Now, who exactly is this 'I' who believes he is struggling with all of this?*

Each time I sat with this question, those small glimpses of stillness I had as a child in the backseat of a smoke-filled station wagon heading towards a state camping ground came up. That mildly detached awareness I experienced as a child converged with the quiet awareness I experience now. And with each remembrance and reconnection of those memories with my current experience, my previously rigid beliefs dissipated.

Beneath the rocky road of cancer and all the beliefs that appeared in my mind and my body, I started sensing a stillness and serenity permeating every situation, object, and thought. I ultimately sensed that tranquility regardless of what I looked at during inquiry. That knowing confirmation of tranquility underneath everything presented the possibility of another choice concerning my interpretations and inclinations towards life.

Creativity Leads to Dreams

Once the urgency of dealing with cancer settled and my energy gradually returned, I decided to continue writing this book. While I didn't know what, I noted something called for resolution before resuming work on the book. One of these moments came when Melanie suggested I contact Katie Curtin[5], a writing coach who Melanie had known for a few years. Katie is all about helping folks express their inner artist, whether that be through writing, painting, photography, drama, mask-making, textile art, and so much more. She introduced me to a regular writing practice and encouraged me to join a writer's group, where we helped each other formulate our ideas for our manuscripts through the offering and receiving of helpful comments.

Katie also sponsors a monthly "Creativity Cafe," where she invites participants to share their expressive works. Being invited as the guest artist one Thursday was a pleasure and a thrill. I presented a few readings from this book, some of my digital art, and even played a few tunes on my guitar. This moment of sharing my creativity merged with memories of freedom while I played guitar in London's Underground many years before.

During one Creativity Cafe, Katie introduced Seema Khaneja, MD[6], a gentle soul who had just written a book describing her journey of healing directed by the principles presented in ACIM.

---

[5] Katie Curtin – Your Creative Soul Coach

[6] https://coachingforinnerpeace.com/

Seema had been inspired by Mary Magdalene and was working with her guidance and words.

Soon after meeting Seema at the Cafe, I had a dream:

After going to sleep, I start dreaming rather suddenly. I find myself in an unremarkable space at a long rectangular table. I am at one end, and Melanie is on my right. I am surprised to see my mother (who passed about ten years prior to this dream) on my left. Seema is at the far end of the table opposite me. And two other women are seated closer to Seema, one on each side of the table. I cannot tell who they are, although I admit my attention is on my mother.

The women speak in unison.

"Have we done everything you asked us to do?"

Their mouths don't move, but I hear this question as clearly as any audible voice. Before or perhaps simultaneously with the next repetition of their query, my mother transfigures into Mary Magdalene, who I remember appeared to Seema in waking life. A feeling of confidence confirms this is Mary Magdalene, even though I don't recall having seen her in my waking life.

I am speechless, and the women ask again, "Have we done everything you asked?"

Instantaneously, memories of my mother's endless insane actions and demands come to mind. But I must answer honestly to myself and the women at the table. I recognize the familiar suspension of hostilities I felt during the dream of my father when presented with the same question. And again, I feel a dissolving, a resolution, a reconciliation, and an opening in my

body. There is a great feeling of relief as something loosens and transforms.

My answer to these women is immediate and profound. "Yes," I reply, and then bow in deep reverence. What else could I possibly add to that? A tear of gratitude comes to my eye regarding Mom/Mary Magdalene. Perhaps this is the first tear of gratitude I have ever shed concerning my mother.

Upon waking, I felt a sense of curiosity and quietness in my room and myself. While these areas of stillness seemed separate at first, soon they merged.

As with my dad, my rocky relationship with my mom continued past her death. I never wanted either of them in my dreams. However, the relationship I thought I had with her changed immediately during this dream. The attenuation was profound and thorough. I now view my mom through a different lens than the one I had for much of my life. There is a felt opening and comfort now when an image of her comes to mind, a connection I had always denied.

For a long time, though, I wondered, "Why did my mother transfigure into a character who I knew as Mary Magdalene?"

A possible answer to that question took a few years to materialize. One day I read about the Catholic Church's long-standing addictive perversion to portray Mary Magdalene as a sinner, a whore, a person possessed by demons, and a potential threat to all the dogma the Church held dear. Despite the Catholic Church reversing its teachings on Mary Magdalene almost sixty years ago, Sunday school teachers and my family insisted and taught all about her alleged failings as I grew up. It turns out that Mary was none of what the Church declared her to be. My current point of view is that my mom was indeed none of the things I insisted she be all those years. In that, I see how my rigid attitudes toward Mom paralleled Mary Magdalene's treatment by the Church.

I came to understand that my parents and other family members didn't force all of their dysfunctionality onto me. On some level, though not usually on a conscious one, I asked them to wear these costumes and play these roles in my life to reflect the particular beliefs and points of view I wanted to explore in this incarnation.

Soon after this dream, the lymphoma cells dancing inside me also posed this question. ***"Have we done all that you asked us to do?"*** The answer to this question wasn't as straightforward; I still felt the pull to continue observing what I needed or wanted to unlearn. Part of this exploration dealt with my shadow side that I continually denied, buried, and fought against in my dreams and waking life. I gradually began reconciliation with my exiled and rejected parts each time I mustered enough courage to explore those dense realms of my persona.

Exploring My Contractions

The lymphoma directed me to keep mining all the persistent or recurrent bodily permutations that still guarded against life and love, to continue digging through the rubble of cast-off parts of myself and see what precious nuggets they held. Despite everything I went through, intermittently, I sensed a guarded and defended me.

I delved into a few of Kiloby's writings on bodily contractions. Visceral sensations and feelings arising during my inquiry ventures became celebrations of coming home. The physical sensations associated with my every thought became more apparent. They rode on ever-so-subtle waves throughout my body. Even the slightest triggered sensation felt more and more like a tsunami. An inner visceral "Yes" or "No" had endless echoes of felt confirmations. With cancer, I learned to use the body's responses to aid in the discernment of all my beliefs, concepts, and points of view.

How did I know I loved the taste of rich, flavorful ice cream? My taste buds signaled the presence of an adequate amount of sugar; my mind said, "Boy, sugar! Do I love this!" and my body confirmed that love with another sensation or feeling. It all went together!

Several times during the upheaval with lymphoma, I started having a mild, twisting contortion deep in my abdomen. I would have associated this spasm with irritation or the beginnings of anger in times past. One evening, the tightening occurred; surprisingly, it wasn't connected to any thought or idea. I wasn't consciously mad at anything. Melanie and I spent time together outside, and everything radiated comfort and relaxation. All was calm. But part of the mind said, '*You need to get angry at something. Anything. Just get angry!*'

With that, I laughed. I wasn't angry. I just sat with the feeling, and it slowly dissipated. My mind worked furiously to slap some label, incident, or memory onto this contraction to define it as anger and declare to the world, *Yes! See how real anger is!* This was quite illuminating for me. And all very peculiar.

How many times have I automatically bought into some sensation or narrative of anger, never questioning its reality? To think I blindly followed that part of my mind all these years in some quixotic mission of self-construction and preservation through one more acquisition of form, even if that form was harmful or destructive.

This same scenario happened several times.

As I watched these, I noticed a sense of the "me" trying to form around the feeling of anger. Again, nothing happened externally that warranted an angry response.

But the "me" revealed itself.

Sometimes, this "me" associates with my name, Bart. Sometimes, as I close my eyes, I see a faint outline of the body, arms, and even my back or bottom—all faint impressions. I sense an activity in one part of the mind, trying to force it all together. It's almost funny to watch. Occasionally, I see cartoon characters holding signs pointing to a sensation waiting for some thought, like a baited hook prepared for a bite. They giggle uncontrollably and acknowledge that it's all just a game where I snare myself.

I notice that different emotions are associated with varying refinements in other body parts. Sometimes, they change or morph into something, showing me how the mind tries to piece everything together to make it real.

Amazingly, yesterday, I called these contractions avoidance, but today, they feel neutral or even gentle invitations to keep moving forward. It just shows me how my mind's perceptions can be reinterpreted in multiple ways. And I don't have to believe in my knee-jerk constructions unequivocally. Can I let it come together and fall apart without demanding action?

After exploring this repeatedly in formal inquiry sessions or just spontaneous silent looking on my part, I saw the “Bart” that I had protected for so long.

Despite all the heartache and turmoil, I now experience an intense love for this cancer and for the experiences it presents. This extends to a love of everything that has happened to me over my lifetime. Reconciliation with a multitude of previous stories and events. Reconciliation with my parents and others in my life. I have met many caring people along the way and had the chance to look at what I have tried to ignore in my body.

Where and in what circumstances could I eventually not find love?

CHAPTER 13
CAN YOU CLEAN THE WINDSHIELD SO AT LEAST I CAN SEE WHERE I AM GOING?

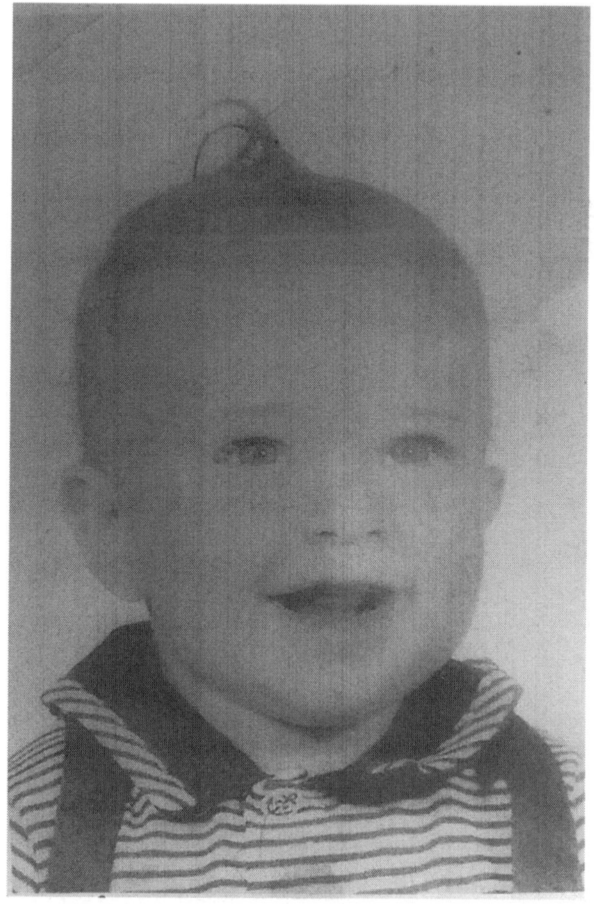

Figure 22 Bart, less than one year old

For most of my life, I detested this picture. I hated this reminder of joyfully running across the yard, eager to spend time with my father in his woodworking shed. From grade school onward, laying eyes on this photo immediately summoned a shield of darkness that demanded pain and revulsion replace the warmth of a joyful heart. I conceived and maintained a theme that joy deserted me early in my life, and in no way would I tolerate photos that said otherwise.

For over 60 years, accepting the innocence in this picture was off-limits. Like the vitamins added to processed foods, I fortified my Iron Man defenses with decades of verifying the world as threatening, brutal, and unpredictable. Even now, after years of insights, dreams, and inquiry, a part of me still tries to deny the delight in my life. It turns out, however, that I can't—that cheerfulness is more an innate part of me than anything I concoct and try to replace it with. I can cover it up, but I can't make it disappear.

My whole narrative surrounding this photograph fell apart one afternoon. No matter how it started, bravery urged me to revisit my underlying hatred of my early beginnings. I retrieved this reminder of a young, carefree Bart from my photographs file on my computer, enlarged it on the screen, and sat gazing at it. At first, the same old irritation surfaced, and I heard a warning:

There is nothing for you in this picture. As you have witnessed, only desperation, sadness, and disappointment await you there. Ok, maybe you did have happiness during one encounter, but how many times must you be reminded of the same old appalling and horrific tales of your past that happened after this picture was taken?

We are trying to protect you and spare you the pain you will find here, I heard.

For the first time, I looked, silently sitting and watching, and let this picture tell me what it meant rather than declaring that I already knew its significance.

With quiet confirmation, a felt opening rose through the silence, followed by a familiar harmony.

So, what crime did this little boy commit that continues to affect you all these years? I heard.

How could he be any other way except joyful and innocent, as this picture represents?

And with that, hardcore beliefs around this snapshot eased, similar to the feelings during the dreams with my mom and dad. This time, the opening of solace and joy was undeniable, and like the opening of a dam's sluices, many expressions of joy flooded my body and memories. A vibrancy in my life unlocked and could not be shut down again. This palpable, childlike aliveness has permeated many of my experiences ever since.

A pronounced sense of connection rushed through me. All of a sudden, it didn't make any sense to deny or block this.

Not in an *Oh, woe is me, that joy is gone, and I may as well give it up.*

But in the feeling and thought, *This innocence and joy have and will always be here.*

Continuing Inquiry

Some situations continue to create the impression that contentment disappears. With each one, I inquire. As reactions arrive, I take them as loving invitations to keep looking at my long-held tendencies.

Take, for instance, shame and guilt.

In our usual evening routine, Mel and I read, perhaps write for a while, and I may go to my office to play guitar or sing a few lines. Carefully arranging her daily flower offerings, she often performs a meditative practice that her teachers call "firing up." This helps move energies throughout her body and allows her to offer these to others.

One evening, as the sun disappeared in the west, I noticed a feeling of shame. I didn't know why, but my mind added that I made too much noise and disrupted Melanie's meditation. Whether I disrupted her or not made no difference, as part of my mind had already passed judgment.

I sent an invitation to the shame; w*hy don't you stay for a while?*

A voice in my head said matter-of-factly that this act of sitting with your shame proves that you indeed have done something, or many things, of which to be ashamed.

Soon, an entire wall of gray plexiglass appeared before me. I couldn't see it with my eyes, but I sure could feel it throughout my head and chest, and my mind's sight confirmed its presence.

What a place to be! Stuck behind this impenetrable barrier. I can't find a way under, over, or around it, as it feels and looks so dense. I also saw a vague picture of my body's physical boundaries.

See, this is solid and, therefore, real. You can't go above it or through it. Shame exemplifies one of the unquestionably real things in this universe.

My upper eyelids drooped as my gaze averted slightly downward and to the right. A forward tilt of my head and a partial frown on my lips helped cement this shameful posture into place. A heaviness throughout my body appeared along with this impenetrable gray mass.

A figure then stood before me. Someone with a pointed finger moved their lips, repeatedly detailing my shameful failings.

I couldn't look at them. I couldn't meet their eyes. In my mind, I said, *Shit. Not again!*

Not moving, an insistence said, *You must now openly declare your shame and thereby confirm its reality before you can move on. Your penance requires that the narrative of your shameful actions repeat incessantly.*

Guilt cropped up at this point with only minor differences compared to shame.

Both emotions boxed me into a position of submission.

This sounded so similar to the Church's dogma of original sin.

The gray, solid shield is still here. I am going to sit with this, leaving myself open to all possible outcomes, and resist the urge to run or to dictate what should happen, I thought.

Wait, I said. *What are these edges I now see?* The supposedly solid gray boundary has changed in shape and impenetrability. Gradually, I sensed the entire shape and found that I now had a possibility to shut this inquiry down or to incorporate this fading figure entirely back into my being—no other words or explanations were required.

Soon, the narrative fell apart, and a connection between shame and the gray shield dissipated. The prison of shame quickly thinned and vanished. And all I did was watch it come and go. When I spoke to Melanie about my self-inquiry adventure, the quizzical look on her face told me that, indeed, I had not interrupted her practice one bit.

Irritations and fears still arise in me and sometimes concern our state and national politics, autocracies in the form of corporations, governments, or even billionaires, media sensationalism, and misrepresentations covering a whole gamut of topics. And I continually notice internal complaints about everyone's driving! These are all things I get to look at if I choose, or alternatively, I can fall back into my conditioned responses.

I work with cancer issues as they come up. Occasionally, a thought in the background pessimistically warns of the next series of blood work or appointments. Oncology consultations still stir up dread. And rather than letting these welded stories and sensations once more cloak my peace of mind, I often choose to entertain that trepidation, watching and feeling as stories emerge. Those tend to revolve around complaints about the long and tedious drive to the clinic or how the lab technician needs three excruciating needle sticks to draw my blood successfully. Not to mention that the results may foretell a much-shortened lifespan filled with all sorts of complication-producing side effects from the next level of chemotherapy.

I know this dread need not rule my life, my responses, or the calmness at my core.

I initiate a conversation with dread through a line of questioning.

Where are you, dread? As I wait for some qualities to come spontaneously to mind.

Where do you reside in my body?

The abdominal area mildly clenches.

If I sit with you long enough, might you be represented by a color or shape?

I get no response, so I ask the question, *Why do you call yourself dread?*

<u>You</u> *call me dread,* is the answer. *I am just a feeling you have cut off from your essence. You always keep running and never want to face me for reasons I don't understand. Closer to reality is that I, this particular sensation, am not associated with any so-called emotion or story. You made all those. I am just an energy. I keep coming up because I want to come home. But don't simply add this to your long list of beliefs. YOU have to experience what these statements mean to you.*

It resonates with me that lingering reactions only ask for attention rather than being buried and ignored. Hoping never to experience them again, I repeatedly stuffed joy, compassion, empathy, anger, sadness, grief, abandonment, and boredom into a bottomless pit. They all became rejected fragments that I further used to repress and invalidate any connection to my body.

Now, I wish to honor these physical modulations and sensations by gently approaching and directly observing them. Occasionally, these contractions morph into an underlying jubilance as I bring my full awareness to them. These discarded pieces of the totality of what I am only want to be seen for what they are without all the song and dance I impose.

Does this elucidation of life supersede all other teachings? No. It is just a concept, and for the time being, this concept meets me right where I currently am in this journey.

The sentiment I labeled dread wasn't created with that name, those associated body parts, or even the stories I tell to define it. I put all this together, and for a long time, this was a helpful, practical, and even life-saving strategy. But now, I recognize that my constant effort in keeping these shadow stories alive has chronically veiled my underlying serenity. My mind's attempt to bolster its position as the one who gives and maintains all meaning for all forms conceals my true nature. What would it be like to experience everything for what it is, not what I demand it to be? I want to allow those scorned parts to reintegrate, enabling lightness of being.

Learning and Integrating

Dynamic accurately describes my ongoing interaction with cancer. As to a definitive reason why I developed this malignancy, I can only relate concepts that come up in this moment. The lymphoma revolves around my lymphocytes, making an abnormally high amount of IgM antibodies, which are the usual first immune responders to anything considered an invader of the body. I acknowledge that the perpetually judgmental part of my mind has always been on high alert, always ready to identify and respond to external and internal assaults on my system. Perhaps the lymphocytes only try to point this out in the most attention-getting way possible. And boy, did they get my attention.

As a young child, I related to the world through giggles and laughter. But gradually, through conditioning—perhaps conditioning I subconsciously sought—I blocked and numbed my sight so that I could no longer experience that more genuine self except in bits and pieces. Part of my exploration and purpose now is to check out each of these blocks as they come up. Tedious? If I want it to be. Playful? It certainly feels that way when my long-held, coveted scripts dissolve.

I rediscovered that I had slowly substituted my steadiness and happiness with fear and pain, convincing myself that I could only find contentment again by building an impenetrable fortress.

I heard that any felt joy was actually pain, since joy threatened the very foundations of the miserable person I had concocted. I dredged up whatever circular reasoning I could find to make an indestructible "me." Eventually, this manufactured ego insisted I resign to the pain in life and never search for happiness again, as experience repeatedly demonstrated that enjoyment always turned to despair. I recounted circumstance after circumstance supporting this.

Reinforcing my pessimism, I withdrew from overtly expressing enjoyment, gratitude, empathy, and compassion, eventually denying they were ever part of me. I began amassing my armory of tendencies.

Meanwhile, the world's wonders patiently waited as I deadened my heart to everything.

Escaping into the cathedral of intellect, I became successful in the eyes of the world, graduating with honors from all levels of schooling. After a few jobs working for others, I seamlessly opened my own medical practice. IRS agents, accountants, lawyers, and patients rejoiced with what I could offer.

But all along, something felt insufficient. My mind said that one more new anything would secure happiness—new patients, cars, tools, or even an increase in salary or more time off. Attempting to remedy this ever-present lack, I physically and mentally pushed myself to find some superficial cure. A significant neck injury, followed years later by the threat of life-ending cancer, jolted me enough to loosen my grip on long-standing alienating beliefs. The angelfish served as a major escort toward this tiny spark of sereneness beyond all my thoughts.

Using inquiry and a mindful awareness of the body, I searched for the delineation of my physical form and the outer world, not only during calm or imperturbation but on occasions when anger erupted. I had always been so wrapped up in the rage that it seemed hard to detect precisely who was angry! Eventually, the certainty of these edges of where my physicality ended and the world started, blurred. Going a little further, I could not prove there was any world or universe outside of my physical senses.

Once again, where or who was that angry, sad, miserable, bored, or left behind person? Even though I looked at this several times, I realized these emotions also connected to deeply-seated bodily memories. These constrictions slowly became pointers guiding me toward the automatic, repetitive behaviors with which I defined myself.

My belief in scarcity and agony wasn't as dense and despotic as I thought. While I tried pinning down the cause of my despair, the pounding of my fists and screaming at the top of my lungs couldn't cement all the elements I had put together any longer. As my authoritative definitions of my misery disintegrated, the sky's blueness filled my heart and mind with a sense of beauty and connection.

Physical pain seems to be a little more of a challenge. My neck continues with intermittent spasms, continual neck crunching, and migraine headaches that routinely occur after minimal activities. I can at least sit with the stabbing, aching, and burning now. Before, I only wanted to medicate them to get them to stop. Rather than running, I place my attention directly into the middle of the pain and wait. The pain can take on a shape, color, and other qualities, including a picture of that particular body part. Often, it transforms into some black ball bouncing slightly back and forth. Do I try to get it to stop, or do I encourage the bouncing? This is an ongoing exploration.

I now openly visit with the sensations I previously used to validate my apparent disengagement from life. There they are, fully present and visible to the inner eye, but without the attached script. Underlying this comes a sense of sadness that, for so long, I worshipped and thanked myself for that disconnection. As I ponder my inclination to numbed-out detachment, a curiosity arises around this wondrous decision-making process. I enter the sensations and rejoice in their glory of being. Not as any specific form, but just as being.

Look at how all of the creation plays together! Just hearing that brings a smile and lightness.

Each time I let things be as they are and allow awareness to show me their nature, a susceptibleness to love, beauty, and ease flourishes. I experience all of these as if watching the sunrise, especially when accompanied by thoughts of Melanie, our children, and my grandchild. A great expansion in the chest and the opening of the belly complements the quieting of all questions. I used to just breathe. Now, I take in the whole universe with each diaphragmatic movement.

Right here and now, I am content, calm, serene, and complete, unlike ever before.

For now …

Lying in bed the other night, my eyes closed for the last time. The transition to sleep, characterized by a relaxation of all my muscles, crept under the covers with me. A resonance emerged along the anterior part of my spine that I instantly recognized as the feeling of "fun." Fun? I wasn't doing anything fun. I was just about to fall asleep. But there it was, fun, at my deepest core. Frankly, never before had I felt this so strongly.

Elation lay under that fun as I remembered my two-year-old self running across the yard. Embodying that delight, I detected small parts of facial expressions and a sense of something pounding on the green grass. As a toddler, I didn't recognize the source of this pounding as my feet yet. Some early physical associations revealed themselves through my memories, showing me the connection between joy and movement. My mind then used these sensations to construct the "toddler Bart" physicality that my parents interacted with each morning.

Wow, I had no idea about this whole construction project! I said to myself.

An utterly fantastic remembrance and experience all at the same time!

I heard the body say, *We are happy to hold these resonances, feelings, and energies for you as long as you need.*

Working with cancer, the idea that my body acted as an encyclopedic reservoir of life struck a chord.

Similar explorations involved the feelings linked with empathy, compassion, gratitude, wonder, completeness, competence, and even greatness—all emotions that I shut down at an early age to save and protect myself. Upon examination, each of these emotions reverberated with an underlying joy. These emotions spontaneously arose and left without any action on my part, and I knew they were always available.

Whether I allow these sentiments to express themselves is my prerogative and need not be dictated by some past liturgical declaration that "these emotions are forbidden and to feel them is a sin."

More recently, something moved through my chest, spreading to the top of my head and down toward my feet. I knew instantly that it represented a sense of purpose, something I never allowed myself. Permitting it to sink in and spread throughout my body was good, and I knew it felt right. I witnessed a confirmation that my purpose involved recounting my journey, as honestly as possible, from early joy to complete shutdown and onward to penetrate the strategies that kept me asleep. This entailed backtracking through my life experience and exploring how I put together myself and my world.

Knowing my purpose for the first time, I feel called to remember, reexperience, and scribe this narrative.

I clearly hear my own voice in my mind joyfully say, ***Don't worry. Don't be afraid. You are only waking up.***

I now feel my purpose as a deep resonance starting in the chest, radiating through the arms and into the entire universe. I know it matters little whether anyone or anything reads these words. Their underlying content has already been freely given to all of creation.

Around that, I feel a sense of perfection, which arrives with fullness, not artificial or controlled, but arising from something other than this physical self. Everything I see in myself, my room, home, family, and the universe is perfect. It is here; how could it not be perfect? Not that the character Bart agrees with all that perfection. Bart himself will never see perfectness. And is that okay?

This resistance to perfection persists. Internal reactions to events invite me to keep looking at how I made this Bart character. Looking at who I was, I glimpse who I am right now, sitting at this typewriter and thinking of lunch a few hours away.

Wait a minute. I thought perfection before God was my goal.

What would it mean to accept that I am already perfect?

These questions stir up incredible bodily sensations beneath which I feel a sense of truth, not in what I still believe and experience but penetrating and encompassing everything in existence. A feeling that there is truth, no matter what I experience, what arises, and what thoughts I think. It is a truth where nothing needs to be irreproachable and a knowing that it's all of no consequence. A sense of a foundationless foundation, never changing, but from which everything comes. That knowing starts deep in my belly and expands to encompass all forms.

It resonates with me that I came here to explore a possible change in my point of view. So far, it has been an odyssey that many may consider negative—the trauma of my crude upbringing, multiple medical issues and subsequent surgeries, depression, divorce, and cancer.

I see my travels differently. To me, the journey entails occasionally stepping back and watching the character of Bart and his interaction with the character called the universe, jumping into the full costume of this grand show, or being the experience of exploration itself—and perhaps combining all three states simultaneously. It is a constant resetting of what this little mind thinks it knows and a connection to something more expansive. It may be gradual learning or unlearning from different teachers as I land on a phrase or saying that resonates and helps open doorways for me to intuit what lies beyond this form.

No thought can ever conclusively define my true nature, but I have an opportunity in how I see myself and the world around me. I color the ultimate neutrality of everything with either fear or love—my self-determination. The most significant part of this realization is that I have a voluntary decision at every level and from every point of view I decide to entertain.

On this earth, I have options, and I more often pick an experience of equanimity, wonder, connection, and love.

I sense something beyond "I" and "not I." Each time I arbitrarily attempt to manipulate pure experience—primarily by pointing out what is lacking or wrong at any particular time—I eventually feel the overwhelming cost of ignorance.

Choosing to incarnate here, I consented to a narrow and particular point of view, effectively limiting creation's expanded perception—like putting blinders on a horse. I vehemently denied consenting to many of my life's occurrences for the longest time. Thus, I blamed my disconnections on others and my human conception and birth.

A symbol of this physical disconnection played out with the cutting of my umbilical cord. What did the severing of the cord feel like, and what preserves the memory of that physical insult in my body?

I once felt the contraction associated with my first breath—just under my rib cage near the top of the abdomen. The next worldly act of separation for me took the form of circumcision. This event reinforced that whatever I brought into this world wasn't good enough and had to be societally mutilated for my own good.

While I don't remember bringing awareness into this world, I know I brought a glimpse of joy, completeness, and curiosity, as those qualities emanate from the pictures of me as a toddler. It is now easy to get lost in that first memory of two-year-old innocence and inquisitiveness as the small yard greeted my feet step by step.

Oh, the pleasure of hearing those toddler footfalls as if it were the first time anyone in the universe freely encountered such an exuberant moment!

Playing with Rigidity and Transparency

And then there are days …

I heard and felt, *You know, Bart, no matter what you do, you're a disappointment to us.*

As heaviness arose, I asked, What did I ever do to disillusion God and the *universe? I hate this feeling of being a failure. It feels so terrible. I just want to run.*

A cold steel bar formed vertically through my chest and belly. Rigid, unbending, supposedly supporting the essence of my manufactured self. It was not pleasant.

Staying with that steel bar sensation, several questions emerged:

What does it mean to be a shit show to my higher self, or worse yet, God? With the way I act, how could I ever be loveable? What action or conviction could redeem the irredeemable person I am?

The questions marched on. *What will that final form be before I forget there ever was form? Who is that one who will be the one who will forget?*

As I sat with these thoughts and rigidity, transparency began to appear, and eventually, it all faded, leaving me with a visceral sense of tenderness.

This insistence of universal disappointment doesn't resonate much anymore, as I recognize that my mind only wants to go off on one of its tangents again. This intellectualism feels good for a while, but weariness soon appears. And when it does float through my awareness, I see that, once more, I have stepped into some rabbit hole of circular thinking, often depicted by a funnel with no end.

I often hear, *Keep going further into that concept, Bart. You're getting so close to narrowing down the universe's secrets to a single sentence or saying.*

With that, my awareness takes a step back and observes the mind in all its intellectual glory.

I occasionally still choose the ego's view of a separated "Bart." Rather than seeing these situations as proof of further separateness, I now regard them as invitations to explore even deeper associations held in my body—contractions that continue pointing me toward a relative truth that I am none of this and all of this.

Pointers to Truth

In writing this book, fears that were long considered genuine and impenetrable now signify road signs and pointers to the next phase of corporality.

What lies over the next horizon? Is it some notion of finality when death enters this body and mind? Do souls reunite on the next level? What other levels of communication await us? Why is this particular universe's point of view 'eat or be eaten'?

A wry smile appears as I enjoy these esoteric thoughts. Quickly, fatigue and discomfort emerge, signaling a total absorption in pretending I am solely a mind that thinks.

These questions and concepts only symbolize the truer nature of everything and everyone I love and interact with here on this earthly plane.

I can choose, and even re-choose, a particular angle or spot from which to view the universe. As a consequence or offspring of consciousness, my mind enables me to explore specific aspects of our infinite connections. But no matter how many different angles I see from, no matter how many other alternative universes I conjure up, and no matter how many various incarnations or bodily levels I fabricate, they all fall short of the truth.

Oddly enough, I feel solace when relaxing into the statement, *"No matter how hard and deep I get into any subject, my mind can only imagine and symbolize what truth is."*

Is there any end to the levels of mind? Probably not—but again, that is just another hole that concepts can crawl in and out of to compare their knowledge and relevance with one another. Another bottomless sinkhole.

When I came here as "Bart," I agreed to use and live by the symbols that help define our particular universe. The concept or object that each symbol identifies is but a representation in and of itself. Even the atoms, with their protons, neutrons, and electrons, are shadows that point to something beyond. And in that, I find wonder and fulfillment—and even this wonder and fulfillment are but feelings representing thoughts that represent yet another thought. All are manifestations of something, but all illustrate nothing at the same time.

I can never find what a symbol points toward. For the longest time, it made some sense to me that quarks and antiquarks were irreducible and impeccably explained the world. Likewise, I had been convinced that only an unquestionable intellectual understanding of myself (perhaps symbolized by a bronze and gold "Bart" statue) could alleviate my fears. Yet each search for this certainty led to one dead end after another.

But don't believe me. Test out your own experience and see where it leads you.

I now find comfort and faith in truth. While my senses might not recognize it, a bodily impulse tells me that I have always resided there. This physical impulse is the love I experience as I pass back and forth between unwavering truth and my existence here as consciousness and mind. That is the love and happiness I feel more and more each day. That feeling of completeness covers everything.

My entire life experience has led me to the awareness and peace that underlies this sentence made up of letters typed on this page. I moved from a belief system that claimed I could eventually know all into a paradigm in which I embrace completeness and love even when life is uncertain and eventually unknowable.

Since my teens, I heard in my head the statement that God would allow only a split second of joy before sending me off to be obliterated. I took this as a punishment and a command never to allow myself to share love in this world. This supposed threat from God terrified me as much as any parental punishment could.

Now, I see this statement not from lack but from love. I view it as a promise to return to peace and completeness, no matter my circumstances. I will feel love as I rest in that return. I once presumed that the emptiness inside me was fear; it is now a loving call to return to truth. Every belief and point of view that I ever held, or could ever hold, can dissolve in that stillness.

Eventually, the concept of "Bart" or even "I" may no longer be needed or make any sense. But for now, I bask in the concept of those bodily impulses toward truth, which tell me that my chosen symbology points to that which is beyond itself. I find comfort in that there is rest so eternal that even a multidimensional mind and consciousness will seem empty.

My Life These Days

Because of this perspective, my felt experience with everything has markedly changed. While a part of me may disagree with another person's point of view, I can empathize with their position in a way that I couldn't for much of my life. Through my deepening compassion, I glimpse another's fear, and then the alive content—aka stillness—under their emotion shines through.

Figure 23 "The real creators of the universe"

I feel a unity with nature now, whereas previously, all connections had been denied. The nighttime stars play with my senses more than ever as I imagine their endless communications with everything else in the universe. The birds that traverse the sky filled with clouds have never been closer.

With Melanie, I see that I have always loved her, and now, when I say that, I can feel it. The words "I love you" have taken on a new subtlety, meaning, and confirmation that seems to cement our relationship. We still have occasional disagreements but can step back and explore the misunderstanding from many angles. And each of those disputes is an opportunity for us both to observe what comes up as a bodily sensation. With everything, there has been a movement from a superficial intellectual understanding of love to an actual embodiment of that love.

I even have a relatively smoother relationship with my first wife. My children are a blessing; each brings a different perspective and quality to my life. Admiration appears as I watch them grow and take on their challenges. While certain tendencies still exist concerning them, I can see how everything they do has a rightness about it.

Recently, I had this dream.

I am riding in the passenger seat in a small car with someone else driving. I think the driver is a man, but I don't know him. I get a glimpse of him only through my peripheral vision. We are on a four-lane highway as I look out the front windshield. Soon, the windshield becomes clouded, fogged, dirty, and drenched by rain. I can't see a thing. I can't tell where the car is headed.

I say out loud, "Can you at least clean the windshield so I can see where I am going?" There is no answer. Soon, everything around me is unrecognizable. I then awaken.

I don't know where this life leads. However, I now choose to have my innate joy and peace as my guide along the path. I know it doesn't matter whether the windshield is clean or dirty, and my mind can complain and be concerned about it all it wants, but that will never alter the innocence that is innately who I am.

I recall the Hiroshima dream I had many years ago when I started this adventure. The shrouded woman in the dream tells me, “Don’t worry. It will come again.” For years, I wondered WHAT would come again. Over time, it occurred to me that my mind allowed the concreteness of my world to thin enough so that I could remember my innate joy and peace. That is what came again. It turns out it never left.

EPILOGUE

Life sends me an almost constant barrage of challenges. Each assigned different degrees of seriousness and attachment by the meaning-making part of my mind. It still demands that each occurrence be given some importance-such as an ongoing ranking and categorizing system.

Some things seem to carry more significance, such as the adventures and plights of my children, relatives, and friends. Others are easier to drop and move on from, but frankly, even the dying grass in the summer heat and drought, of which I have little control, sometimes pulls at me and whips up a dry, emotional windstorm.

My lymphoma has been relatively calm for about two years. We all watched the IgM levels (the tumor marker) rise until the laboratory couldn't give us an absolute figure, only a general, "It's above 7000 again." And considering that our average IgM level is less than 300, 7000 can be alarming. This high IgM level indicated the presence of a large number of lymphoma cells in my body, leading to various symptoms. At first few suspicious symptoms surfaced, so my oncologist let the IgM increase. Gradually, however, more apparent symptoms appeared, and it was hoped they would improve. They didn't. This included an intermittent cough with occasional blood in my sputum, extreme fluctuations in body temperature (chilled to the bones or sweating buckets), tiredness, sensitivity to dairy products, and further weight loss. Particularly concerning and debilitating, my muscle mass was gradually turned into IgM and then stored throughout the body, especially the lungs.

I was started on an oral medication, which unfortunately didn't improve my overall disease process. Six months into this treatment plan, I weighed in for my oncology appointment at 147 lbs. My oncologist took one look at me and said, "This medicine is clearly not working for you." Perhaps the oral med's side effects were causing more detriment and hastening my demise. An additional clue of my worsening condition was evidence of lymphoma cells and IgM antibodies in my lungs.

Things even progressed to the point that I needed some home Oxygen, as my room air saturation was below 90%, compared to normal, above 96%.

My oncologist immediately scheduled me for hospital admission to receive inpatient plasma exchange or PLEX, which removes most of my blood plasma (containing many IgM molecules) and restocks my circulatory system with fresh plasma from generous donors. While highly irregular and aggressive, four consecutive treatments were performed. This meant that during each of the four PLEX treatments, about 3.7 liters of my plasma was extracted from me and tossed into the biohazard bin. The goal was to reduce my IgM level enough so that a newer chemo infusion could be tried in hopes of wiping out more of the lymphoma cells.

I questioned rather forcefully the insane hospital rituals of 3 AM blood draws and 4 AM vital sign checks. How would any patient get any rest with that schedule, all in the name of having information for the morning rounds?

Melanie shared with me that it seemed I was going through a sort of soul-searching and life reflection while in the hospital those five days. She tells me I expressed deep empathy for many patients and other caregivers throughout my career, empathy I'd never felt towards them. I connected with many of my pain patients on a level even more profound than when I underwent neck surgeries. She said my heart seemed to continually crack open again and again throughout this stay. Some of this is fuzzy in my memory, but perhaps an echo of it remains.

After the PLEX, my lungs felt immediately better, and I could at least coexist with my living space without supplemental oxygen and persistent coughing. While the new IV chemo agent reduced my IgM even further, the toll on my bone marrow became apparent about halfway through the protocol. Yet, my body lived on, a testament to the remarkable resilience of the human spirit in the face of adversity.

So here I am, progressing through a new phase of this dance with cancer. Several times, my blood counts were so low that further IV therapy needed to be postponed. When does it become clear that the body is acting as a mouthpiece of the mind as it tries to say, "Enough is enough"?

That, along with everything else in life, invites me to ask more unanswerable questions. This leads to more rabbit holes of endless deep dives into the cause and purpose of everything. Just what was the plan before the big bang? Did I even have a say in all of that? Is adding one more landing pad of questionable understanding helpful? These questions could engage me in an endless thought-based exploration of life and its mysteries.

I could continue saying that my upbringing and all the dysfunction I mimicked as a child are legitimate causes for being disgusted at the world, myself, and others. Nothing can change any of that, so I may as well resign myself and even revel in a life of outrage, blaming this experience or that person. But I choose not to. I choose to accept my past and move forward with understanding and empathy.

From Bart's perspective, this exploration continues. I am tired of fighting my past, memories, situations, and myself. I am tired of experiencing some bodily contraction and playing through the same old zombie-like, unexamined, and unquestioned responses.

In other words, I know now I have a choice. I can insist that I always know and can always explain everything, or I can rest in not knowing. I choose the latter more and more. I'm becoming increasingly comfortable with uncertainty, realizing it's not about what I know but the power of my choices.

Through my exploration of dreams, non-ordinary states, and self-inquiry, I am now creating an ever-expanding space for joy and peace in me. I am deeply grateful for the support and love surrounding me on this journey.

Made in the USA
Middletown, DE
28 July 2024

58038108R00199